Colin Powell

Biographies
IN AMERICAN FOREIGN POLICY
Joseph A. Fry, University of Nevada, Las Vegas
Series Editor

The Biographies in American Foreign Policy Series employs the enduring medium of biography to examine the major episodes and themes in the history of U.S. foreign relations. By viewing policy formation and implementation from the perspective of influential participants, the series humanizes and makes more accessible those decisions and events that sometimes appear abstract or distant. Particular attention is devoted to those aspects of the subject's background, personality, and intellect that most influenced his or her approach to U.S. foreign policy, and each individual's role is placed in a context that takes into account domestic affairs, national interests and policies, and international and strategic considerations.

Volumes Published

Lawrence S. Kaplan, *Thomas Jefferson: Westward the Course of Empire*

Richard H. Immerman, *John Foster Dulles: Piety, Pragmatism, and Power in U.S. Foreign Policy*

Thomas W. Zeiler, *Dean Rusk: Defending the American Mission Abroad*

Edward P. Crapol, *James G. Blaine: Architect of Empire*

David F. Schmitz, *Henry L. Stimson: The First Wise Man*

Thomas M. Leonard, *James K. Polk: A Clear and Unquestionable Destiny*

James E. Lewis Jr., *John Quincy Adams: Policymaker for the Union*

Catherine Forslund, *Anna Chennault: Informal Diplomacy and Asian Relations*

Lawrence S. Kaplan, *Alexander Hamilton: Ambivalent Anglophile*

Andrew J. DeRoche, *Andrew Young: Civil Rights Ambassador*

Jeffrey J. Matthews, *Alanson B. Houghton: Ambassador of the New Era*

Clarence E. Wunderlin Jr., *Robert A. Taft: Ideas, Tradition, and Party in U.S. Foreign Policy*

Howard Jablon, *David M. Shoup: A Warrior against War*

Jeff Woods, *Richard B. Russell: Southern Nationalism and American Foreign Policy*

Russell D. Buhite, *Douglas MacArthur: Statecraft and Stagecraft in America's East Asian Policy*

Christopher D. O'Sullivan, *Colin Powell: American Power and Intervention from Vietnam to Iraq*

Colin Powell

American Power and Intervention from Vietnam to Iraq

Christopher D. O'Sullivan

ROWMAN & LITTLEFIELD PUBLISHERS, INC.
Lanham • Boulder • New York • Toronto • Plymouth, UK

ROWMAN & LITTLEFIELD PUBLISHERS, INC.

Published in the United States of America
by Rowman & Littlefield Publishers, Inc.
A wholly owned subsidiary of The Rowman & Littlefield Publishing Group, Inc.
4501 Forbes Boulevard, Suite 200, Lanham, Maryland 20706
www.rowmanlittlefield.com

Estover Road
Plymouth PL6 7PY
United Kingdom

British Library Cataloguing in Publication Information Available

Library of Congress Cataloging-in-Publication Data:

O'Sullivan, Christopher D.
  Colin Powell : American power and intervention from Vietnam to Iraq / Christopher
D. O'Sullivan.
     p. cm. — (Biographies in American foreign policy Joseph A. Fry)
  Includes bibliographical references and index.
  ISBN 978-0-7425-5186-2 (cloth : alk. paper) — ISBN 978-0-7425-6535-7 (electronic)
  1. Powell, Colin L. 2. Generals—United States—Biography. 3. African American
generals—Biography. 4. United States. Army—Biography. 5. Statesmen—United
States—Biography. 6. United States. Dept. of State—Biography. I. Title.
  E840.5.P68O885 2009
  327.730092—dc22
  [B]   2008046759

Printed in the United States of America

∞ ™ The paper used in this publication meets the minimum requirements of
American National Standard for Information Sciences—Permanence of Paper
for Printed Library Materials, ANSI/NISO Z39.48-1992.

To my father, Gen. Curtis "Hoop" O'Sullivan

Contents

~

Chronology

1962 August: Powell receives orders for South Vietnam.
   August 25: He marries Alma Johnson in Birmingham, Alabama.
   September: He attends a five-week adviser course at Fort Bragg and is promoted to captain.
   December 25: He arrives in Saigon to serve as adviser to the Army of the Republic of Vietnam.

1963 January: Powell arrives in Quang Tri province.
   March 23: His son Michael Kevin is born.
   July 23: He steps on a Punji trap and is awarded the Purple Heart.
   November 1: He returns to Saigon; his tour of duty is complete.
   November 1: South Vietnamese president Ngo Dinh Diem is assassinated.
   November 22: He arrives in Nashville and hears of JFK's assassination.

1964 January: Powell attends advanced airborne training.
   August: Gulf of Tonkin Resolution is passed.

1966 Spring: Powell attends the Infantry School as a major.

1967 Fall: Powell attends Command and General Staff College at Fort Leavenworth.

1968 June: Powell graduates second in his class from Command and General Staff College.
   July 21: He returns to Vietnam for a second tour.
   July 27: He is assigned to the Third Battalion (First Infantry) American Division.
   November 16: He is injured in a chopper crash and receives a medal for life saving.

1969 July: Powell's second tour in Vietnam ends.

1970 August: Powell is promoted to lieutenant colonel.

1971 May: Powell receives an MBA in data processing from George Washington University.
   July: Powell is appointed to the Office of Assistant Vice Chief of Staff of the Army.

1972 May: Powell is selected as a White House fellow in the Office of Management and Budget (OMB).

1973 February: Powell becomes special assistant to the deputy director of the OMB.
   August: He serves as commanding officer of an infantry battalion in Korea.

1974 September: Powell returns to the United States.

1975 August: Powell attends the National War College at Fort Mc-
Nair.

1976 February: Powell is promoted to colonel.

April: He becomes brigade commander with the 101st Airborne at Fort Campbell.

1977 May: Powell is appointed to the Office of the Special Assistant to the Secretary and Deputy Secretary of Defense.

1979 June 1: Powell is promoted to brigadier general at age forty-one.

1981 January 20: Ronald Reagan is inaugurated.

February 4: Powell is appointed senior military assistant to the deputy secretary of defense.

March: He becomes assistant division commander of the Fourth Infantry Division at Fort Carson.

September 1: Reagan dispatches U.S. Marines to Lebanon.

1983 June 29: Powell is promoted to major general.

July: He is appointed military aide to Secretary of Defense Caspar Weinberger.

October 23: Marine barracks in Beirut are bombed.

October 25: The United States invades Grenada.

1984 November: Weinberger announces the "Weinberger Doctrine."

1986 March 25: Powell is appointed to the command of V Corps in West Germany as lieutenant general.

July 2: Powell is sworn in as commanding general of V Corps in Frankfurt.

October 11–12: The Reagan-Gorbachev summit is held at Reykjavik.

December 18: Powell is appointed deputy national security adviser.

1987 January 2: Powell arrives at the White House as deputy national security adviser.

February 28: Gorbachev offers to eliminate intermediate nuclear forces.

November 5: Powell becomes Reagan's sixth and final national security adviser.

December 8–9: The Washington summit is held.

1988 May: The Moscow summit is held.

December: The Governor's Island summit is held.

1989 January 20: Reagan leaves office.

January: Powell is appointed commander of U.S. Army Forces Command, or FORSCOM, as a four-star general.

October 1: Powell begins his tenure as chairman of the Joint Chiefs of Staff.

December 20: The United States invades Panama.

1990   August 2: Iraq invades Kuwait.

1991   January 16: The air war against Iraq begins.

February 23: The ground offensive against Iraq begins.

March 3: The Iraqi military signs a cease-fire.

March 6: Bush proclaims a "new world order."

March 6: Iraqi forces crush an uprising by Shiites and Kurds.

May 23: Powell is reappointed for a second term as chairman of the Joint Chiefs of Staff.

1992   November 19: Powell meets with president-elect Bill Clinton for the first time.

December 3: The United States launches humanitarian intervention in Somalia.

1993   September 30: Powell ends his second term as chairman of the Joint Chiefs of Staff.

He is awarded a second Medal of Freedom by President Clinton.

October 3: U.S. forces engage in combat with Somali militias.

1994   September 16: Powell travels to Haiti as part of the Carter Mission to restore Jean-Bertrand Aristide.

December: Powell turns down President Clinton's offer of a senior appointment.

1995   September 16: *My American Journey* is released.

November 8: Powell announces that he will not run for president in 1996.

1996   August 12: Powell speaks at the Republican National Convention in San Diego.

2000   July 31: Powell speaks at the Republican National Convention in Philadelphia.

December: The Supreme Court ends the recount in Florida.

December 16: Powell accepts Bush's appointment as secretary of state.

2001   January 17: Powell is confirmed as secretary of state.

February 16: U.S. air strikes against Iraq begin.

April 1–3: U.S.-Chinese tensions develop over the downing of an American spy plane.

August 6: Bush receives a briefing titled "Osama bin Laden Determined to Attack the U.S."

September 11: The World Trade Center and Pentagon are attacked.

September 12: NATO invokes Article V of the North Atlantic Treaty.

October 19–20: U.S. forces intervene in Afghanistan.

December 12: Bush announces that the United States will break the 1972 Antiballistic Missile Treaty.

2002   April 8–17: Powell goes on a Middle East mission.

May 6: The Bush administration announces it will not honor the International Criminal Court protocol.

September 16: Iraq agrees to weapons inspections.

October 11: Congress votes during midterm elections to authorize the use of force against Iraq.

November 2: UN Security Council Resolution 1441 for Iraqi disarmament is passed.

2003   February 5: Powell presents the administration's case for war in a UN speech.

March 19: The United States launches the invasion of Iraq.

May 1: Bush declares major combat operations in Iraq over.

2004   April 28: U.S. soldiers are revealed to have tortured and killed Iraqi POWs.

November 12: Powell announces that he will resign in January.

2005   January: Powell leaves the State Department and is replaced by Condoleezza Rice.

September: Powell admits to regretting the UN speech of February 2003.

2006   December 17: Powell publicly says U.S. forces in Iraq are broken and that he doubts sending more troops, as the Bush administration desires, will make any difference.

~

Acknowledgments

The writing of this book has benefited from the work of many scholars working in the field of American foreign relations, but I am also indebted to the
following people. Appreciation must begin with Andy Fry for his unparalleled editing skills. Andy is the very definition of a generous and dedicated
series editor. Jeffrey L. Matthews also demonstrated remarkable insight and
thoroughness as a reader and provided me with numerous useful observations
and suggestions. The staff at Rowman & Littlefield, particularly Niels Aaboe,
Michelle Cassidy, David Fagan, Elaine McGarraugh, and Jen Kelland did
an outstanding job editing the manuscript and preparing it for publication.
Carolyn Jones of the *San Francisco Chronicle* also provided helpful suggestions
on the manuscript. David S. Foglesong offered illuminating insights into
U.S.-Soviet relations during the Reagan years, and Andrew Bacevich, Lawrence Wilkerson, and Lawrence Korb generously shared their perspectives
on subjects such as Colin Powell, the Powell Doctrine, the Vietnam Syndrome, and American foreign policy. Also of assistance were the archivists
at the Ronald Reagan Presidential Library, particularly Lisa Jones and Steve
Branch; the staff at the George H. W. Bush Presidential Library, particularly
Bonnie Burlbaw; and the staff at the William J. Clinton Presidential Library,
particularly John Keller. Mairi MacDonald introduced me to the oral history
collections on American foreign policy at the Library of Congress. John Kent
and the Center for International Studies at the London School of Economics provided me with a visiting fellowship for research on American foreign
relations in the extensive holdings of the British Library of Political and

Economic Science, and the Andrew W. Mellon Foundation provided me with a generous grant to do research in Washington, D.C., in the summer of 2007. The J. William Fulbright program and the Jordanian American Commission for Educational Exchange supported me during a year of teaching the history of American foreign relations at the University of Jordan in Amman, where many of the ideas for this book began to come together. I would like to thank my many students at the University of Jordan for their challenging questions and fascinating observations about American foreign policy in the Middle East. Manaf Damluji, my esteemed friend and research colleague from the University of Jordan, shared with me an invaluable Iraqi perspective on Powell, Bush, and the Iraq War. His insights were always much appreciated. I would also like to acknowledge the contributions of students at the University of San Francisco who have taken my courses on the history of American foreign relations, as well as the many people at Sonoma State University who attended my Bernard Osher lectures on the recent history of American foreign relations, particularly Drs. Deborah and Charles Eid and Jeanne Johnson of the Johnson Family Foundation, who provided me with grants and other financial support for the lecture series and research. Finally, I would like to thank my wife, Maeve, for her love, friendship, and good humor on three continents.

Introduction

Few figures in the past quarter century have played a more significant role in American foreign policy than Colin Powell. As national security adviser in the Ronald Reagan administration, chairman of the Joint Chiefs of Staff under George H. W. Bush and Bill Clinton, and secretary of state during George W. Bush's first term, he played a prominent role in four administrations, Republican and Democrat, spanning two decades. Using the medium of biography, this exploration of Powell's career and character reveals several broad themes crucial to American foreign policy and yields insights into the evolution of American foreign and defense policy in the post-Vietnam and post–Cold War eras.

This book explains Powell's diplomatic style and its place in the American foreign policy tradition. Over the past two decades, he has been engaged in the most important foreign and defense policy debates, such as the uses of American power in the wake of Vietnam, the winding down of the Cold War and the quest for new paths for American foreign policy, the interventions in Panama (1989) and the Persian Gulf (1991), the controversies over interventions in Bosnia and Somalia in the early 1990s, and the aims and goals of U.S. diplomacy after September 11. Powell also played a central role in the restoration of the military's reputation after Vietnam and was the first African American national security adviser, chairman of the Joint Chiefs, and secretary of state, as well as a major figure as the United States went to war with Iraq after September 11.

Powell wielded power at the highest levels of the most important foreign policy bureaucracies: the Pentagon, the White House, the Joint Chiefs, and the State Department. Of the seven seats on the National Security Council (NSC), he has held three. He has also served ten presidents in a career spanning fifty years. He entered the military when Dwight D. Eisenhower was in the White House. Dispatched to Vietnam when John F. Kennedy took the fateful decision to expand his adviser program in 1962, Powell returned for a second tour at the end of the Johnson years, when there were more than five hundred thousand troops in Southeast Asia and the war had become a quagmire. He began his apprenticeship in the Beltway bureaucracy as a White House fellow under Richard Nixon and served in the Pentagon during the Gerald Ford and Jimmy Carter administrations. Under Reagan, he became a special adviser to Secretary of Defense Caspar Weinberger and, later, national security adviser. As chairman of the Joint Chiefs at age fifty-two, he was at the center of the major foreign policy challenges faced by presidents George H. W. Bush and Bill Clinton. When he accepted the appointment as secretary of state in December 2000, he was poised to become one of the most powerful cabinet officials in decades.

At the time of his nomination, the media observed that he overshadowed the president-elect. He was one of those cabinet appointees who, like William Jennings Bryan in 1912 or Herbert Hoover in 1920, possessed an impressive stature prior to taking office. One has to go back to Charles Evans Hughes's appointment in 1921 or George C. Marshall's appointment in 1947 to find a secretary of state entering office with as much prestige, moral authority, and promise. There may not have been any American since Marshall or Eisenhower with as much credibility on matters of defense and foreign policy.

The Vietnam Syndrome and the Powell Doctrine

Powell is perhaps the ideal biographical subject for exploring the so-called Vietnam Syndrome and the repercussions of that war for American foreign policy. He has said that Vietnam taught him to distrust civilian experts with little or no military experience, and in the years after the war, he grew increasingly critical of the way it was conducted, with several administrations concealing from the American people the war's true costs and consequences. Powell came away from that experience convinced that a successful foreign policy required the backing of the American public. These lessons may have influenced his actions when confronted by Donald Rumsfeld, Dick Cheney, and the neoconservative faction in the George W. Bush administration. The lessons Powell took from his Vietnam experience certainly contributed to his thinking, first as an aide to Weinberger and later on his own, about the establishment of a set of criteria for the deployment of troops abroad, subsequently known as the "Powell Doctrine." Advocating overwhelming force, the Powell Doctrine called for the formulation of clear political and military objectives, articulated in advance, along with an all-out effort to guarantee public backing for military intervention. To his critics, the doctrine was unduly restrictive, particularly at a time when the United States was likely to engage in smaller conflicts not requiring overwhelming force.

The Search for a Foreign Policy Consensus after the Cold War

Powell's career also offers a vehicle for examining the numerous challenges facing American foreign policy since the Cold War. He served as national security adviser (1987–1989) as America's role in the world was being redefined and transformed. He worked closely with other moderates, such as Secretary of State George Shultz and Secretary of Defense Frank Carlucci, to ensure that the more ideological Reagan made the most of Soviet leader Mikhail Gorbachev's "new thinking" in foreign policy. His tenure as chairman of the Joint Chiefs during the first Gulf War brought him, through the medium of television, into millions of American households. He was no ordinary chairman. The first African American in the post, Powell was also the youngest ever, the first to have previously held a cabinet-level job, and the first to serve a full term since the passage of legislation expanding the powers of the position. But disputes arising during his tenure—particularly with Secretary of Defense Dick Cheney—left a residue of mistrust that, for all the outward appearances of unity, had profound consequences during the Bush II administration.

The end of the Cold War had other consequences for Powell, his career, and his eponymous doctrine. With the receding of Cold War tensions, the United States was less restrained militarily and more eager to project its power around the world in places as far-flung as Panama, Kuwait, Iraq, Somalia, Bosnia, Kosovo, and Afghanistan. Moreover, the United States no longer seemed restricted to fighting limited wars, and the chances of success for such interventions appeared to be greater following the collapse of the Soviet Union. Despite the end of the Cold War and the demise of the USSR, the quest for empire remained on the table. Perhaps this should have reinforced the necessity of applying the criteria of the Powell Doctrine. That it did not become one of the critical factors leading to the debacle in Iraq after 2003.

Exploring the Powell "Phenomenon"

Many believed Powell could one day become the first African American president. The 1995 publication of his best-selling memoir, My American Journey, sparked a political frenzy. The book sold more than one million copies. He developed a standing in the nation far beyond what one might expect of a retired chairman of the Joint Chiefs, as demonstrated by the sprouting of hundreds of "Powell for President" clubs seeking to draft him to challenge Clinton in 1996. His emphasis on his meritocratic rise made many Americans, white and black, feel better about themselves and their country.

Beyond the compelling biography, Powell's character and personality remained something of an enigma. Admired by millions, he could be an aloof and distant public figure. While many Americans projected their aspirations and hopes for the nation onto him, his innate reserve often left the public, and even his closest associates, uncertain about his beliefs. Although conservative in outlook, Powell was never sufficiently ideological to wear the "Vulcan" or "neoconservative" label. Instead, he represented the closest thing to foreign policy continuity over the past two decades. When he became secretary of state in 2001, he saw his role as bridging the foreign policies of the new administration and those of the previous three.

Outwardly, Powell's constancy and loyalty rarely wavered, but, behind the scenes, he often struggled with his ambivalence about those he served. As Reagan's national security adviser, he expressed distress at the president's lack of engagement and scant interest in matters of state. As George H. W. Bush's chairman of the Joint Chiefs, Powell was often dismayed by Bush's penchant for personalizing foreign policy and took offense at the president's use of racially charged "wedge" issues at home. Although he respected Clinton as the commander in chief, Powell felt incompatible with him and his new foreign policy and defense team, particularly in the wake of the "don't ask, don't tell" imbroglio over gays in the military. Nevertheless, he developed a strong personal relationship with Clinton and waited until the end of his term as chairman to retire. As George W. Bush's secretary of state, he consistently defended the administration's actions and became the moderate and reasoning face of an increasingly ideological foreign policy often out of sympathy with views he once professed. Shultz, who had patiently outmaneuvered his more ideological colleagues to ultimately gain influence over Reagan by 1987–1988, provided a model. Powell, too, believed that an ideological and disengaged president could be persuaded to follow his lead. An exploration of Powell's struggles from 2001 to 2004 reveals much about the turmoil and infighting within the administration, as well as the origins and conduct of the war in Iraq.

His identification with the institutions he served, including the U.S. Army, usually triumphed over other factors in his life, such as his race or social origins, in shaping his worldview. He was an institutional man in an era when Americans' faith in institutions was in decline. Some of the forces supporting George W. Bush, such as powerful and ideologically driven media corporations and think tanks, politically mobilized religion, and corporate power, were unfamiliar and even alien to Powell, with his Jamaican-Bronx origins, his formative years at the City College of New York (CCNY) and experience with the Reserve Officers' Training Corps (ROTC), his devotion to the army, and his commitment to public service. His austere style and personal moderation were incompatible with the increasingly right-wing, populist, Christian, and Southern-based Republican movement that comprised so much of Bush's base of support. Powell often revealed ambivalence about his place in this constellation. His support for the Republican Party had less to do with ideology than the party's perceived identification with military values and "strong" national security policies, as well as his loyalty to political mentors dating back to the Nixon administration.

Iraq and the "Fog of War"

Throughout his tenure at the State Department, Powell maintained his disdain for ideologues. Some observers surmised that, to Powell, the shadow of Robert McNamara and his know-it-all whiz kids hovered over the tensions in the administration. His skepticism of civilian hawks, stemming from Vietnam, but also from his years in the Reagan administration, set him apart from Cheney, Rumsfeld, Paul Wolfowitz, and John Bolton.

Powell's qualified support for alliances, treaties, and international institutions also put him at odds with the vice president and secretary of defense, as well as with appointees in his own State Department. His Atlanticism and support for alliances—which he had inherited from his years working with Weinberger and Shultz, his command of V Corps in the NATO forces in West Germany in the mid-1980s, and his stints as national security adviser and chairman of the Joint Chiefs—left him isolated in an administration dubious of the usefulness of European and NATO allies and inclined toward unilateralism.

Powell's military-managerial leadership style served him well at the Pentagon, as national security adviser, as chairman of the Joint Chiefs, and in leading the State Department bureaucracy. But it ultimately left him vulnerable to ideological assaults from administration hard-liners and their surrogates in the right-wing media and think tank community. His preferred method of bureaucratic infighting remained patience and discretion, but his opponents did not play by the same rules, and the loyalty Powell so prized was rarely reciprocated. Clashes between Powell and Rumsfeld grew increasingly bitter. It was usually a one-sided contest: Powell, seeking the high ground, often refused to take his critics' bait. This proved a fatal mistake. In a post–September 11 climate of national hysteria and heightened nationalism, Powell found it increasingly difficult to make a reasoned and nuanced case for diplomacy. After he did weigh in at the United Nations in February 2003 prior to the invasion of Iraq, his arguments were later revealed to have been deeply flawed. Seeking to garner the support of an ambivalent public and skeptical allies, the case for war was stretched perilously thin. Powell, more than anyone else in the administration, put his reputation on the line and made statements that later proved false. Did he truly believe such claims? Did he make faulty assertions based upon bad intelligence? Or was he part of the faction that was determined to go to war regardless of the facts?

Powell's reputation for probity and honesty and much of the credibility he had built up with the public over two decades was badly damaged by his role in making the case for war, a war that proved to be a major departure from his own doctrine and his previously stated beliefs about thorough planning, clarity of mission, cooperation with alliances, public candor, the deployment of overwhelming force, and exit strategies. Ultimately, the so-called Rumsfeld Doctrine of using smaller, lighter units prevailed. Powell's departure from the administration in January 2005 represented a stark admission of defeat, not only for Powell the man but also for his doctrine.

Powell once criticized Lyndon Johnson for deciding, in the midst of the war in Vietnam, not to seek reelection and retiring to Texas. He lamented that "packing it in and going home to the ranch was not an option available to career officers, or to American draftees, for that matter." And yet, in the end, Powell, too, departed during a war, one—largely because of his UN speech—he had done much to initiate, leaving behind 150,000 U.S. troops with no clear resolution in sight.

CHAPTER ONE

~

The Education
of a Soldier, 1937–1980

The first four decades of Colin Powell's life were formative, but it was his experiences in Vietnam, in particular, that shaped his thinking and had the most profound impact on his public career. Although his early years with the Reserve Officers' Training Corp (ROTC) and the U.S. Army are certainly relevant to his story, his two tours in Vietnam, as well as the years immediately following them, began the process of molding the man and shaping his views of the Vietnam Syndrome and what would later come to be called the Powell Doctrine. Moreover, his selection for various war colleges and elite training programs, coupled with his appointments in the Pentagon and other areas of the federal bureaucracy, began the process of Powell's being recognized as an efficient and talented public servant.

Colin Luther Powell was born in Harlem on April 5, 1937, during the Great Depression. He was raised in the Hunts Point neighborhood of the South Bronx. Hunts Point, later depicted as a drug- and gang-ravaged slum in the 1981 film *Fort Apache, The Bronx*, was a decidedly different place during Powell's youth. In the 1940s and 1950s, it was a thriving multicultural community of close-knit families. Powell's father, Luther, came to New York from Jamaica aboard a United Fruit Company steamer in 1920, at the height of the first wave of Jamaican immigration to the United States, which had begun in 1900 and was halted by restrictive legislation in 1924. As many as fifty thousand Jamaicans settled in the United States during that period. Powell's mother, Maud Ariel McCoy, known as "Arie," came from slightly better economic circumstances. She possessed a high school education and had worked in a lawyer's office in Jamaica prior to emigrating. Like many Jamaicans, the family's ethnic mix included some African, English, Irish, Scottish, Arawak Indian, and even Jewish ancestry.[1]

Powell grew up in a tightly woven network of kinship, within a protective circle of immediate and extended family. His mother and father were hardworking immigrants. Although they, like many others, struggled during the Depression and after, by Powell's own admission they were never really in want. Powell attended Morris High School in the South Bronx. Despite his immigrant parents' urgings that he work as hard in school as they did at their jobs, he was a solid C student. He later described himself as a bit of a mamma's boy, lacking in ability and having an aversion to science and math. He dabbled in track and field at Morris High but showed neither a particular aptitude in athletics, nor promise in much of anything else, and later admitted to having been "amenable, amiable, and aimless."[2]

In 1954, he enrolled at City College of New York (CCNY), which had been the gateway to the middle class for generations of immigrants. The campus had been known for leftist sympathies in the decades before Powell's arrival and for its active Socialist, Communist, and Trotskyite groups. Powell was oblivious to this fevered political history. "I went to college for a single reason: my parents expected it," he remembered years later. "I don't recall having had any great urge to get a higher education. I don't even remember consciously thinking the matter through. I just recall that my parents expected it of me. And in those days when your parents expected something, it was what you had to do. In my family, especially, you did what your parents expected of you."[3]

Despite his dislike of science and math, Powell began as an engineering major but immediately encountered difficulties. "My parents said engineering was the best field to choose," he later wrote. "I quickly learned that I had no aptitude for engineering. . . . One hot afternoon, the instructor asked me to visualize a cone intersecting a plane in space. It was at that point that I decided to drop out of engineering." He changed his major to geology because it seemed less daunting. He also enrolled in ROTC. "I had noticed a bunch of fellows wandering around Amsterdam and Convent avenues in uniform," he recalled. "It was the local ROTC detachment. I had a certain interest in the military. My generation, after all, had essentially spent its elementary school years watching World War II and then, after a brief postwar hiatus, its teenage years watching and hearing about the Korean War. So if you were of that generation, the military had made a very indelible impression upon you." Powell recounted that he maintained an average "that barely crept above

'C' (the only way it crept above 'C' was four straight years of 'A' in ROTC, which, thank goodness, counted on your academic record.)"[4]

Powell recognized that CCNY "might not have been West Point," but it did possess the largest ROTC contingent in the United States, with fifteen hundred cadets. Moreover, he had finally discovered something that commanded his interest. He loved the cadets' spit and polish and developed into a good soldier, becoming cadet colonel of the Pershing Rifles during his senior year and graduating first in his ROTC class in 1958. "As an incidental dividend I received a B.S. degree in geology for mastering the rock formations under Manhattan," he observed dryly. "At 21, therefore, I was on my way to the Army."[5]

During ROTC summer training in Fort Bragg, North Carolina, in 1957, Powell experienced his first real encounter with racism. He learned that he had to use toilets marked "colored" and suspected he may have been passed over as "Best Cadet" because of his race. Despite that experience, he had decided on a career in the military. His family needed no further persuasion after he explained the army's generous pensions and benefits. It was a propitious time to enter the Cold War military, which was in the process of building a vast bureaucracy requiring an ever-expanding officer pool. Moreover, President Harry Truman had integrated the armed forces ten years before. Powell acknowledged that the army had become a good place for a young and ambitious black man. "Beginning in the fifties," he later wrote, "less discrimination, a truer merit system, and leveler playing fields existed inside the gates of our military posts than in any Southern city hall or Northern corporation."[6]

After graduation from CCNY, he spent two months in Ranger School at Fort Benning, Georgia. Many of the military's posts were in the South, posing a problem for blacks. The bases were comparative oases, often surrounded by the bigotry and segregation of the pre–Civil Rights South. Powell soon discovered the racial rules of Fort Benning's neighbor, the city of Columbus: he could shop at Woolworth's, but he could not eat at the lunch counter or use the restroom. He could walk the streets but not look at a white woman. Under such circumstances, Powell welcomed his assignment to West Germany as an infantry officer.

Upon returning to the United States in 1960, Powell was assigned to Fort Devens, Massachusetts. The following year, 1961, proved to be a turning point in his life. First, his three years in the army were up. He could have left the military but elected to make it a career. Second, Powell met Alma Johnson, a speech pathologist from Birmingham, Alabama. The two were married in August 1962 and eventually had three children. The year 1961 also marked a turning point for the nation. America had a young new president, John F. Kennedy, in the White House. More importantly, the U.S. commitment to faraway South Vietnam took on a new meaning. Kennedy and his advisers, particularly the president's favorite general and future chairman of the Joint Chiefs, Maxwell Taylor, saw Vietnam as a place to demonstrate the president's inaugural pledge to pay any price and bear any burden in the defense of freedom.

Initially, Kennedy's strategy for supporting South Vietnam included everything short of combat troops, and his administration embraced a doctrine of counterinsurgency. Under Taylor's tutelage, Kennedy grew increasingly enthusiastic about psychological warfare, intelligence gathering, and Special Forces. Powell's training at Fort Bragg and subsequent deployment to South Vietnam reflected these trends in Kennedy's thinking. The Special Forces assumed heightened importance as the vanguard of the New Frontier's efforts to wage the Cold War.

Kennedy, much like his two predecessors and two successors, largely ignored the broader historical forces at work in Southeast Asia that had fueled the war. American policymakers remained baffled by the root causes and historical contexts of the war, such as nationalism and decolonization, and instead tended to see the conflict as part of a global Communist strategy. Many years after the fall of Saigon in 1975, Powell reexamined his own feelings about the war. He concluded that American political leaders had led the country into a war for "the one-size-fits-all rationale of anticommunism, which was only a partial fit in Vietnam, where the war had its own historical roots in nationalism, anticolonialism, and civil strife beyond the East-West conflict."[7]

In 1962, U.S. Special Forces were advising the Army of the Republic of Vietnam in its struggle, not only against the forces of Communist North Vietnam, but also against the North Vietnam–supported insurgency in the South. As a professional soldier, Powell looked forward to his deployment to Vietnam with enthusiasm. Kennedy had raised the U.S. commitment of advisers from thirty-two hundred to eleven thousand, and in 1962 Powell was part of a growing, but still relatively small, mission. He prepared for his new assignment with five weeks of specialized training at Fort Bragg's Unconventional Warfare Center. He arrived in Saigon on Christmas Day 1962, a critical time for the American effort there. Kennedy had dramatically increased U.S. military assistance to the South Vietnamese government of President Ngo Dinh Diem, but Diem's regime proved unsteady and was losing Kennedy and his advisers' confidence.

After what Powell described as an official "indoctrination" in Saigon about the importance of the American endeavor in Vietnam, he arrived in A Shau, a tropical forest along the Laotian border, where he served as an adviser to a South Vietnamese infantry battalion. He essentially commanded a battalion in the Army of the Republic of Vietnam, and his first impression was, "What the hell am I doing here?" The answer to his question had been only partially provided by the briefing in Saigon. But, in a way that aptly encapsulated the absurdity of the American experience in Vietnam, Powell learned the more prosaic reasons why he had been posted to A Shau. When, in January 1963, Powell met Capt. Vo Cong Hieu, the commander of the Second Battalion, the Vietnamese officer explained that A Shau was a "very important post."

"What's its mission?" Powell asked.

"It's a very important outpost," Captain Hieu repeated.

"But why is it here?" Powell persisted.

Hieu explained that the outpost was there to protect an airfield.

"What is the airfield here for?" Powell asked.

The airfield was there, the Captain explained, to protect the outpost.[8]

Years later, Powell bitterly referred to this exchange as symptomatic of the larger problems America faced in Vietnam. He believed that ill-considered and illogical notions conceived in Washington, many of which had scant application in an environment like Vietnam, marked the war. He derisively recalled "the secure-hamlet nonsense, the search-and-sweep nonsense, the body-count nonsense, all of which we knew was nonsense, even as we did it." Powell, who described himself as a "true believer" in the American mission in Vietnam, acknowledged that his anticommunism and staunch support for the war blinded him to the realities of the American involvement.[9]

Frequently under fire during his first tour, Powell was wounded while on patrol when he stepped on a Punji trap—a concealed and camouflaged sharpened stake—which entered his left foot and pushed through the top of his boot. He was awarded the Purple Heart. His first tour ended in November 1963, and he departed Vietnam shortly after the murder of President Diem in a bloody coup. South Vietnam was thereafter wracked by instability. Although Powell could not have known it at the time, Diem's murder set in motion a series of events that deepened the American commitment to South Vietnam and, ultimately, led to Powell's return five years later. "In spite of my misgivings, I was leaving the country still a true believer," he remembered of his first tour. "I had experienced disappointment, not disillusionment. I remained convinced that it was right to help South Vietnam remain independent, and right to draw the line against communism anywhere in the world. The ends were justified, even if the means were flawed."[10]

Powell returned to the United States on November 22, 1963, the day President Kennedy was assassinated in Dallas. His time home between his two tours in Vietnam (he returned to Saigon in July 1968) coincided with most of Lyndon Johnson's presidency. It was a time of significant turmoil in the United States, as the opposition to the war in Vietnam increased and the struggle for black civil rights reached its crescendo. Powell grew painfully aware of the juxtaposition of his service to his country in Vietnam while American blacks struggled at home for the most basic civil and political rights.

He returned to Fort Benning for nearly three years and then was selected in 1967 for the army's Command and General Staff College in Leavenworth, Kansas, where he graduated second out of a class of 1,244. Now a husband and a father of three, Powell felt uneasy as his second Vietnam tour approached. He had little of the enthusiasm and thirst for adventure that had characterized his first assignment. As he prepared for his second tour, the Tet Offensive of January–March 1968 had a devastating impact on how Americans perceived the war, shaking support for the war to its very core. Although technically an American victory, the very fact that the Communist forces could launch such a widespread offensive undermined the Johnson administration's argument that the United States held the upper hand in the conflict.

Powell arrived in Saigon on July 27, 1968. He had the rare experience of participating in two vastly different chapters of the Vietnam War. As a Special Forces adviser with the rank of captain in 1962 and 1963, he represented a key component of Kennedy's Vietnam mission. Returning as a major in 1968, he was part of Johnson's Vietnam misadventure, a different war altogether. He was assigned to the Twenty-third Infantry Division as executive officer of the Third Battalion, First Infantry. The war, and South Vietnam, had been transformed over the previous five years. There had been approximately eleven thousand American troops in Vietnam when he departed in November 1963. Now, only six months after the Tet Offensive, there were five hundred thousand. The streets of Saigon, previously flowing with pedicabs, were now clogged with U.S. Army vehicles. During his first tour, the U.S. presence in South Vietnam was understated. Now, U.S. personnel were everywhere. Powell observed that American barracks, storage depots, airfields, hospitals, and military jails dominated the once-charming colonial city. "Saigon now resembled an American garrison town more than the Paris of the Orient," he remembered. Things had also changed for the American soldier. Approximately twenty-five thousand Americans had already died in Vietnam, but Washington's objectives were no closer to fulfillment. Morale was poor. "Fragging" incidents, where troops killed their own officers, often by tossing a fragmentation grenade near them while they slept, occurred with increasing frequency. As an infantry officer, Powell had legitimate concerns about fragging and made sure not to sleep in the same spot every night. He soon discovered the potential benefits of good press coverage for one's career. This was a lesson he took to heart, and to the top ranks of the army, over the course of the next quarter century. After seeing Powell in an *Army Times* photo of the top Leavenworth graduates, the commanding general of the American Division assigned him to his staff.[11]

His appointment to the American Division was a mixed blessing. American had a reputation as one of the worst divisions in the army. Soon, charges of human rights abuses surfaced. A massacre of Vietnamese villagers by U.S. troops, at My Lai, had occurred in March 1968, several months prior to Powell's return to Vietnam. The division was more interested in crafting a defense against the charges than in investigating the incident. Powell, as the division's deputy operations officer, maintained that relations between U.S. forces and the Vietnamese people were "excellent," and he waved away queries by characterizing My Lai as an isolated instance of abuse.[12] He noted that all new soldiers arriving in South Vietnam received instructions in civic affairs and the importance of treating the Vietnamese with courtesy, as well as another hour-long course on the Geneva conventions and the proper treatment of prisoners. "Although there may be isolated cases of mistreatment of civilians and POWs this by no means reflects the general attitude throughout the division," Powell reported. "In direct refutation of this portrayal is the fact that relations between American soldiers and the Vietnamese people are excellent." Two reporters who investigated the massacre and the army's response to it concluded that Powell's report constituted part of the cover-up and that Powell had demonstrated "all the signs of a soldier who had triumphed in the battle of military paperwork" and "wrote what his superiors clearly wanted to hear."[13]

Since Vietnam is a major part of Colin Powell's story, understanding his views on that war is essential. It is widely acknowledged that Powell's experience in Vietnam profoundly influenced the rest of his career, as well as his approach to the question of American overseas military intervention when he was chairman of the Joint Chiefs and secretary of state. Although all of Powell's biographers have addressed the issue, it is nonetheless difficult to understand the specific impact of his Vietnam experiences fully. His most detailed reflections about Vietnam were written roughly three decades after the events he describes. He was also writing in a radically changed context in the mid-1990s when America had become deeply ambivalent—but also increasingly forgetful—about the war. Powell was certainly influenced as much by the way the war had been perceived and contextualized as by his actual experiences and recollections.

When his memoir appeared in 1995, Powell's comments on the Vietnam War drew much interest, particularly for any insight they provided into his views on intervention and the use of force. Writing two decades after the end of the Vietnam War, Powell sought to demonstrate that he had learned numerous lessons from his Vietnam experiences that had later proved useful to policy making. His views on Vietnam are also relevant because Powell ultimately became, at least between the two wars with Iraq in 1991 and 2003, the recognized public authority on the connection between Vietnam and debates over intervention in the post-Vietnam era. Although, as is explored in the next chapter, the Powell Doctrine owed much to its predecessor, the Weinberger Doctrine, it was Powell, using supposed lessons learned in Vietnam, who often, if inconsistently, sought to play a restraining role in the Bush I, Clinton, and Bush II administrations.

The lessons and legacies of Vietnam have been vehemently debated. The war roiled American society, confronting many Americans with unpleasant realities about their country and the costs and consequences of its foreign and defense policies. There is no agreement even today over why the war happened and its consequences or ultimate meaning. The war was no doubt a turning point in U.S. foreign policy, as the consensus supporting America's Cold War containment strategy had fragmented, and détente emerged as an alternative. There was also much discussion in the years after the war of a "Vietnam Syndrome" that allegedly inhibited American adventurism abroad. Vietnam cast a shadow over the debates about intervention in Central America in the 1980s, the war in the Persian Gulf in 1991, and the conflict in the Balkans in the early 1990s. Recent controversies, such as the occupation of Iraq, have only further complicated the legacy of Vietnam and its supposed "lessons."[14]

The conflict in Vietnam involved five administrations from Truman to Ford, but its consequences and legacies stretched beyond this. It consumed the presidencies of Johnson and Nixon. It divided the Democratic Party on foreign affairs for decades and fueled the political appeal of Ronald Reagan, whose rhetoric was intended to vanquish much of the memory of Vietnam. It also divided American society over who served and exposed stark class and economic differences in a nation that prided itself on its egalitarianism. As the demands for more troops grew, the policy of granting deferments from the draft became increasingly controversial. Many with connections scurried for safe havens. "The whole system of deferments and angles for escaping the fighting may have been technically legal," Powell later wrote. "But it was class-ridden, undemocratic, and unjust."[15]

Powell became especially critical of the way America provided the troops for Vietnam. He believed that the draft's inequalities symbolized the overall unfairness of the way America waged war in Vietnam. "Losses in the war were perceived as if they were happening only to the military and their families," Powell wrote. "They were not seen as sacrifices shared by the country for a common purpose, as in other wars."[16] Favoritism also reigned in determining the highly sought after slots in the National Guard, which was almost a guarantee of remaining stateside. African Americans comprised only 1 percent of Army National Guardsmen. Powell asserted that "the policies determining who would be drafted and who would be deferred, who would serve and who would escape, who would die and who would live—were an antidemocratic disgrace." He remained angry that so many of the sons of the "powerful and well placed" wrangled slots in reserve and National Guard units.[17]

Powell believed "the military failed to talk straight to its political superiors or to itself. The top leadership never went to the Secretary of Defense or the President and said, 'This war is unwinnable the way we are fighting it.' Many of my generation, the career captains, majors, the lieutenant colonels seasoned in that war, vowed that when our turn came to call the shots, we would not quietly acquiesce in halfhearted warfare for half-baked reasons that the American people could not understand or support. If we could make good on that promise to ourselves, to the civilian leadership, and to the country, then the sacrifices of Vietnam would not have been in vain."[18]

Powell lamented that the Johnson administration sought to fight the war in Vietnam with as little inconvenience to the country as possible. "Taxes to finance the war had not been raised. Better-off kids beat the draft with college deferments." He acknowledged that the United States had seriously misunderstood its adversary in Vietnam and had underestimated its will to fight and its true war aims. Moreover, the United States had severely limited its prospects in Vietnam by misusing intelligence and failing to understand Vietnamese society. The military and civilian leadership had "bowed to groupthink pressure and kept up the pretenses, the phony measure of body counts, the comforting illusion of secure hamlets, the inflated progress reports."[19]

Powell has inferred that the war might have been winnable from a military standpoint. This is paradoxical because he also observed that U.S. officials failed to see that the war had causes beyond communism, such as nationalism and anticolonialism. He never addressed how the United States could have prevailed in a war where the other side was motivated by such factors. His critique of the conflict assumed that, if America had fully mobilized to win, had been more forthright with the public, and had done more to give the American people a better sense of the mission in Vietnam, the outcome could have been more favorable for the United States. He overlooked, however, the possibility that had all of these things been done, the American people might have become even more dubious about U.S. involvement in Vietnam.

Powell later wrote that he learned from his Vietnam experience that war should be "the politics of last resort." He believed that if the United States did go to war, it should be for reasons that the American people could support. The country should fully mobilize its resources to fulfill that mission "and then go in to win." In Vietnam, he argued, "we had entered into a halfhearted half-war, with much of the nation opposed or indifferent, while a small fraction carried the burden." He lamented that "you do not squander courage and lives without clear purpose, without the country's backing, and without full commitment."[20] At the same time, Powell's critique focused narrowly on the decision making of the military, the relationship between the military and the civilian leadership, and the ways the military failed to fight the war to win. Never does he venture beyond this critique to examine the broader implications of America's Cold War containment policy in Vietnam.

Powell returned stateside in 1969 and received permission to enter the MBA program at George Washington University, graduating in May 1971. He was next assigned to the Pentagon as an aide to the vice chief of staff of the army. The army was enduring a historic crisis, and it was an interesting time to be at the Pentagon. Gen. Maxwell Taylor had quipped that the army had been sent to Vietnam to save that nation, but the army had to be withdrawn in order to save the army. Nixon was pursuing the strategy of "Vietnamization" by which the United States began to turn the primary responsibility for fighting the war over to the Army of the Republic of South Vietnam. To a veteran like Powell, who had been involved in training the South Vietnamese forces in 1962 and 1963, it was frustratingly obvious that the U.S. effort in Vietnam had come full circle.

While he was at the Pentagon, a study conducted by the Army War College surveyed five hundred lieutenant colonels who had served in Vietnam. The survey revealed harsh criticisms of the senior army leadership as being out of touch and unable to face its failures. The colonels depicted an army beset by racial strife, generational differences, and disciplinary problems.

That the army was on its way to becoming an all-volunteer force by 1973 reflected the depths of the crisis provoked by the problems of the Vietnam-era draft. Most of the nation's elite had avoided service in Vietnam, while those drafted tended to be the least powerful and least connected. Powell's new boss, Gen. William E. DePuy, was in the vanguard of reformers who sought to recreate the army out of the crisis of Vietnam. As head of the Army's Training and Doctrine Command, he wanted reforms in structure, leadership, and ethical climate. DePuy had gathered some of the most promising lieutenant colonels as a kind of brain trust. Powell had expected to be installing computer systems in the Pentagon. Instead, as an analyst on the general's staff, "I was exposed at a key point in my career to the Army's best and brightest."[21]

DePuy ordered Powell and his colleagues to "start thinking the unthinkable"—a restructuring of the army to only five hundred thousand troops. Powell and his fellow officers were astonished. The suggestion seemed draconian. The army had not numbered that few since 1940. In the Vietnam theater alone, the military had deployed 543,000 troops. Although the army never had to face the radical cuts DePuy and others had anticipated, it did see a major reduction of its overall troop strength from a high of 1.6 million at the height of Vietnam to just under 800,000. Working for DePuy had a huge impact on Powell. "Just as the Army retrenched in the wake of Vietnam, all of the armed forces would have to contract after the Cold War ended," he wrote. "When faced with this reality as Chairman of the Joint Chiefs of Staff, I had already completed my graduate education in force-cutting twenty years before under Bill DePuy."[22]

Powell's biggest career break came when he was selected for the prestigious White House Fellows program for 1972. Although Powell showed little initial interest in the program and his superiors in the Pentagon had to order him to apply, his application made the case that, owing largely to Vietnam, the American military had become alienated from the American people. As an example of this, Powell need have looked no further than his alma mater, City College of New York, where the ROTC program, which once had been the largest in the country with fifteen hundred cadets, had dwindled to only eighty-one by 1972 and was subsequently discontinued.

Through the White House Fellows program, Powell, a self-described "fledgling student of power," learned not only how government worked but how he could work the government to advance his career. Shrewdly anticipating that budgeting would prove crucial to the future army, he was assigned to the Office of Management and Budget (OMB). Beyond the prestige of obtaining the fellowship and the advantages such an opportunity could confer on his career, Powell made numerous professional contacts, including Frank Carlucci, then deputy to OMB director Caspar Weinberger, known as "Cap the Knife" for his budget-cutting prowess. "The people I had met during that year [shaped] my future in ways unimaginable to me then," Powell wrote. He also learned valuable lessons about working in the federal bureaucracy and completed the fellowship convinced that government service often entails compromise: "People have to trade, change, deal, retreat, bend, compromise, as they move from the ideal to the possible."[23]

Perhaps the most valuable part of Powell's fellowship year was the trips throughout the United States and the world, including to the Soviet Union and China. These trips, particularly those to Communist countries, softened some of his more simplistic views. He claimed to have discovered "the common humanity of all people" and that the peoples of the Soviet Union, for example, were "not political ideologues. They were the Soviet equivalent of my own family, a mother buying groceries for supper, a tired father heading home after a hard day at the ministry mailroom, kids thinking more about the soccer prospects of Moscow against Kiev than about spreading Marxism globally."[24]

During a trip to Atlanta with the fellows program, Powell met Georgia governor Jimmy Carter. He was impressed when the "boyish forty-nine-year-old with a blinding smile" mesmerized the fellows with his vision of the New South. For Powell, who had endured his own unpleasant experiences in the South and whose previous conceptions of Southern politicians ran from Bull Conner to George Wallace to Lester Maddox, Carter represented a new vision of the South and the country. This memory of the Georgia governor stayed with Powell, and he voted for Carter for president in 1976.[25]

Powell returned to military duty after the fellowship, commanding a battalion of seven hundred in Korea, but was soon recalled to the Pentagon. He then spent part of 1975 at the National War College at Fort McNair, where, only months after the fall of Saigon, significant soul-searching was underway. Powell, too, thought about what went wrong in Vietnam. While reading Carl von Clausewitz, the nineteenth-century military theorist, he discovered confirmation for many of the things he believed about Vietnam. He was particularly taken by von Clausewitz's comment that "no one starts a war, or rather no one in his sense should do, without first being clear in his mind what he intends to achieve by that war and how he intends to achieve it." ("Mistake number one in Vietnam," Powell thought.) This led to von Clausewitz's second rule: political leaders must set a war's objectives, while armies achieve them. "In Vietnam," Powell observed, "one seemed to be looking to the other for the answers that never came. Finally, the people must support a war. Since they supply the treasure and the sons, and today the daughters too, they must be convinced that the sacrifice is justified. That essential pillar had crumbled as the Vietnam War ground on."[26]

After graduation from the National War College in 1976, Powell took command of the Second Brigade of the 101st Airborne Division at Fort Campbell, Kentucky, where he commanded three battalions, totaling more than twenty-five hundred troops. But soon he was back inside the Beltway. He returned to Washington at an opportune time for a young and ambitious officer. Moreover, he observed that many of the officers he served with were older than he, having already peaked professionally, lacking the breaks, the good timing, or the sheer luck that he had enjoyed. Despite the perception of retrenchment in the wake of Vietnam, the postwar army offered numerous opportunities for young officers like Powell. This was made possible by ever-increasing defense budgets, the growing professionalization of the military, the expansion of the pool of officers, and the increasing employment of military officers in many parts of the federal bureaucracy. Opportunities continued to arise. In early 1977, somewhat to his astonishment, he was interviewed by Carter's national security adviser, Zbigniew Brzezinski, for a job with the National Security Council. He instead joined the Office of the Secretary of Defense as special assistant to Harold Brown. The secretary of the army, Clifford Alexander, the first African American ever to hold the position, tripled the number of black generals during his tenure, and in December 1978, Powell received a promotion to brigadier general. Powell had become the youngest general in the army at forty-one. After a brief stint in the Department of Energy, he returned to the Pentagon in 1979, becoming, after 1981, an aid to Frank Carlucci, who held the number two job at the Pentagon under Reagan's new secretary of defense, Caspar Weinberger.

At this point in his career, Powell had had an opportunity to observe and learn from a variety of leaders and leadership styles in both the military and civilian sectors. Wisely, he did not seek to emulate the flamboyant, Patton-esque style, which was not suited to his temperament. Powell's approach remained low-key, seeking to balance authority and persuasion. He had once been told by one of his superior officers that he was not likely to have a conventional army career.[27] Although Powell always worried about being perceived as a political officer, he was becoming that species of general, not unlike Gen. Alexander Haig. Although their styles and personalities were vastly different, Haig had in some ways paved the way for Powell's rapid ascent through the bureaucracy.

Powell was the youngest general in the army, but his future career path was hardly guaranteed. His rise to national prominence required a number of additional lucky breaks, as Powell himself has acknowledged. First, his past association with Weinberger and Carlucci led to his appointment as Carlucci's assistant in 1981 and his return to the Pentagon as Weinberger's military aide in 1983. The fallout from the Iran-Contra scandal led to his return from military duty to become Carlucci's deputy at the National Security Council in 1986. Moreover, Weinberger's retirement in October 1987 led to Carlucci's becoming secretary of defense and Powell's replacing him as national security adviser.

These first forty-four years of Powell's life provided the template for his meteoric rise over the next two decades. His Jamaican origins and ROTC background afforded him a critical distinctiveness. His distinguished service in Vietnam set him apart from most of those with whom he would be working over the next two decades. Few senior appointees in the Reagan, Bush I, Clinton, and Bush II administrations had served in Vietnam, and it became apparent that even many from Powell's own generation had studiously avoided combat. While Powell's service in Vietnam set him apart, it was what he ultimately made of that experience that distinguished him from other veterans of that war. His Vietnam years became the foundation of the Powell Doctrine, and later his Vietnam experiences also provided him with examples for selectively advocating against interventions during the Bush I and Clinton administrations, though, curiously, less so in the Bush II administration. Moreover, Powell's tenure in the federal bureaucracy in the 1970s established the professional patterns and connections that would serve him so well in the Reagan administration throughout the 1980s. Gradually, owing to his contacts and reputation, he rose through the Reagan administration, seen as a figure known for his moderation and competence during a presidency that was often lacking in both.

Notes

1. Quoted in Colin Powell, *My American Journey* (New York: Ballantine, 1995, 2003), 8.

2. Quoted in Powell, *My American Journey*, 12.

3. Powell to Hank Cohen, October 7, 1988, with attachment: Powell draft speech to CCNY alumni, folder 10, box 92477, Powell files, Ronald Reagan Presidential Library.

4. Powell to Hank Cohen: draft speech to CCNY alumni.

5. Powell to Hank Cohen: draft speech to CCNY alumni.

6. Quoted in Powell, *My American Journey*, 61.

7. Quoted in Powell, *My American Journey*, 144.

8. Quoted in Powell, *My American Journey*, 78–79.

9. Powell, *My American Journey*, 84–85, 100–101.

10. Quoted in Powell, *My American Journey*, 101.

11. Powell, *My American Journey*, 126–29.

12. James Mann, *Rise of the Vulcans: The History of Bush's War Cabinet* (New York: Viking Press, 2004), 43.

13. Quoted in Michael Bilton and Kevin Sim, *Four Hours at My Lai* (New York: Penguin, 1992), 213.

14. Robert K. Brigham, *Is Iraq Another Vietnam?* (New York: Public Affairs, 2006), 149–67; Lloyd C. Gardner and Marilyn B. Young, eds., *Iraq and the Lessons of Vietnam: Or, How Not to Learn from the Past* (New York: The New Press, 2007).

15. Powell, *My American Journey*, 566.

16. Quoted in Powell, *My American Journey*, 125, 128.

17. Quoted in Powell, *My American Journey*, 144.

18. Quoted in Powell, *My American Journey*, 143–45.

19. Powell, *My American Journey*, 122, 142–44.

20. Powell, *My American Journey*, 143–44.

21. Powell, *My American Journey*, 151.

22. Powell, *My American Journey*, 152.

23. Powell, *My American Journey*, 161–72.

24. Powell, *My American Journey*, 165.

25. Powell, *My American Journey*, 166.

26. Quoted in Powell, *My American Journey*, 200.

27. Powell, *My American Journey*, 221.

CHAPTER TWO

~

From the Pentagon to the White House, 1980–1987

Colin Powell's career has been closely associated with the Powell Doctrine as well as with the so-called Vietnam Syndrome—the assertion that in later years America and its policymakers were reluctant to use military force owing to fears aroused by the fallout from Vietnam. In his 1995 memoir, Powell explained in detail how Vietnam, or the Vietnam Syndrome, shaped his beliefs about the uses of American power. As a result of the Vietnam Syndrome (particularly after the end of the Cold War between 1989 and 1990), many anticipated that America would have fewer rationales for defense spending or military interventions. Yet, actual events after the fall of Saigon, particularly after Ronald Reagan's election in 1980—a period of increasing foreign intervention and the use of force—raise questions over whether a Vietnam Syndrome actually existed.[1]

The American electorate in 1980 opted for the candidate who pledged to reverse the trends of the half-decade following the end of the Vietnam War. Between the Reagan administration's September 1982 decision to intervene in the Lebanese civil war with twelve hundred U.S. Marines and the war in Iraq, which began in 2003, the United States had been involved in numerous military interventions or confrontations. Powell played some role in nearly all of them. He was a military aide to Secretary of Defense Caspar Weinberger during the early years of Reagan's effort to overthrow the Nicaraguan government (1981–1988), the bombing of the U.S. Marines barracks in Lebanon (1983), the invasion of Grenada (1983), and the air strikes against Libya (1986). He was national security adviser during the latter part of the ongoing proxy war with Nicaragua and the naval confrontations in the Persian Gulf with Iran (1987–1988). He was chairman of the Joint Chiefs during the invasion of Panama (1989), the first war with Iraq (1991), the dispatch of U.S. forces to Somalia (1992–1993), and the initial debates over whether to intervene in the former Yugoslavia (1992–1993). And he was secretary of state during the beginnings of the wars in Afghanistan (2001) and Iraq (2003).

During the years of Powell's service as a senior official, running from his appointment as national security adviser in 1987 to his resignation as secretary of state in 2004, the United States cited threats that served to justify new weapons systems, continuing high levels of military spending, and overseas interventions. These threats ostensibly provided compelling justifications for interventions even in the years after the demise of the Soviet Union and the end of the Cold War. Moreover, many of these interventions demonstrated the public support and political advantage presidents could manufacture by resorting to force as commander in chief.

Reagan pursued a foreign policy largely based upon the restoration of American military power. Although Reagan held strong instincts about world affairs, and during political campaigns conveyed convictions, he was often uninterested in policy details and lacked sufficient focus or knowledge to give subordinates clear directions. According to his first secretary of state, Gen. Alexander Haig (1981–1982), Reagan's real thoughts about his own foreign policy were difficult to know. Owing to Reagan's detached managerial style, his foreign policy appointees exerted more influence than in previous administrations. It initially seemed as if General Haig would emerge (as he once memorably described himself) as the "vicar" of Reagan's foreign policy. The former protégé of Henry Kissinger, apparently with Reagan's encouragement, made a bid for leadership of the administration's foreign policy.[2] Instead of Haig's becoming the dominant figure, intense infighting ensued among senior officials. Haig lamented that he could rarely get near enough to Reagan to discuss matters with him in any depth, and when he did, Reagan revealed little. Haig discovered that Reagan was incurious about foreign policy and had little understanding of the connection between presidential ideas and the formulation of policies to carry them out. To Haig's rising anger and frustration, he often learned of new initiatives through the newspapers. Reagan's foreign policy advisers regularly pursued their own objectives; as a result, the Central Intelligence Agency and the National Security Council launched their own foreign policies. Freelancers of various sorts were attractive to the president, provoking, in the words of Reagan's third national security adviser, Robert McFarlane, "guerilla warfare within the administration" as every official "tried to put his personal agenda in front of the President."[3]

By the summer of 1982—only a little more than sixteen months into the administration—Reagan already had a new national security adviser and a new secretary of state. Years before the revelations about the Iran-Contra controversy, foreign diplomats in Washington fretted that they could not recall a comparable degree of foreign policy chaos. Even McFarlane acknowledged that the administration's foreign policy and national security machinery were effectively useless. This drift continued under Haig's successor, George Shultz, who waged bureaucratic warfare against other senior officials. The defense buildup, heavy emphasis on covert operations, and alarmist ideological rhetoric about the Cold War hardly constituted a foreign policy—for which some feared that covert operations had become a substitute.[4] Ideological obsessions tended to disfigure the administration's worldview. What should have been relatively minor concerns—such as Nicaragua and Lebanon—loomed increasingly large, making it difficult to distinguish among genuine national interests as opposed to mere ideological fixations.

The Vietnam Syndrome and the Evolution of the Powell Doctrine

Powell began the Reagan years at the Pentagon, reunited with Frank Carlucci from his White House fellowship years. Carlucci was serving as deputy secretary of defense to the new defense secretary, Caspar Weinberger, a diminutive San Francisco–bred lawyer who had become the steward of the largest peacetime defense buildup in world history. Weinberger also became one of the most important backers of Powell's career. Shortly after Reagan's election, the new secretary of the army, John Marsh, offered Powell the post of undersecretary of the army. Powell was dubious of Marsh's intentions. He noted that Marsh "hoped to place a qualified minority executive in a senior position in an organization composed almost of 40 percent minority soldiers." Instead, Powell decided to remain Carlucci's aide until the spring of 1981, when he returned to military duty.[5] "Was Colin Powell exceptional?" former secretary of the army, Clifford Alexander, recalled. "No. There were a number of black generals who were equally as good as Colin Powell. By working in the Pentagon, he was visible to the Republican leadership. And Colin, who is smart and competent, did quite well, in part because of proximity."[6]

Reagan's new militarism was in many ways a response to the Vietnam Syndrome, but the defense buildup may have been based on several miscalculations rather than a coherent strategic vision. Reagan had pledged to outspend the Carter administration on defense. During the 1980 campaign, he spoke ominously of a "window of vulnerability" between Soviet and U.S. capabilities. This charge, although a campaign tactic later revealed to be untrue, nonetheless sparked enthusiasm throughout the Pentagon bureaucracy. Powell believed that Vietnam had created a breach between the U.S. military and the American people and that the Reagan-era buildup would contribute to healing that division. He thought the Carter administration had let America's defenses slide and that Reagan would restore order and prestige to American foreign policy and the armed forces. Despite Carter's providing the then unimaginable sum of $134 billion for defense in his final budget, Powell contended that the military suffered from poor morale and underfunding.

Weinberger, who had earned the nickname "Cap the Knife" as a budget-slashing head of the Office of Management and Budget in the Nixon administration, transformed himself into "Cap the Shovel" by obtaining more than had been budgeted for the Pentagon. Powell described the budget increases of Reagan's first year as "Christmas in February." He recalled, "The chiefs began submitting wish lists. . . . They went from their wish lists to their dream lists, pulling out proposals they never expected to see in the light of day. The latest figures went to the Office of Management and Budget, and the word came back, not enough. OMB's conclusion was based on no strategic analysis; the Reagan White House was simply telling the Pentagon to spend more money. The military happily obeyed. Manna, they realized, does not fall from heaven every day."[7]

Defense spending nearly doubled, but often the spending was not related to a larger, coherent strategy. Pentagon scholar Dale Herspring has concluded that "the somewhat incoherent fashion in which the money was allocated meant that a considerable part of it was wasted. . . . Ultimately, one could argue that the armed forces were in equally bad shape when Reagan left office as when he entered, even if some of the equipment and weapons were newer."[8] Powell observed that even First Lady Nancy Reagan began to see Weinberger's enthusiasm for unrestrained defense spending as a liability to Reagan's legacy.[9]

Powell left the Pentagon in 1981 for an assignment as an assistant division commander at Fort Carson, Colorado, an apprenticeship for command of a full division. He was devastated when his superiors at Fort Carson described him in their evaluations as someone with a bright future as a "staff officer" or "trainer" rather than as a commander of troops. His evaluators concluded that he had the makings of a "staff officer in a major command headquarters" but that he was not suited for a top command. They considered this "more Colin's forte than command at this time." Although stung by this assessment, after a stint at Fort Leavenworth, he returned to the Pentagon in the summer of 1983 to serve as Weinberger's military aide, emerging as an influential adviser to the secretary of defense.[10]

According to Carlucci, Powell became one of the few people in all of Washington who could persuade the stubborn Weinberger to change his mind. For the next three years, Powell had an insider's perspective on the battles for control of Reagan's foreign policy, ostensibly a valuable education for a self-described student of power. Some observers believed the clash between Shultz and Weinberger was one of the nastiest in recent Washington history. Fascinated by the way they vied for power, Powell watched, sometimes with amusement, sometimes in dismay, the constant plotting and infighting. Observers remembered that the Shultz-Weinberger rivalry went beyond normal Washington enmities. McFarlane, a witness to numerous Washington turf wars dating back to the Nixon administration, believed the Shultz-Weinberger struggle to be the worst he had seen, describing it as "extreme, endemic and ultimately corrosive."[11]

Many presumed the defense buildup would help avoid the possible deployment of U.S. forces. This proved illusory. The large increases in military spending had brought Washington no closer to resolving the question of when to use military force. On the contrary, the buildup may have created new pressures for interventions as a means of demonstrating the Pentagon's worth. The debates within the administration over whether to intervene in tiny Lebanon in 1982, for example, were some of the most bitter, in part because they pitted Weinberger against Shultz. Because Reagan rarely offered a clear sense of what he desired in Lebanon, various departments and agencies clashed violently over the preferred policy. Beirut became the focal point of several Reagan-era foreign policy blunders. Developments there led to the ill-conceived deployment of U.S. Marines, along with an aerial and naval bombardment of the city of Beirut and its environs. At the urging of McFarlane and Shultz, although strongly opposed by Weinberger, twelve hundred U.S. Marines were deployed to Beirut in September 1982, ostensibly to provide peacekeeping but also to establish an American military presence. In hindsight, Powell believed that the lessons of Vietnam had gone unheeded. He was scornful of the rationales for the deployment, believing the troops had been dispatched "for the fuzzy idea of providing a 'presence.'"[12]

The administration drifted into dangerous waters, taking sides in a civil war and aggressively backing Israel's Lebanese Christian allies. At Shultz's urging, Reagan agreed to air strikes and a naval bombardment of Beirut, destroying completely the cover of the Marines, who were there to form part of a mere "presence mission," not, as it turned out, to take part in a Lebanese civil war. McFarlane persuaded Reagan to have an offshore American battleship, the *New Jersey*, begin firing sixteen-inch shells into the neighborhoods of Beirut, aiming to punish the Shiite population of the city. Powell believed this made little sense militarily. He recalled in dismay that these artillery barrages were carried out "World War II style, as if we were softening up the beaches on some Pacific atoll prior to an invasion."[13]

The deployment to Lebanon led to the attack on the U.S. Marine barracks when, on October 23, 1983, a truck loaded with twelve thousand pounds of TNT exploded, killing 241 Marines while they slept in their barracks, a death toll that constituted 20 percent of the entire deployment. "What we tend to overlook in such situations is that other people will react much as we would," Powell shrewdly observed of the Beirut debacle. "When shells started falling on the Shiites, they assumed the American 'referee' had taken sides against them. And since they could not reach the battleship, they found a more vulnerable target, the exposed Marines at the airport."[14] Following the bombing, several Americans living in Beirut were taken hostage, including the CIA station chief, William Buckley. The administration grew increasingly desperate to free Buckley, whose capture threatened to pull back the veil on covert operations in the region, including an ill-conceived CIA-sponsored hostage-taking scheme. The Reagan administration's efforts to obtain the release of the hostages led to the launching of the secretive Iran-Contra initiative that supplied Iran with weaponry and directed part of the profits to the Contras fighting to overthrow the left-leaning Sandinista government in Nicaragua.[15]

The Lebanon debacle provided another important chapter in Colin Powell's education. He later wrote that "the shattered bodies of Marines at the Beirut airport were never far from my mind in arguing for caution." Feeling strongly that lives should not be risked unnecessarily in the service of vague goals, Powell believed civilian officials should ask themselves whether they could face the families of dead soldiers and explain to them that they had died as a symbol of American strength or to provide a "presence."[16] In response to calls for the withdrawal of the remaining Marines, Reagan and Shultz objected that an evacuation would "allow the terrorists to win." Nonetheless, after several months, Reagan announced in February 1984 that U.S. forces were not being "withdrawn" but merely "redeployed" out of Lebanon. "It was one of the worst defeats of the Reagan administration," McFarlane recalled.[17]

As officials in Washington scrambled to limit the fallout from the debacle in Lebanon, the subsequent U.S. invasion of the tiny Caribbean island of

Grenada provided cover. At the time of the invasion, Grenada was an island of eighty-four thousand people, defended by a poorly armed militia of two thousand, with no navy, no airpower, and no means of resisting an invasion. What had raised the hackles of the Reagan administration? Grenada, hoping to attract more tourism by expanding its runways to allow for larger planes, had invited a Cuban construction battalion to aid in the building of an international airport. Shultz and Weinberger deemed Grenada a potential beachhead for Cuban expansion in the Caribbean, and the Pentagon recognized that the island was no match for the mightiest military power in the world, now in the third year of a defense buildup. Considering Grenada's size and its nonexistent defenses, it should have been an easy operation. Instead, it took a week to subdue resistance on the island, with many problems owing to poor planning and preparation in the Pentagon and bitter interservice rivalries. Excellent media management obscured many of these problems, and the invasion was covered in positive, strongly patriotic hues. The public euphoria that greeted the invasion also distracted attention from the Beirut debacle. "The invasion of Grenada was a perfect opportunity," observed David Ignatius of the *Washington Post*. "It allowed Reagan to win one in near-perfect laboratory conditions and thereby erase some of the bad taste left by the bombing of the Marine headquarters in Beirut the same week."[18] Moreover, Grenada turned out to be astonishingly good public relations. With a media blackout in place, reporters simply ran wild with whatever scant information the Pentagon parceled out. The resulting coverage increasingly equated the invasion of Grenada with the 1944 Allied assault on Normandy and anticipated the coverage of the Gulf War of 1991. Lost in the celebration was the fate of Grenada itself, where the subsequent American promotion of "democracy" included $675,000 from the CIA to bolster pro-U.S. parties on the island.[19]

Perhaps most importantly to the White House, public opinion polls demonstrated that the invasion of Grenada had sufficiently distracted the American people from the debacle in Beirut and that Reagan had not suffered any political damage from the failure of the Middle Eastern deployment. On the contrary, Grenada, not Beirut, became a major part of Ronald Reagan's legacy. An outpouring of nationalism followed the invasion, and a wave of popular culture played on the American desire to stand tall in the world. Reagan and his advisers skillfully tapped into this with appeals to patriotism. Most of this amounted to little more than Cold War agitprop, but Grenada was yet another step in reshaping America's self-image after Vietnam.[20] Much of the popular culture of the 1980s—including the Tom Clancy novels, the movie *Top Gun*, and the Chuck Norris films—revealed a strident nationalism, tapping undercurrents of unresolved anger about the American defeat in Vietnam. The series of *Rambo* films starring Sylvester Stallone were emblematic of this genre, bringing to the big screen Reagan's revisionist rhetoric regarding Vietnam.[21]

Many in the administration came to believe that a mere reassertion of American power would reestablish America's place in the world. But it remained unclear precisely what senior officials thought about the vexing question of intervention in the wake of Vietnam. Most officials supported military intervention if there was a strong probability of complete success, such as in tiny Grenada. Other situations, such as the intervention in Lebanon and the debate over whether to commit U.S. forces to Nicaragua, demonstrated a reluctance to use force in areas where the United States could not guarantee success. Grenada did not distract everyone from the tragedy in Beirut, and the Lebanon debacle prompted serious rethinking in Washington, particularly by the sober-minded Weinberger, who had been deeply shaken by the large loss of life. "I've never seen Cap look as sad as he did after the Marines were killed," Powell recalled.[22]

Weinberger sought to use the tragedy in Beirut to lay down a series of rules—ultimately known as the "Weinberger Doctrine"—for the deployment of American forces. Weinberger sought to put the brakes on the growing enthusiasm for militarism that had emerged from the Grenada invasion. For Weinberger, building up America's defenses was one thing, but using American forces for adventurism abroad was another matter altogether. Dismissive of Weinberger's concerns, Shultz thought he was letting the Vietnam Syndrome paralyze him. Shultz called instead for an aggressive antiterrorism policy, including military interventions. But Weinberger regretted that he had not been more adamant about the removal of the Marines. "I was not persuasive enough to persuade the President that the Marines were there on an impossible mission," Weinberger recalled. "When that horrible tragedy came, I took it very personally and still feel responsible in not having been persuasive enough to overcome the arguments that 'Marines don't cut and run,' and 'We can't leave because we're there,' and all of that."[23] Weinberger had wanted to address this shortly after the October 1983 Beirut bombing, but the White House feared reminding people of the debacle during the 1984 presidential campaign.

In late November 1984, three weeks after Reagan's landslide reelection, Powell accompanied Weinberger to the National Press Club, where the secretary, in what he believed was his most important speech, offered six criteria designed to avoid debacles like Vietnam and Lebanon. It was an astonishing speech for any secretary of defense, particularly the U.S. official most closely associated with the Reagan-era defense buildup. First, Weinberger argued, the United States should commit forces only if the United States' or its allies' vital interests were at stake. Second, if the United States decided it had to commit forces, it should do so with all the resources necessary to win. Third, U.S. forces should be deployed only with clear military and political objectives. Fourth, American officials should be ready to change the commitment if the objectives changed. Fifth, the armed forces should be asked only to take on commitments that could gain the support of the American people and the Congress. And, sixth, U.S. forces should be committed only as a last resort.[24]

Powell took many of the Weinberger strictures to heart when he became chairman of the Joint Chiefs under Bush I and Clinton. Powell noted that

Figure 2.1. Powell meets with National Security Adviser Adm. John Poindexter, while President Reagan and White House Chief of Staff Donald Regan look on, February 20, 1986. At the time this photo was taken, Poindexter and Don Regan were deeply immersed in the labyrinthine details of what would become known as the Iran-Contra scandal, where the administration secretly dispatched arms to Iran's Ayatollah Khomeini in exchange for the release of hostages held in Lebanon. The scandal would lead to the resignation of both Regan and Poindexter and a yearlong investigation of the scheme's complicated details. It would also bring President Reagan to the brink of ruin. The scandal would directly benefit Powell by provoking widespread personnel changes in the Reagan White House and forcing the restoration of a more moderate and professional national security team. Photo credit: Ronald Reagan Presidential Library.

"in the future, when it became my responsibility to advise the president on committing our forces to combat, Weinberger's rules turned out to be a practical guide."[25] In time, Weinberger's parentage of the rules was forgotten, as the media increasingly referred to them as the "Powell Doctrine." Powell understood that Vietnam remained a shadow over the entire Lebanon debacle. "Weinberger was a lot like Reagan," Powell told *Washington Post* reporter Lou Cannon, "in that World War II was wonderful, all the soldiers were brave and honorable, all the sisters were virtuous and the American people were singing songs and honorable. Then Vietnam, yuck, because these six tests had not been met with respect to vital interest, national purpose, people behind us and all of that. [Weinberger] never wanted to ever preside over anything like a Vietnam involvement by U.S. forces, whereas [Shultz] saw the U.S. forces as a flexible tool of diplomacy. Why do we pay for all this stuff if we can never use it short of World War III? The answer was somewhere [in] between. . . . But Beirut wasn't sensible and never did serve a purpose. It was goofy from the beginning."[26]

The Consequences of Iran-Contra: Powell's Rise

Powell's political skills were becoming formidable. Owing to his service to the secretary of defense, and despite his poor performance review at Fort Carson, he used his Washington connections to skip a division command and go directly to commanding a corps, V Corps, in Germany. This appointment also allowed him to leave Washington at precisely the right time, just as the Iran-Contra initiative was gathering momentum. Although he admitted he felt uneasy about skipping a division and going directly to a corps, he saw it as an opportunity to erase the memory of the performance rating he had received at Fort Carson. "I was determined to prove that I was an able commanding general and not a Pentagon-bred political general."[27] But, once again, the political dimension of Powell's career prevailed, and he was summoned back to Washington, this time to assist in rebuilding the National Security Council after the most damaging scandal of the Reagan era.

The Iran-Contra affair is a significant part of Powell's story. It led to a Reagan administration housecleaning and cleared the path for Powell's rise. Not only did the fallout from the scandal bring him back to Washington from Germany in December 1986 to serve as deputy to the new NSC adviser, Frank Carlucci's, but it also facilitated Powell's promotion to national security adviser himself less than a year later, in November 1987. "If it hadn't been for Iran-Contra," he later admitted, "I'd still be an obscure general somewhere. Retired, never heard of."[28] In the broader history of American foreign policy, Iran-Contra is an example of White House foreign policy making gone disastrously wrong. In 1981, Reagan had pledged to return to a cabinet form of government. In reality, what transpired was administrative anarchy, with officials following their own paths, often without the knowledge of the president. The Iran-Contra affair was also a response to the Vietnam Syndrome and the Weinberger Doctrine. In reaction to Weinberger's criteria, various officials turned to covert operations and a reliance upon surrogates to achieve their foreign policy objectives. The NSC and the CIA took foreign policy into their own hands, something both agencies proved ill equipped to do.

The administration's curious fixation on relatively small matters such as Nicaragua and Lebanon often grew into huge crises, overwhelming policymakers and often subordinating other issues, like relations with the USSR and China and the pursuit of peace in the Middle East. Reagan described Nicaragua, a tiny Central American republic of only 4.5 million people, as a Soviet, or even terrorist, beachhead, a "second Libya right on the doorsteps" of the United States, and a "safehouse, a command post for international terror." As Reagan's public statements about Nicaragua became increasingly apocalyptic, the CIA carried out its own foreign policy and covert operations throughout Central America.[29]

Iran was another obsession. Reagan had railed publicly against making deals with terrorists, and Shultz claimed the administration had been a leader in stopping international arms sales to Iran. Nevertheless, in the vain hope of achieving progress on freeing the hostages held in Beirut, Reagan authorized the sale of weapons to Iran in the hope that Iran would wield influence over the Shiites of Lebanon. Further complicating matters, Iran was engaged in a ghastly death struggle with neighboring Iraq, and Reagan had also been supplying Iraq's Saddam Hussein with materiel and intelligence. Reagan was thus assisting both Iran and Iraq—although both were seen as adversaries of the United States and its interests in the Middle East.[30]

McFarlane, along with aides John Poindexter and Oliver North, kept the Iran initiative a secret, particularly from Congress and four of the eight members of the NSC. Sloppy amateurism undermined this dubious scheme from the start. Officials placed funds in the wrong Swiss bank accounts, and when some participants skimmed from the transactions, more than $33 million went missing. One conspirator kept $200,000 to purchase a Porsche and two weeks at a weight-loss clinic. Shultz's assistant secretary of state, Elliot Abrams, lied to Congress about his involvement in setting up a Swiss bank account with $10 million provided by the sultan of Brunei.[31]

It was perhaps fitting that Nicaragua was the setting for the unraveling of the initiative. In the autumn of 1986, a CIA cargo plane illegally supplying the Contras was shot down, resulting in the capture of a crew member and the discovery of evidence linking the flight to the White House. It was soon revealed that North and his associates had outsourced their scheme to unreliable go-betweens. "We have been dealing with some of the sleaziest international characters around," Shultz warned Reagan. A number of things about North's past behavior should have raised warnings about his reliability. But North thrived and rose not only because of poor administrative oversight but also because he presented himself as the embodiment of the very icons and heroes that 1980s popular culture celebrated.[32]

The Iran-Contra scandal also derived from the administration's ideological approach to the world: officials became convinced that their convictions took precedence over the law (or even good sense). Powell occasionally got a whiff of the paranoia at the White House, such as when he received a request from North for a permit to carry a gun. Baffled by the request, he wondered why North needed a gun on the staff of the National Security Council, and why he needed to route the request through his desk at the Pentagon. When an aide told Powell that North believed "people [were] out to get him," an incredulous Powell asked, "Who?" In his 1995 memoir, Powell described North and Poindexter as the "midnight moles" at the White House. He observed that "the NSC had filled a power vacuum and had become its own Defense Department, running little wars, its own state department, carrying on its own secret diplomacy, and its own CIA, carrying out clandestine operations."[33]

Reagan's public comments on Iran-Contra only did more damage, as did the revelation that he was soliciting advice from Richard Nixon about containing the scandal. One poll showed that only 14 percent of the public believed the president's explanations. The scandal revealed a lack of candor and accountability on the part of the major participants including Reagan, Vice President Bush, Shultz, and Weinberger, all of whom gave conflicting and contradictory accounts of the initiative and their roles in it. Both Reagan and Bush protected themselves by claiming ignorance of key aspects of the policy. "Ronald Reagan had made his public mea culpa. But in his heart of hearts he remained pure," Powell recalled. Powell believed Reagan remained unrepentant. "For all the near destruction of his presidency, Reagan would have gone for another hostage-freeing scheme at the drop of a Hawk missile."[34]

Powell was only a peripheral player. He had effectively sidestepped most of the controversy and continued to rise. For Powell, Iran-Contra was a close call, perhaps closer than he cared to acknowledge. He understood that he could face problems stemming from the scheme, and at one point he even looked into the legal implications of the arms transfers. He later enjoyed a reputation as an honest broker in the wake of the scandal, but he could be quite lawyerly in his explanations of his own role. In his 1995 memoir, he acknowledged, "I had played a part in getting the Army's TOW antitank missiles transferred to the CIA, which then shipped them to Iran."[35] He argued that while it had been revealed that he was privy to detailed information about arms shipments to Iran, he was aware only of "proposals" to ship the missiles. The independent counsel in the case found, in words echoing the earlier description of Powell's role in the handling of the My Lai investigation nearly twenty years before, that Powell's deposition testimony was "misleading" and that his performance "hardly constituted full disclosure."[36]

Powell saw the initiative as McFarlane's "bid for Kissingerian immortality." He maintained that arms for hostages was merely a flawed policy, "not a criminal act liable to bring down the presidency. Senior officials cannot fall on their swords every time they disagree with a President." It was not so much that Powell opposed the initiative in principle. Rather, he opposed "the risking of the administration's credibility in a reckless cause."[37] Powell was correct that the administration's credibility had been shaken. "Mr. President," Shultz told Reagan, "if I'm telling you something you don't know—and I don't know very much—something is wrong here. . . . Our credibility is shot. We've taken refuge in tricky technicalities of language to avoid confronting the reality that we lied to the American people."[38] CIA director William Casey sensed that the Iran-Contra imbroglio could be an opportunity to dispose of Shultz by pinning responsibility for the initiative on the secretary of state. The stoic Shultz, whom State Department employees called "Buddha," fought back aggressively against Casey's effort to saddle him with the blame. The scandal ultimately played into Shultz's hands by aiding him in his effort to change the composition of the administration in ways that favored his own objectives.

The administration also faced the problem of what to do about the position of national security adviser, as the credibility of the fourth occupant of the job, Poindexter, had been completely shredded by his role in the scandal. Even some administration insiders believed Reagan had appointed people who lacked qualifications for their posts. Casey pushed for the return of Carter's hard-nosed national security adviser, Zbigniew Brzezinski, as a check on Shultz. But Shultz, fearing the prospect of such a strong-willed national security adviser, advocated Weinberger's former deputy—and Powell's former mentor—Carlucci. He was given the thankless task of rebuilding the machinery of the National Security Council and restoring confidence in the administration's foreign policy.[39] "I told [Reagan] I was a manager, not a visionary," Carlucci recalled. "I thought I could put the NSC back into shape, but I was not going to conceptualize a whole new foreign policy for him, if that's what he was looking for. He didn't really respond, in typical Ronald Reagan fashion. He probably told a joke or two. The conversation may have lasted fifteen or twenty minutes."[40]

In selecting his deputy, Carlucci needed someone he could trust, such as Powell, his longtime aide and associate dating to his White House fellowship with the OMB in 1972. Carlucci sensed in Powell a "savvy understanding of the process. When you get a person who is that astute you want to use him in bigger things." Carlucci, whom Powell referred to as his "godfather of godfathers," told him he was not looking for a foreign policy expert but rather an enforcer or gatekeeper. "I wanted somebody Ronald Reagan would be comfortable with," Carlucci recalled. "I knew Colin was that kind of person as well. He fit the bill to a 'T' and I was very comfortable with him." Powell had remained close to Carlucci in the years since their service together at the Pentagon in 1981. According to Carlucci, Powell often sought his advice on how best to handle Weinberger, and he had kept Carlucci abreast of what was going on in the Pentagon.[41]

Powell, who often bemoaned his frequent civilian assignments, had concerns about how the appointment might impact his military career. But he was learning the game of Beltway politics. He engineered the appointment in such a way as to enhance his military career, not detract from it. "There is only one way I can make this departure honorable," Powell warned Carlucci, "the only way I'll be able to face my fellow officers." He explained that the appointment could not come from Carlucci but instead had "to be a request directly from the commander in chief. That's the one thing my world will understand." Carlucci set to work, and two days later Reagan called Powell and dutifully went through the talking points Carlucci had prepared. Powell was once again heading back to Washington, having commanded V Corps for only five months.[42]

When Powell returned to Washington in December 1986 to become Carlucci's deputy, he lamented that had he stayed on with V Corps, he "might have had a shot at promotion to four stars and command of all U.S. Army forces in Europe." Powell wrote this in 1995, by then knowing full well that taking this appointment had led to him becoming, in short order, national security adviser, then by 1989, chairman of the Joint Chiefs. By 1995, he was seriously considering a bid for the presidency. Even Carlucci corrected Powell: "Colin, you're going to wind up as chairman, take my word for it."[43]

As Carlucci's deputy at the NSC, Powell came to be seen as the antidote to North and Poindexter. His colleagues regarded him as a safe presence at a time when previous military officers on the staff had been just the opposite. He represented a far more preferable public face than North or Poindexter for the rehabilitation of not only the NSC's reputation but also that of the military. He became known not for his ideological zeal but for his pragmatism and competence. This embodied an important part of his appeal, both then and later.[44] Still, not everyone was impressed. Reagan's first national security adviser, Richard Allen, saw Powell as "a man of great caution who rarely [took] a position on anything but was a good staff man at the time [and] did the job."[45] Moreover, several State Department officials complained to Shultz that Powell, as Weinberger's former executive assistant, might strengthen Weinberger's hand. They warned Shultz that, in his support for Powell and Carlucci, he had turned the NSC staff over to Weinberger and the Pentagon, but Shultz reassured them that he could work with the new appointees.[46]

Powell's return to Washington brought a change in perspective. As Weinberger's military aide at the Pentagon between 1983 and 1986, he had been absorbed with helping Weinberger formulate and promote his doctrine. Now, at the White House, Powell would be helping Carlucci restore the NSC after many years of turmoil, as well as working to bring stability to Reagan's dysfunctional policy system.

At the time of Carlucci's and Powell's appointments, Reagan's foreign policy was in crisis. Perhaps its only unvarnished achievement was the successful summit with Soviet leader Mikhail Gorbachev at Geneva in November 1985, but the disorganized and hastily arranged follow-up summit the following year at Reykjavik had undermined progress even there. A June 1987 *Washington Post*/ABC News poll found that 69 percent of the American people thought Reagan was lying about Iran-Contra. His approval rating dropped twenty-six points in the first month of the scandal, and only 28 percent approved of his handling of foreign policy. The subsequent Tower Commission Report depicted Reagan as frequently confused, remote, and uninformed and cited his hands-off leadership style as one of the chief reasons for the scandal. It described the NSC staff as a secret cell within the government and revealed the chaos at the heart of the administration, criticizing Shultz and Weinberger for their elaborate efforts to distance themselves from the mess. The Iran-Contra special prosecutor Lawrence Walsh went further than Tower, charging that Reagan's detachment allowed for illegal activities on a grand scale.[47]

Both Carlucci and Powell were quick studies. They aimed to rehabilitate not only Reagan and his foreign policy but also the National Security Council system, which now carried the stigma of spiraling out of control in the Nixon, Carter, and Reagan administrations. Powell saw his and Carlucci's role as rescuing Reagan's foreign policy from the "political karate of a handful of zealots." Powell observed that McFarlane, Poindexter, and North had "worked for a President who did not like to step between his powerful cabinet members and make hard choices." Now, Powell faced the daunting challenge of interacting with this chief executive. He discovered that Reagan became extremely uncomfortable in "improvised situations" and that the president frequently did not take much interest in matters of state. Powell once observed that Reagan had an "actor's memory"—once he got something into his head, it was almost impossible to change his mind.[48] "My impression was of a man who was in a daze," Carlucci recalled of Reagan. "He didn't know what had hit him, didn't understand it, and he couldn't get past the Iran-Contra thing for a long time."[49] At this point in his presidency, he seemed increasingly vague and confused, his administration held together by miracles of staffing. Former Senate majority leader Howard Baker, the new White House chief of staff, having replaced Don Regan, created a more structured environment around Reagan—much as James Baker had done in the first term. Howard Baker had to confront the administration's central problem on his first day. At the announcement of his appointment, Attorney General Ed Meese phoned him in a state of agitation. "Howard," Meese said, "I think you better get over to the White House. There's no one in charge."[50]

Unnerved by Reagan's decision-making style, Powell observed that when Carlucci presented the president with a series of options, Reagan might say nothing until Carlucci offered his own recommendation. Carlucci could not recall any instance where Reagan rejected their advice, but the president might not commit himself beyond acknowledging that he had heard the briefing. After one such session, a frustrated Carlucci asked Powell, "Was that a yes?" Carlucci recalled that "Colin would simply brief him. 'Sir, this is what we're doing, if you have no objections.' Invariably, he wouldn't. The concept was to try and keep the issues off his desk. . . . That was the way foreign policy was basically conducted."[51] Powell later wrote that "the President's passive management style placed a tremendous burden on us," and he and Carlucci felt uneasy implementing decisions in such confusion and uncertainty.[52] "Colin, you and I are going to have to figure out what the right thing to do is, what Ronald Reagan would want done," Carlucci concluded. "We're going to have to impute decisions because we're not going to get crystal clear decisions from him. We're not going to usurp authority onto ourselves, that was the failing of our predecessors. But we have to think through very carefully what the Reagan policy should be."[53]

Carlucci was not content with merely restoring the old NSC system, which, he believed, should ideally function as an advisory and policy coordinating body, not, as had recently been the case, an agency for carrying out clandestine and even illegal operations. He, like Shultz, wanted Reagan to achieve substantive foreign policy objectives before he departed the White House. When Carlucci replaced Weinberger at the Pentagon in the fall of

Figure 2.2. Powell's appointment as national security adviser, November 5, 1987. Caspar Weinberger (L), President Reagan, and Frank Carlucci (R) look on. As this photo illustrates, Powell had suddenly been transformed from a typical behind-the-scenes staff man into an official making policy pronouncements in front of the cameras. It was at this moment, in November 1987, that Powell, who had previously developed a reputation as an excellent staff assistant, emerged into the public eye in his own right. More importantly, he was promoted to national security adviser at the very moment that Reagan's foreign policy began to achieve an internal consensus to focus on several large objectives, including arms control and better relations with the Soviet Union. With George Shultz at the State Department and with Carlucci now replacing the stubbornly hawkish Weinberger at the Pentagon, a revitalized foreign policy troika of Powell, Shultz, and Carlucci would steer Reagan toward a new détente with Soviet leader Mikhail Gorbachev. Photo credit: Ronald Reagan Presidential Library.

1987, Powell moved up to become the national security adviser. Other matters were increasingly breaking Shultz's way. The right-wing ideologue Jeane Kirkpatrick had already left the administration in 1985, and FBI director William Webster became CIA director after Casey's death in the spring of 1987. The public face of the Reagan foreign policy team had been transformed. The pieces were slowly falling into place for Shultz, who, after four and a half years on the job, finally had a team designed to aid him in steering Reagan in the direction of substantive arms-control agreements during the last year of his presidency.[54] Most importantly, as of March 1985, Mikhail Gorbachev had arrived on the scene as the new Soviet leader. The Cold War would never be the same.

Figure 2.3. Powell, as national security adviser, briefing the president at the Reagan's ranch in Santa Barbara, November 25, 1987. White House Chief of Staff Howard Baker listens. Powell and Baker provided the White House with something it had not had for several years: quiet, understated professionalism. Throughout his political career, Reagan remained a hands-off administrator with little interest in the details of governing; thus, his political fortunes often depended on the quality of his staffing. When it was bad, such as during the years 1985 and 1986, it nearly led to the president's impeachment. When it was good, such as during the 1981–1984 period, or again during the last two years of Reagan's presidency from 1987 to 1988, the administration could effectively accomplish a number of its political objectives. Adult supervision had returned to the Reagan White House. Both Powell and Baker once again proved the dictum that there is no limit to how much an official can accomplish if he remains unconcerned about who takes the ultimate credit. Photo credit: Ronald Reagan Presidential Library.

For Powell, it was a truly remarkable advance during a relatively short period of time. The tumult of the first six years of the Reagan administration had facilitated his rise from an obscure aide to the deputy secretary of defense, to the corridors of power in the White House with daily access to the commander in chief. His association with Weinberger proved lasting, as Powell would subsequently champion the cause of the Weinberger Doctrine, which in time became the Powell Doctrine.

From his assignments at the Pentagon and later at the NSC, Powell had enjoyed a front-row seat observing the administration's bitterest battles over intervention and the meaning of the Vietnam Syndrome. Powell had come away from these struggles with immense respect for George Shultz as a talented bureaucratic operator and moderate voice on issues such as U.S.-Soviet relations. On the questions of intervention and the lessons of Vietnam, Powell demonstrated a greater affinity with Weinberger. While Powell shared with Shultz his moderation and realist desire to solve problems, reduce tensions, and reach arms-control agreements, he more closely mirrored Weinberger in his antipathy toward the view of military intervention as the one-size-fits-all cure for the problems plaguing Reagan's foreign policy. Moreover, as deputy national security adviser, and later as national security adviser in his own right, he became a central figure in some of the most important international events as the Cold War ended. Here, Shultz's influence was most relevant, whereas Weinberger's lessons did not become as apparent until the debates over the Gulf War in 1990 and 1991 and Bosnia in 1992 and 1993.

Notes

1. The essential memoirs touching upon Reagan's foreign policy are Alexander M. Haig Jr.'s *Caveat: Realism, Reagan, and Foreign Policy* (New York: MacMillan, 1984); Robert C. McFarlane, *Special Trust* (New York: Cadell and Davies, 1994); George Shultz, *Turmoil and Triumph: Diplomacy, Power, and the Victory of the American Ideal* (New York: Simon and Schuster, 1993); and Caspar Weinberger, *Fighting for Peace: Seven Critical Years in the Pentagon* (New York: Warner Books, 1990). These should be supplemented by scholarly explorations such as David E. Kyvig, "The Foreign Relations of the Reagan Administration," in *Reagan and the World*, ed. David E. Kyvig (Westport, CT: Praeger, 1990); Frances Fitzgerald, *Way Out There in the Blue: Reagan, Star Wars and the End of the Cold War* (New York: Touchstone, 2000); William M. LeoGrande, *Our Own Backyard: The United States in Central America, 1977–1992* (Chapel Hill: University of North Carolina Press, 1998); Mark P. Logan, *The Reagan Doctrine: Sources of Conduct in the Cold War's Last Chapter* (Westport, CT: Praeger, 1994), and James M. Scott, *Deciding to Intervene: The Reagan Doctrine and American*

Foreign Policy (Durham, NC: Duke University Press, 1996). Michael T. Klare, *Beyond the "Vietnam Syndrome": U.S. Interventionism in the 1980s* (Washington, DC: Institute for Policy Studies, 1982), examines the many interventions in the wake of Vietnam.

2. Interview with Richard Allen, Ronald Reagan Oral History Project, May 28, 2002, Miller Center for Public Affairs, University of Virginia.

3. Haig, *Caveat*, 92–93, 142–43; McFarlane, *Special Trust*, 174.

4. Interview with George Shultz, Ronald Reagan Oral History Project, December 18, 2002, Miller Center for Public Affairs, University of Virginia; McFarlane, *Special Trust*, 174–88.

5. Colin Powell, *My American Journey* (New York: Ballantine, 1995, 2003), 250.

6. Quoted in Henry Louis Gates Jr., "Powell and the Black Elite," *New Yorker*, September 25, 1995, 72.

7. Powell, *My American Journey*, 249, 304.

8. Quoted in Dale R. Herspring, *The Pentagon and the Presidency: Civil-Military Relations from FDR to George W. Bush* (Lawrence: University Press of Kansas, 2005), 295.

9. Powell, *My American Journey*, 337.

10. Quoted in Powell, *My American Journey*, 261.

11. Interview with Frank Carlucci, Ronald Reagan Oral History Project, August 28, 2001, Miller Center for Public Affairs, University of Virginia; author interview with Lawrence Korb, March 17, 2006; David J. Rothkopf, *Running the World: Inside the National Security Council and the Architects of American Power* (New York: Public Affairs, 2005), 228–30; McFarlane, *Special Trust*, 323–28.

12. Quoted in Powell, *My American Journey*, 280–81.

13. Quoted in Powell, *My American Journey*, 280–81.

14. Quoted in Powell, *My American Journey*, 281.

15. On the Iran-Contra affair, see Theodore Draper, *A Very Thin Line: The Iran-Contra Affairs* (New York: Hill and Wang, 1991). See also Peter Kornbluh and Malcolm Byrne, eds., *The Iran-Contra Scandal: The Declassified History* (New York: The New Press, 1993); John Tower, Edmund Muskie, and Brent Scowcroft, *The Tower Commission Report* (New York: Times Books, 1987); Lawrence Walsh, *Firewall: The Iran-Contra Conspiracy and Cover-Up* (New York: W. W. Norton, 1997).

16. Powell, *My American Journey*, 281.

17. McFarlane, *Special Trust*, 273.

18. David Ignatius, "Reagan's Foreign Policy and the Rejection of Diplomacy," in *The Reagan Legacy*, ed. Sidney Blumenthal and Thomas Byrne Edsall (New York: Pantheon Books, 1988), 175.

19. Bob Woodward, *Veil: The Secret Wars of the CIA, 1981–1987* (New York: Simon and Schuster, 1987), 290.

20. Gil Troy, *Morning in America: How Ronald Reagan Invented the 1980s* (Princeton University Press, 2005), 241; Michael Schaller, *Reckoning with Reagan: American and Its President in the 1980s* (New York: Oxford University Press, 1992), 146–47.

21. Andrew J. Bacevich, *The New American Militarism: How Americans Are Seduced by War* (Oxford: Oxford University Press, 2005), 111–17.

22. Quoted in Lou Cannon, *President Reagan: The Role of a Lifetime* (New York: Public Affairs, 2000), 389.

23. Interview with Caspar Weinberger, Ronald Reagan Oral History Project, November 19, 2002, Miller Center for Public Affairs, University of Virginia.

24. Weinberger, *Fighting for Peace*, 445–57.

25. Quoted in Powell, *My American Journey*, 293.

26. Quoted in Cannon, *President Reagan*, 354.

27. Powell, *My American Journey*, 305.

28. Henry Louis Gates Jr., "Powell and the Black Elite," *New Yorker*, September 25, 1995, 67.

29. Schaller, *Reckoning with Reagan*, 147; Richard Reeves, *President Reagan: The Triumph of Imagination* (New York: Simon and Schuster, 2005), 218–21.

30. Bruce W. Jentleson, *With Friends Like These: Reagan, Bush and Saddam, 1982–1990* (New York: Norton, 1994).

31. Reeves, *President Reagan*, 384; Draper, *A Very Thin Line*, 368–71.

32. Quoted in Shultz, *Turmoil and Triumph*, 828; Constantine C. Menges, *Inside the National Security Council: The True Story of the Making and Unmaking of Reagan's Foreign Policy* (New York: Simon and Schuster, 1988), 357–61.

33. Powell, *My American Journey*, 279, 321–23, 330.

34. Powell, *My American Journey*, 325, 336.

35. Powell, *My American Journey*, 300, 317.

36. Lawrence E. Walsh, *Iran-Contra: The Final Report* (New York: Random House, 1994), 438–39.

37. Quoted in Powell, *My American Journey*, 297–301.

38. Quoted in Shultz, *Turmoil and Triumph*, 828.

39. Bernard Weinraub, "New N.S.C. Chief Is Said to Plan a Near-Total Overhaul of Council," *New York Times*, December 16, 1986.

40. Interview with Kenneth Adelman, Ronald Reagan Oral History Project, September 30, 2003, Miller Center for Public Affairs, University of Virginia; Shultz, *Turmoil and Triumph*, 842–43; interview with Frank Carlucci, Ronald Reagan Oral History Project, August 28, 2001, Miller Center for Public Affairs, University of Virginia.

41. Interview with Frank Carlucci, Ronald Reagan Oral History Project.

42. Quoted in Powell, *My American Journey*, 319.

43. Interview with Frank Carlucci, Ronald Reagan Oral History Project.

44. Don Oberdorfer, "Colin Powell: A Key Figure in Policy at the Revamped NSC," *Washington Post*, March 23, 1987.

45. Interview with Richard Allen, Ronald Reagan Oral History Project, May 28, 2002, Miller Center for Public Affairs, University of Virginia.

46. Shultz, *Turmoil and Triumph*, 843.

47. Shultz, *Turmoil and Triumph*, 863; Walsh, *Firewall*.

48. Powell, *My American Journey*, 321–23, 336, 367; interview with William Webster, Ronald Reagan Oral History Project, August 28, 2002, Miller Center for Public Affairs, University of Virginia.

49. Interview with Frank Carlucci, Ronald Reagan Oral History Project.

50. Quoted in Reeves, *President Reagan*, 386.

51. Interview with Frank Carlucci, Ronald Reagan Oral History Project.

52. Quoted in Powell, *My American Journey*, 323.

53. Interview with Frank Carlucci, Ronald Reagan Oral History Project.

54. Interview with George Shultz, Ronald Reagan Oral History Project.

CHAPTER THREE

~

National Security Adviser at the End of the Cold War, 1987–1989

Colin Powell's elevation to deputy national security adviser, and later to the position of national security adviser itself, entailed many challenges he had not anticipated. Powell's career to 1986—entailing service as a professional soldier with two tours in Vietnam, selection for some of the army's most prestigious officer-training programs, service in numerous Pentagon bureaucratic roles, including close proximity to one of the most powerful secretaries of defense—appeared to have set him on a course to address the challenges of intervention, the Vietnam Syndrome and, eventually, the Weinberger Doctrine. He was fortunate that many of the most intense debates about the Vietnam Syndrome and intervention, in Lebanon, Nicaragua, El Salvador, and Grenada, for example, had occurred in the years prior to his accession to national security adviser. The period of Powell's service as national security adviser, a little more than a year from the end of 1987 to the close of the administration in January 1989, was largely consumed with issues related to U.S.-Soviet relations, arms control, great-power summitry, and the winding down of the Cold War. These were areas to which he had not previously given much thought, but he proved to be a quick study and acquitted himself with aplomb under often trying circumstances.

Mikhail Gorbachev's rise to power in the Soviet Union set in motion a series of events that left the world changed forever. For Ronald Reagan, having spent the first five years of his presidency without a face-to-face meeting with a Soviet leader, Gorbachev's accession to power in March 1985 led to five meetings over the course of the final three years of his presidency.

Gorbachev's revolution presented an interesting challenge for someone like Powell. At one of their meetings, Gorbachev posed a question to Powell that would stay with him for the remainder of his time in the White House, as well as for the next few years of his military career: what will you do when you've lost your best enemy? Powell replayed the question over and over in his mind. How *would* the American military, let alone American foreign policy, respond to Gorbachev's initiatives? The containment of the Soviet Union had been the chief focus of U.S. foreign and defense policy for four decades. If Gorbachev changed the dynamic, what would the United States do? Having spent most of his adult life in the army or the Pentagon, Powell's views on the Cold War and the Soviet Union had been rather conventional. But Powell, like George Shultz, deserves much credit for keeping personal ideological views out of the emerging U.S. relationship with Moscow. He not only admired Gorbachev's energy and dynamism but saw him as a new kind of Soviet leader.[1]

Like Shultz, Powell sensed Gorbachev's impatience to reform the Soviet system and society through glasnost (openness) and perestroika (restructuring). Gorbachev also linked his domestic reforms to radical changes in Soviet foreign policy. New thinking at home also meant new thinking abroad. Gorbachev was determined to lead a revolution in Soviet foreign policy, one that would ultimately end the Cold War. Initially, he moved cautiously for fear of provoking the hard-liners in the Kremlin and the Soviet military. Gorbachev recognized that too many unilateral concessions on his part might put him in jeopardy and endanger his reforms. Moreover, his early steps were contingent on gaining assurance that the United States would not aggressively exploit a period of Soviet internal reform and readjustment.[2]

With or without U.S. cooperation, Gorbachev was determined to make sweeping changes in Soviet foreign and defense policy over his nearly six years in power. Faced with this revolution in Soviet foreign policy, Shultz and Powell saw an opportunity for U.S. cooperation on arms control and other matters. Powell also sensed that part of Gorbachev's impatience stemmed from the Soviet leader's fatalistic belief that he might not be afforded much time to implement his revolution. Powell was impressed that Gorbachev seemed to foresee that he would push his reform agenda as far as Soviet politics and society would allow before sweeping him aside as a spent force. As Gorbachev's wife, Raisa, once observed, "The thing about innovations is that sooner or later they turn around and destroy the innovators."[3]

The Reagan administration was not prepared for Gorbachev's arrival on the world stage. Lacking a consistent strategic conception, the administration had instead substituted political slogans such as "peace through strength" or "evil empire" for a policy. Reagan simply did not have a coherent approach to the USSR. This was not entirely Reagan's fault. The leadership of the Soviet Union was in a state of uncertainty during Reagan's first four years, with Leonid Brezhnev declining and dying in 1982, succeeded by the ailing Yuri Andropov, who died in 1984, followed by the near-comatose Konstantin Chernenko, who died in early 1985, to be succeeded by Gorbachev.

Gorbachev's new diplomatic offensive began almost as soon as he took power. At the beginning of 1986, he launched a major overture, proposing the abolition, in stages, of all nuclear weapons. Shultz had been encouraged by the Soviet leader's moves, and Reagan, too, desired the elimination of nuclear weapons, but the Pentagon led by Casper Weinberger remained suspicious. The new Soviet leader's utterances did not match the administration's assumption that all Soviet leaders were alike. The youngest full member of the Politburo since the Stalin era, Gorbachev was just fifty-four (twenty years younger than Reagan) when he became the leader of the Soviet Union. He spoke with conviction about transformational change in both domestic and foreign policy. New evidence, much of it from Soviet sources, reveals that Gorbachev contemplated abandoning the Cold War.[4]

Gorbachev prompted a whole new dynamic in U.S.-Soviet relations, particularly in arms control. Although there had not been a superpower summit during the first four years of Reagan's presidency, one was arranged only eight months after Gorbachev's accession. Five summits occurred in quick order, beginning with Geneva (1985), then Reykjavik (1986), Washington (1987), Moscow (1988), and New York (1988). In one sense, Gorbachev rescued Reagan's presidency from Iran-Contra. During the depths of the scandal, Reagan's approval rating had fallen below 50 percent and public approval of his foreign policy to 33 percent. Both figures began to rise after the December 1987 Washington summit with Gorbachev.[5]

National Security Adviser, 1987–1989

It had been a meteoric rise for Powell, but what kind of national security adviser would he be? He did not see himself as another Henry Kissinger or Zbigniew Brzezinski, "with their Ph.D.s and international relations backgrounds."[6] Instead, he aimed to be a steady, trusted public servant, exactly what many desired after the first six years—prior to the arrival of Frank Carlucci and Powell—of ideological zeal and reckless adventurism.[7] No longer Weinberger's or Carlucci's assistant, Powell began emerging from the shadows. In a town with its share of outsized egos, he conveyed a different impression: low-key, understated professionalism.[8] "He was a consensus builder," recalled NSC official Clarke McCurdy Brintall. "He could bring people together, opposing factions together. He would answer his mail. If you left a telephone call, he would return the telephone call. There was a great sense of closeness and rapport working with the NSC at that time."[9] Moreover, he had an appropriate sense of ego and little ideological rigidity. "Colin Powell and [NSC aide] John Negroponte did not want the NSC to run everything," recalled NSC official Robert Pastorino. "They wanted the NSC to coordinate. They didn't want the NSC to make the decisions and carry them out. They wanted the NSC to coordinate, which is the way it was first set up. . . . It was an obvious reaction to the previous time when McFarlane and Poindexter were perceived as running it differently."[10]

He also understood his role in the administration. Shultz approvingly observed of Powell that "in the services I think people get trained about roles. They understand when you're a General in charge and when you're advising and so on. It's part of their training to see if you're in this role, you do this, if you're in that role, you do that. So it came much easier to him."[11] Moreover, Powell was comfortable with himself. Reagan biographer Lou Cannon observed that Powell soon distinguished himself as "among the most moderate, realistic, and thoughtful of Reagan's aides."[12] He also began to understand the power of the media, observing that "we had entered an age where TV images formed perceptions, and these perceptions eclipsed reality." Powell quickly mastered the art of Washington spin and developed a reputation for skill with reporters. "They get to pick the questions," Powell said of the media. "But you get to pick the answers."[13]

To some, more important than the Iran-Contra scandal itself was what it said about the Reagan White House. The Tower Commission Report revealed the administration's inner turmoil, problems Powell and Carlucci knew intimately. The report further exposed Reagan's lax management style.[14] None of these findings came as a surprise to Powell, who had already served a one-year apprenticeship under Carlucci prior to taking the job himself. As Weinberger's aide and then Carlucci's deputy, he had observed the many disputes and conflicts between State and Defense, between State and the NSC, and between the CIA and State.

The Tower Commission only scratched the surface. As the multitude of memoirs from this period reveal, the Reagan administration was often at war with itself. The president's poor administrative skills meant that a void existed at the center of the administration, often filled by scheming advisers who had unprecedented power and influence. Powell observed in Reagan an overreliance on advisers and a lack of good judgment about their character. He noted that Reagan frequently demonstrated a level of trust in subordi-

Figure 3.1. Powell briefing President Reagan, November 25, 1987. Powell, like Carlucci before him and White House Chief of Staff Howard Baker, had to address one of the more significant presidential health crises in American history. As the Reagan years drew to a close, Powell faced the challenge of working with a president who was rapidly aging while in office and showing signs of mental fatigue. Powell handled this challenge with much grace and consideration toward the president. It was during his time as Reagan's last national security adviser that Powell developed a well-deserved reputation for professionalism, discretion, and a businesslike, understated competence. Photo credit: Ronald Reagan Presidential Library

nates "that could be a little frightening."[15] This was compounded by the administration's ideological coloration, with different officials pursuing what they believed to be Reagan's desires with a zeal that often propelled them into controversy, or worse.[16]

Powell was also dealing with one of the more serious presidential health crises in the nation's history. By all accounts, from both members of the administration and outside observers, Reagan was aging rapidly. Even as governor of California in the 1960s, he had been a hands-off administrator without much interest in the details of government. He preferred to govern by instinct, ideological certitude, and timely anecdote. Reagan's aging in the White House accentuated these tendencies. Years before specialists detected evidence of Alzheimer's, some observers believed, through careful study of Reagan's public performances, that America's oldest president was declining mentally. Those around Reagan evidenced sympathy, concern, and some alarm.[17] "Ronald Reagan clearly was not a detail person," Carlucci recalled. "You could never tell how much of an issue he was absorbing."[18]

Reagan came into sharper focus for Powell when he arrived at the White House as Carlucci's deputy in late 1986, and more so after his appointment to replace Carlucci. He came to understand that Reagan had to be handled with care and that sudden changes threw the president off balance, with potentially disastrous results. Powell had been troubled by Reagan's inattention to detail and his inability to settle debilitating disputes among advisers. He also detected a kind of "quasimystical streak" in Reagan that went beyond consulting an astrologer. Reagan had his own private version of reality, which frequently conflicted with the reality around him. Powell revealed that Reagan saw Chernobyl as "a biblical warning to mankind," and Reagan's frequent comments about possible invasions from outer space made Powell particularly uneasy. Whenever Reagan raised the subject, Powell rolled his eyes and warned his staff, "Here come the little green men again."[19]

Although he was understandably grateful to Reagan for accepting Carlucci and Shultz's suggestion to elevate him to national security adviser, Powell's true feelings about the fortieth president were complex. He admired Reagan for his ability to simplify matters, for the good cheer he exuded, and for his impeccable tailoring. But he also observed that Reagan's warmth had a kind of manufactured quality, that he could appear "warm" as if on cue, while remaining distant and detached. Powell described this as Reagan's "impersonal intimacy." He also felt Reagan could be inconsiderate. Unlike previous officials he had served under, such as Weinberger and Carlucci, Powell observed that Reagan and the first lady rarely thanked their staffs or advisers or showed gratitude of any kind.[20]

Powell believed, as Carlucci did before him, that Reagan's detachment and remoteness made the job of national security adviser especially difficult. "The President himself never spoke to me about the job," he recalled, "never laid out his expectations, never provided any guidance; in fact, he had not personally offered me the position or congratulated me on getting it. After ten months in the White House, I was not surprised." Like previous advisers, Powell was also challenged by Reagan's failure to set clear foreign policy objectives. Senior officials, seeking guidance or even a sign of what Reagan desired of them, often left the Oval Office disappointed. Former secretary of state Alexander Haig once described the Reagan White House as a mysterious ghost ship, where one heard the creak of the rigging and the groan of timbers and sometimes even caught a faint glimpse of the crew, but it was impossible to know who was really at the helm.[21]

Powell emerged as the most prominent black official in Reagan's administration, but he has said little about Reagan's record on race and civil rights. His ambivalence about Reagan and race formed part of the paradox of his serving in Republican administrations. Many of Reagan's associates have attested to the president's lack of personal racism, but his public record and actions on the questions of race and civil rights were far from sympathetic. Powell may have been unaware of the effective use Reagan had made of racial appeals dating back even before he became governor of California in 1966. Reagan launched his political career upon the rhetoric of racial backlash. His emergence onto the national political stage in the 1964 presidential campaign of Barry Goldwater revealed his opposition to black voting rights, which he saw as humiliating to white Southerners. Reagan became a master at maintaining a sunny disposition as he exploited anxieties about race, integration, and civil rights.[22] While running for governor of California, he made opposition to civil rights a cornerstone of his candidacy, and some of his campaign commercials struck ominous notes concerning integration. His opponent in that race, Gov. Pat Brown, supported California's Rumford Fair Housing Act of 1963, which sought, in accordance with federal civil rights laws, to reduce barriers in housing based on race. Reagan, who had supported a white backlash initiative against the act in 1964, pledged to fight it, and his denunciations of the act enabled him to make large inroads into the white electorate.[23] As governor, he became known for his skepticism regarding civil rights and for his appointment of people hostile to black voting rights. When launching his 1980 campaign for president with a speech about "states' rights," he chose, of all places, the tiny hamlet of Philadelphia, Mississippi, where three civil rights workers had been brutally slain in 1964. For black Americans, Reagan's gesture was, in the words of *Washington Post* columnist William Raspberry, a bitter symbolism.[24]

As president, Reagan aimed to weaken the enforcement of civil rights and equal opportunity laws and speculated that Martin Luther King Jr., one of Powell's heroes, would one day be exposed as a Communist sympathizer.[25] His frequent attacks on "welfare queens" and support for the apartheid regime in South Africa were consistent with his record. In a 1995 interview with Henry Louis Gates Jr., Powell acknowledged some discomfort with the administrations he had served and their records on race and civil rights. "The problem with Reagan, Bush and Weinberger and their ilk is that they just never knew," Powell told Gates. "They were never sensitized to it. They never had to live with it. They were never close to it. And the cold political calculus is that the Republicans said, 'We can't get these people, so why spend a dime trying?'"[26]

Powell, Reagan, and Shultz

Carlucci had made an impressive start on rebuilding Reagan's dysfunctional National Security Council system, but Powell still inherited a deeply troubled office. The NSC suffered from serious management issues that had nearly brought down the administration. Reagan appointed six national security advisors in eight years. The job became known as the administration's Bermuda Triangle, and one official quipped that Reagan "changes them like he changes his underwear."[27] A history of these Reagan-era appointments reads like the story of the six wives of Henry VIII, who are remembered with the mnemonic "divorced, beheaded, died, divorced, beheaded, survived." Only the fifth and sixth, Carlucci and Powell, achieved any degree of success.[28]

By the time Powell became national security adviser in November 1987, the Reagan foreign policy team had undergone a transformation. The hard-line Weinberger, long opposed to negotiations with Gorbachev, had departed, to be replaced at the Pentagon by the more pragmatic Carlucci. Shultz and Carlucci had suggested that Reagan elevate Powell to become the new national security adviser. Shultz liked Powell and believed he could build a functioning foreign policy team with him. "I had a hard time with them until Colin Powell," Shultz recalled. "Then with Colin everything worked sort of by the book, was good."[29] Shultz moved to forge a working group with Powell and Carlucci. Shultz told Reagan that "with Carlucci, Powell, and me in the key foreign and security policy posts, that would be by far the best team, and in fact, the first genuine team, assembled in the entire Reagan presidency."[30] The three began meeting at seven every morning without aides. Carlucci recalled that "those meetings were the key to the effective functioning of foreign policy in the last year and a half of the administration."[31]

After the Iran-Contra debacle, Shultz, Carlucci, and Powell strove to make the arrangement work. "Everything that was going on we knew, we shared," Shultz recalled.[32] "Ronald Reagan has had the landing lights on and the flaps down for the last year," Shultz told Carlucci. "Now we're going to have to step up to the plate on foreign policy. The only way it's going to work is for the three of us to agree."[33] Powell saw Shultz as the primary figure in the administration's foreign policy and never hesitated to defer to Shultz or Carlucci if the maintenance of the relationship required it.[34]

Powell, Shultz, and Carlucci were pragmatists who modulated their essential conservatism when it suited their objective of pushing Reagan in the direction of improved U.S.-Soviet relations and an arms-control agreement with Gorbachev. In pursuit of this goal, Powell, Shultz, and Carlucci had to contend with administration hard-liners, many of whom not only distrusted Gorbachev but also feared the consequences of the Cold War's end. Beginning with his 1976 crusade to deny the Republican nomination to President Gerald R. Ford, Reagan had elicited from many of his followers an uncompromising hostility to détente. All too often, Reagan's brand of anticommunism tended toward the apocalyptic. The very forces mobilized by the Reagan revolution proved difficult, once unleashed, to rein in, making it harder to shift course when global circumstances changed and the administration began to seek rapprochement with the USSR.

Confusion over Reagan's true objective further complicated the process. During the previous seven years of his administration, Reagan had sided with various advisers on different matters, leaving Shultz frequently infuriated and on the verge of resignation. At times, such confusion embarrassed Powell, who might inadvertently appear to be at odds with his own president.[35] There was no telling what Reagan might say publicly, and Powell no doubt knew that Reagan could be responsible for some bizarre comments, as when he told the press in October 1987 that he believed domestic "Communists" were behind his recent political misfortunes, or when he told a reporter he believed the revival of the McCarthy-era House Un-American Activities Committee should set things right.[36]

Powell also had to deal with unresolved matters from the previous seven years of Reagan's foreign policy. The consequences of the Reagan Doctrine were one such problem. The doctrine had stemmed from the conviction that every foreign policy challenge was linked to Cuba or the Soviet Union. "Our choosing sides in conflicts around the world," Powell observed, "was almost always decided on the basis of the East-West competition." Relying on proxies was another way to avoid U.S. intervention—a concession to the Vietnam Syndrome—and complemented the Weinberger Doctrine by avoiding the deployment of U.S. troops. But aspects of the Reagan Doctrine revealed the seamier side of Reagan's foreign policy. The proxy wars in the developing world caused immense suffering, as the United States allied itself with some shady characters—Manuel Noriega in Panama, Jonas Savimbi in Angola, Mobutu Sese Seko in Zaire, and the apartheid regime in South Africa—many of whom were put on the U.S. payroll in the defense of "freedom." Powell recalled, "Cold War politics sometimes made for creepy bedfellows."[37]

Few regions were as affected by the Reagan Doctrine as Central America, where the administration aimed to overthrow the left-leaning Sandinista regime in Nicaragua. Many in the administration believed their own hyperbolic rhetoric about Nicaragua. Reagan told the nation that Nicaragua was a sanctuary for terrorists. He sought to mobilize public support by warning that the Sandinistas might march on Texas. The administration launched a secret public relations campaign—called "White Propaganda"—with $440,000 appropriated from the State Department's Office of Public Diplomacy to place anti-Sandinista and pro-Contra op-ed pieces in the *Wall Street Journal, New York Times,* and *Washington Post.* Powell inherited the unenviable task of salvaging what remained of the tattered Nicaragua policy.[38] The policy had not only run aground but very nearly sank Reagan's presidency when over-zealous White House staffers sought to keep it alive through illegal means. Moreover, the Central American nations themselves had now seized the initiative, backing a peace plan of their own that increasingly marginalized Reagan's militarist approach to the region.

Powell, working closely with Shultz, was a central figure in modifying Reagan's Central America policy by seeking congressional support. But Powell's own views of the Contras often seemed confused and contradictory. He believed "in the justice of the Contra cause" and that they were "fighting for democracy" while acknowledging that many of them were "unregenerate veterans of the corrupt regime of Anastasio Somoza." He rationalized that "in the old days of the East-West polarization, we worked with what we had."[39] For the most part, he saw the Contras as leverage. Shultz, too, had few illusions about them. Both believed the Contras might prove useful in pressuring the Sandinistas, but little more. Over Nicaragua, Powell also struggled with hard-line enthusiasts for the Contra cause, such as Republican congressman Richard B. "Dick" Cheney of Wyoming, who frustrated Powell with his uncompromising approach to the issue.

Powell and Summit Diplomacy

Managing the many problems of Reagan's Central America policy paled in significance compared to the looming challenge of U.S.-Soviet relations. Soon after his November 1987 promotion to national security adviser, Powell tackled the daunting problems of preparing for Gorbachev's imminent visit to Washington, where Reagan and the Soviet leader were scheduled to sign the Intermediate-Range Nuclear Forces (INF) Treaty. He fretted that Reagan might not be up to meeting Gorbachev. The Reykjavik summit of October 1986 had been something of a fiasco. The administration was unprepared for the complex matters discussed at Reykjavik. One obstacle in Iceland had been Reagan's passionate attachment to the Strategic Defense Initiative (SDI), or Star Wars, which he imagined as a space-based defense against nuclear missiles. As so often happened in this administration, Reagan had announced SDI in March 1983 without consulting Weinberger, Shultz, the Joint Chiefs, or Paul Nitze, his chief arms-control negotiator, most of whom came to see it merely as a bargaining chip. Although the scientific community was dubious of SDI, the subject obsessed Reagan. He grew emotionally attached to SDI even if only he believed it could work.

In her perceptive history, *Way Out There in the Blue*, Frances Fitzgerald exposed the paradox of Reagan's enthusiasm for SDI. For several years prior to Reykjavik, Reagan's arms-control advisers had pursued a strategy of using SDI as a bargaining chip to extract concessions from the USSR on offensive weapons. Instead, at Reykjavik, Reagan had offered the USSR major concessions on offensive weapons in exchange for a nonexistent SDI. Gorbachev pointed out that only laboratory research into defenses was allowed under the 1972 Antiballistic Missile Treaty, but Reagan ignored Gorbachev's protestations that he could not make exceptions to the treaty that could imperil him with his own hard-liners. The summit collapsed in disappointment and acrimony.

Powell wanted to avoid the kinds of problems that plagued the Reykjavik meeting and its aftermath. One factor playing into his desire for a successful summit was the great change in circumstances since the October 1986 Reykjavik meeting. For Powell, the good news was that, although the substantive results of Reykjavik were less than clear, Reagan's approval rating momentarily jumped to record highs. But that had been just before the Iran-Contra revelations and the many months of hearings investigating the scandal throughout the summer of 1987. Reagan's approval rating thereafter fell to an all-time low of 42 percent after his unsteady public performances attempting to explain Iran-Contra. Compounding Reagan's problems, his nominee for the Supreme Court, Robert Bork, had been rejected in the Senate 58–42, the largest vote against a high court nominee in history, and the Wall Street crash of late October 1987 further undermined public confidence in the administration. Now, Reagan needed Gorbachev more than Gorbachev needed Reagan.

Carlucci believed that summit diplomacy gave Reagan "a new lease on life" during the darkest months of his administration.[40] For Reagan, there appeared to be little to lose. One *New York Times*/CBS poll reported that only 16 percent of Americans had an unfavorable view of Gorbachev. Many in the White House were beginning to conclude that a summit in Washington with the Soviet leader, leading to an arms treaty, was Reagan's best chance of recovering his presidency and establishing a historical legacy other than Iran-Contra. But another rocky summit might just finish Reagan off politically for the remaining year of his presidency.

The pressure on Powell was immense. Substantive agreements had to be reached. Controversy had to be avoided. And, most importantly, Reagan had to be at the top of his game. Powell understood that with Shultz's deft handling of the news media and Reagan enveloped in a protective cocoon of staffers determined to deflect public criticism, blame would fall on him, as national security adviser, if the summit faltered. It had proved convenient for Shultz and Reagan to lay the blame on White House Chief of Staff Don Regan for Reykjavik and on Robert McFarlane, John Poindexter, William Casey, and Regan for Iran-Contra. The administration was skilled at manufacturing scapegoats to shield Reagan from responsibility for previous political disasters. Powell thus understood that there were numerous potential perils. But he also possessed certain advantages. The summit would be held in Washington, the first since the Nixon-Brezhnev meeting of 1974 (when another American president in crisis reached out to a Soviet leader for rescue). Reagan, who never traveled well and had been known to doze in the presence of world leaders, would at least be sleeping in his own bed.

Powell anticipated that Gorbachev would be sharp and that Reagan would have to be both well briefed and well rested. He thus grew increasingly alarmed with Reagan's inadequate preparations for the summit. Every time he sought to brief the president, Reagan lost focus. Once, the president insisted on talking about a set of cufflinks he was going to give Gorbachev, rather than discussing briefing materials on the substance of the summit.[41] Powell also became exasperated when Deputy White House Chief of Staff Ken Duberstein demanded that the INF Treaty signing occur at 1:45 p.m., rather than at the previously scheduled morning time. As was later revealed, Nancy Reagan had been consulting astrologers throughout Reagan's political career, and one particular astrologer, the San Francisco socialite Joan Quigley, had influenced many of the administration's decisions, including those involving foreign policy and diplomacy.[42] A dismayed Carlucci demanded that Powell explain the scheduling changes. "Colin, what the hell is this?" Carlucci asked. "Why does this have to be set at that particular time?" "Frank," Powell replied, "you don't want to know."[43]

At the beginning of the Washington summit in early December 1987, Powell's worst fears were initially realized. Gorbachev spoke first. By all accounts, it was a masterful performance. He spoke without notes, addressing the complicated and substantive issues of the summit. Powell recorded his first impressions of the Soviet leader: "Bright. Fast. Quick turning radius. Vigorous. Solid. Feisty. Colorful Speech." Gorbachev used arms-control terminology like "MIRV" and "depressed trajectories." Powell conceded that Gorbachev, who knew the throw weights and technical details of various weapons systems, understood more about some U.S. weapons than he did. Powell held his breath when it was Reagan's turn to speak. It was a lamentable performance. The president began by telling a pointless and unfunny joke about the Soviet Union. No one in the room laughed. Gorbachev stared ahead, expressionless. Powell wanted to disappear under the conference table. "It was offensive," he lamented.[44] "The President's performance continued to reveal his thin preparation," Powell observed of the first day of the summit. "On diplomatic questions he would turn to Shultz and say, 'Well, George, you might want to say a word about that.' On military matters, he turned to Carlucci: 'Frank, I'm sure you would like to address that point.'" Powell recalled, "The meeting was a disaster." Afterward, the American participants retreated to the Oval Office where Shultz gave Reagan a scolding. "Mr. President," Shultz said, "that was a disaster. That man is tough. He's prepared. And you can't just sit there telling jokes." Powell shared Shultz's concerns, but he also worried about Reagan's self-esteem. During his year in the White House, Powell had learned that Reagan, like many professional entertainers, possessed a delicate ego. To bounce back from his poor showing, Reagan needed restored confidence. Powell ordered his staff to work overnight to provide Reagan with a simpler set of talking points, which improved the situation but did not resolve it.[45]

Powell continued to observe Gorbachev throughout the summit and admired the Soviet leader's intellectual dexterity. Gorbachev could make detailed presentations on complicated issues "out of his head, displaying total command of his material." But Powell also noted Gorbachev's quick, unscripted wit and occasional flashes of anger, demonstrating that he was not merely concerned with public relations. Gorbachev had also become quite adept at handling Reagan and his tendency to wander. "Though Gorbachev was clearly superior in mastery of the issues," Powell observed, "there was not a trace of condescension in his manner."[46]

One problem for Powell during the Washington summit was that he could not be everywhere at the same time. While he was away working on the final communiqué, Reagan told Gorbachev a story he had read in *People* magazine about a morbidly obese, twelve-hundred-pound shut-in. A puzzled Gorbachev responded by asking about the location of the nearest men's room, gesticulating to the Soviet ambassador, Anatoly Dobrynin, as he left the room.[47]

For the most part, Powell, with the sympathetic understanding of Gorbachev, managed to minimize such gaffs and keep the meetings focused on arms control. The meeting's crowning achievement was the signing of the INF Treaty on December 8, which eliminated all ground-launched intermediate- and shorter-range nuclear missiles. In the wake of the Washington

Figure 3.2. Powell meets Soviet leader Mikhail Gorbachev for the first time at the Washington summit, December 8, 1987. Agreeing with Secretary of State George Shultz's assessment, Powell shrewdly understood that Gorbachev was a world-historical leader, the kind of figure who appears on the world stage once in a generation. Powell, like Shultz and Frank Carlucci, worked to guarantee that the Reagan administration took maximum advantage of the unique historical opportunity Gorbachev's leadership presented. The three American officials worked against the clock, as Reagan's presidency neared its end, to secure arms-control agreements and the restoration of détente with the Soviet Union. It also did not hurt that Reagan, by the end of 1987, desperately needed Gorbachev. After the loss of the Senate in the 1986 midterm elections, the revelations from the Iran-Contra scandal throughout the spring and summer of 1987, the epic stock market crash of October 1987, and the resounding rejection of Reagan's Supreme Court nominee that same month, Reagan's presidency was looking increasingly tattered and lacking in energy and imagination. Great-power summitry with Gorbachev offered Reagan an opportunity to stand tall on the world stage, but it also gave the president the opportunity to change the subject to peacemaking after several years of bad news. Photo credit: Ronald Reagan Presidential Library.

summit, it was becoming clear that the United States had a remarkable opportunity to reach agreements with the new Soviet leader, maybe even to address some of the most contentious issues of the Cold War. Powell, following Shultz's lead, sensed this.

It would not be easy. Some of Reagan's most zealous conservative defenders predicted the end of Western civilization if Reagan continued on his present course. Others beside the right-wing media and think tank community were alarmed. Numerous administration officials also feared the consequences of

Shultz's objective of establishing a new détente. Powell struggled to prevent the hard-liners in the administration from derailing the new détente. They were trying to reverse the trends of the rapprochement, hoping to revive Reagan's Cold War rhetoric of the past.

While preparing for the upcoming Moscow summit during a visit to the Kremlin in February 1988, Powell received a revealing briefing about Gorbachev's goals and aims from Anatoly Dobrynin, the Kremlin's diplomatic éminence grise. He explained to Powell that Gorbachev, a trained lawyer, wanted to make the Soviet Union a nation based upon the rule of law "instead of a place run by party hacks." He warned that Gorbachev's reforms were "driving the generals crazy" and explained that because Gorbachev wanted to focus on domestic reforms, he did not want Cold War tensions

Figure 3.3. Powell briefing President Reagan, along with White House Chief of Staff Howard Baker and Deputy Chief of Staff Ken Duberstein, April 18, 1988. The team of Baker and Powell at the White House, along with George Shultz at the State Department and Frank Carlucci at the Pentagon, gave Reagan's last year in office a decidedly moderate hue. One could have imagined these officials advising previous Republican presidents such as Richard Nixon or Gerald Ford, both of whose administrations were deemed dangerously moderate by the Reaganite true believers. There was no doubting that the moderates were now in the ascendancy. They would lead Reagan toward a number of eleventh-hour foreign policy triumphs in 1988, after two disastrous and controversial years that nearly cost him his presidency. Photo credit: Ronald Reagan Presidential Library.

creating obstacles. Powell did not discount what Dobrynin told him. He understood more clearly than most that Gorbachev and his senior advisers sought to give the Americans the clearest picture possible of their aims and goals to avoid unforeseen surprises.[48]

The unpleasant surprises came from Washington, not Moscow, demonstrating that Powell still had much to learn about Washington politics. The hard-liners desperately wanted to extend the Cold War, and Reagan delivered an old-fashioned Cold War speech in April 1988. Moreover, some in the administration may have been seeking to placate the harshest right-wing critics in advance of Reagan's upcoming trip to Moscow. Neither Powell nor Reagan, who Powell claims was truly committed to the strategy of "moving away from confrontation and toward cooperation with the Soviet Union," noticed the tone of the speech, which harkened back to the ideological posturing more typical of the president's first term.[49]

When Gorbachev and Powell met in April 1988 in Moscow, Gorbachev expressed concern with the tone of Reagan's recent speech on the state of U.S.-Soviet relations. Was he missing something, he asked Powell? The Reagan speech had put Gorbachev in a difficult position in Moscow and exposed him to criticism from his own hard-liners. Gorbachev told Powell that they should resist people "who want to put sticks in the spokes of Soviet-American normalization." But, having come this far with Reagan, Gorbachev would not allow anything to derail his objectives. Powell was relieved that the general secretary did not exploit Reagan's remarks as Nikita Khrushchev had the downing of an American U-2 spy plane just prior to his summit with President Dwight D. Eisenhower in 1960. Powell reassured Gorbachev that Reagan remained committed to détente.

Gorbachev told Powell he was moving forward and that no disruptions by hard-line opponents of détente could change that. Gorbachev cited former president Richard Nixon's recent attack on the INF Treaty. "Nixon has taken a break from the labor of writing his memoirs to take part in political debates," Gorbachev told Powell and Shultz. "The dead should not be allowed to take the living by the coattails and drag them back to the past." Powell thought to himself, "Very perceptive, Mikhail." Gorbachev explained to Powell and Shultz his objectives of glasnost and perestroika, warning that he was impatient to do as much as he could before he was turned out of office. "He was going to change the USSR in ways we never imagined," Powell recalled. "He was saying, in effect, that he was ending the Cold War." At one point in the discussion, Gorbachev looked directly at Powell and smiled: "What are you going to do now that you've lost your best enemy?"[50]

Powell began to imagine a world without the Cold War, but he observed how difficult it was for others to accept the possibility of change. The U.S. intelligence community had downplayed the profound changes in the USSR and continued to believe the Soviets would be a permanent enemy. Both Powell and Shultz began to ignore such so-called experts, particularly the CIA. On the way back to the United States, Powell stopped in London to brief Margaret Thatcher on the summit. He informed the prime minister that Gorbachev had told him, "I'm going to do as much as I can for as long as I

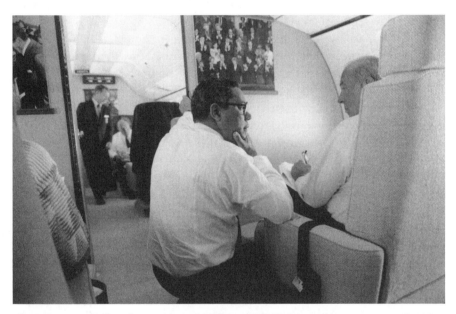

Figure 3.4. Powell and Secretary of State George Shultz confer en route to the Moscow summit, May 29, 1988. Shultz was often called "Buddha" for the sense of calm and stoicism he projected. Powell respected Shultz for his skill at bringing a degree of realism and pragmatic problem solving to the Reagan administration. Although Powell owed much of his career to Shultz's chief rival in the administration, Secretary of Defense Caspar Weinberger, Powell valued Shultz's guidance and saw the elder statesman as a successful example of how a statesman could achieve his objectives. When Powell became secretary of state in 2001, he sought to follow Shultz's example of providing realist alternatives for a president too often inclined to embrace extreme ideological positions. While Shultz was largely successful in patiently outlasting his rivals and steering Reagan in a more moderate direction toward détente, Powell failed spectacularly in his later efforts to get George W. Bush to resist unilateralism, preemptive war, and the siren call of neo-imperialism. Photo credit: Ronald Reagan Presidential Library.

can. I will make it irreversible. And then someone else will come and replace me when I've worn myself out."[51]

In Moscow for the May 1988 Reagan-Gorbachev summit, Powell obtained fresh evidence of Soviet defense realities during meetings with high-ranking Soviet military officials.[52] Moreover, the Moscow summit was seen as another triumph. Owing to slick public relations, it was perceived as even better than the Washington summit, although it lacked the substance of the INF Treaty, which had been agreed to at Washington. The Moscow meeting did, however, continue the pattern of good relations between Moscow and Washington and set the stage for Gorbachev's dramatic appearance before the United Nations in December 1988, at which occasion he declared what amounted to a unilateral end to the Cold War.

The UN speech was remarkable for Gorbachev's announcement of sweeping, across-the-board, unilateral cuts in armaments. The thunderous applause that greeted Gorbachev's arrival at the UN General Assembly impressed Powell. The content of Gorbachev's speech impressed him even more, as the Soviet leader declared, with no quid pro quo from Washington, that the Soviets would reduce their armed forces by five hundred thousand. Powell, who had now observed Gorbachev at close range over the past year, said, "[T]here was no doubt in my mind that he meant what he said." After the speech, Gorbachev turned to Reagan, Vice President George H. W. Bush, and Powell at Governor's Island and said, "In 1985, when I said there was going to be a revolution, everybody cheered. They said, yes, we needed a revolution. But by 1987, our revolution was on, and the cheering began to die down. Now, in 1988, the revolution still goes on, but the cheering has stopped."[53]

Conclusion

Assessments of Powell's time as national security adviser are almost universally positive. Although he held the post for only a little more than a year, he achieved much during his tenure. Most observers credit him with playing a constructive role after Iran-Contra in rebuilding Reagan's tattered national security personnel.[54] "Colin Powell played a central role and had considerable responsibility for cleaning up other people's messes," concluded NSC scholar David Rothkopf.[55] Powell and Shultz also worked harmoniously to steer Reagan toward the agreements with Gorbachev and responded shrewdly to Gorbachev's overtures and initiatives. Near the end of the administration, during a dinner held in Shultz's honor, Powell joked that "the NSC adviser and the secretary of state had not gotten on so well since the days when Henry Kissinger held both jobs simultaneously." Kissinger, sitting at the dais, roared with approval. There was much truth in Powell's comment.[56] Reagan biographer Lou Cannon concluded that Powell had been "a conspicuous success in a job where many failed during the Reagan administration."[57]

Reagan's record on the management of his foreign policy was troubled. For the first six years of his administration, chaos frequently reigned in the White House and within and between departments and agencies. His lax management style exacerbated this problem, as he was incapable of giving his subordinates clear direction or even adjudicating disputes among them. By any standard of assessment, his national security apparatus was a total failure, as several of his six national security advisers have attested. Until the arrival of Carlucci, it was never clear to Shultz or Weinberger (or Reagan) what the NSC staff might be up to. Its machinations compounded the chaos and inconsistency of Reagan's foreign policy.

Reagan and his admirers claimed that merely by enhancing American military power, he had made the world a more ordered place. Yet, for all of America's power, the world remained chaotic, and it soon became apparent that all the military spending in the world could not establish order or ensure peace. Moreover, massive military spending often had unintended consequences. The economic boom of the time was driven by massive budget deficits, doubling the national debt in the first six years. These massive deficits also created systemic problems as they distorted exchange rates, undermined American international competitiveness, and devoured capital that might otherwise have gone toward investment. All of these developments contributed to the economic downturn of 1990 to 1992.

Nor was defense spending related to any overarching strategy. Alliances were frayed, the peace process in the Middle East languished, and what should have been relatively minor concerns, such as Lebanon and Nicaragua, paralyzed the administration. Owing largely to orthodox Cold War geopolitical assumptions, the Reagan administration insisted upon treating challenges like Lebanon and Nicaragua as part of the East-West confrontation rather than local conflicts with local causes. The Reagan Doctrine's reliance upon proxies to fight wars in the developing world often provoked more, not less, instability, particularly in Central America, Africa, and Afghanistan. The Reagan Doctrine was often implemented covertly, with Casey's CIA and McFarlane's and Poindexter's NSC staffs freelancing throughout the world. Such schemes almost brought the administration to ruin. The intervention in Lebanon led to a chain reaction that nearly crippled Reagan's presidency. The administration's enthusiastic backing of Islamic militants in Afghanistan, some of whom later comprised elements of the Taliban and al Qaeda, had major repercussions for Reagan's successors, as did the decision to tilt toward Iraq's Saddam Hussein in his war with Iran. The administration's Middle East policy was a naive muddle, shredded by regional crises. A "strategic partnership" with Israel as part of a new Cold War approach to the region created new realities in the region and throughout predominantly Muslim countries. Reagan's policies often strained relations with European allies. Moreover, the very fact that the Reagan administration issued a record-setting forty-one UN Security Council vetoes, twelve of them to protect the white-ruled apartheid regime in South Africa, further demonstrated its ideological marginalization from the mainstream of world politics.

The Reagan administration neither orchestrated nor shaped the events that led to Gorbachev's rise and his reform effort. American policy toward the USSR had been rhetorical, posturing, and without real substance. There is scant evidence that the Soviet Union ever attempted to match the Reagan-era defense buildup. On the contrary, the Soviets were, as Gorbachev hinted to Powell, prepared to end the Cold War regardless of the U.S. course, as long as they could obtain assurances that the United States would not exploit their predicament. Certainly, Gorbachev's speech at the United Nations demonstrated his belief that he had finally achieved mastery over his own hard-liners and no longer needed reciprocal concessions from the Americans.[58] The administration's eventual response to Gorbachev's initiatives, after halting beginnings, was commendable. With the distractions out of the way, such as the Iran-Contra scandal and the retirement or marginalization of many hard-line advisers, much could be achieved. Although some might argue that "the breakthroughs were largely the result of aggressive Soviet diplomacy rather than American efforts,"[59] Shultz and Powell deserve credit for ensuring that the United States did not miss the opportunity Gorbachev presented. And Reagan, to the shock and dismay of many of his supporters, turned out to be far more receptive to better relations with the Soviet Union than many believed he could ever be. Ultimately, it was in dealing with Gorbachev that the administration shone, and Powell was rightly proud to have seen the new détente as one of the major achievements of his career. From what we know of the seven years prior to Powell's arrival, nothing was foreordained about the new détente. It required the efforts of officials like Shultz, Carlucci, and Powell.[60]

There is certainly some irony in the leader of the Soviet Union's bailing Reagan out. After all, Reagan had built much of his following upon hyperbolic rhetoric about the USSR. As Francis Fitzgerald shrewdly observed, "The price of Reagan's restoration was precisely what the conservatives had so strenuously attempted to avert for a decade: a general sense in the United States that there was no serious Soviet threat and the Cold War was coming

Figure 3.5.   A contemplative Powell at the Moscow summit, May 29, 1988. Looking back on Powell's extensive career, the new détente of 1987 to 1989 stands out as one of his most important achievements, and the warm feelings produced by the Reagan-Gorbachev Moscow summit of May–June 1988 marked one of the crowning moments of those years. While many commentators would later heap praise upon Powell for his role as chairman of the Joint Chiefs during the 1990–1991 Gulf War against Iraq, his work as Reagan's sixth and final national security adviser was in many respects more lasting and historic. But Powell's support for the new détente during these years would also create unanticipated problems. Not everyone was pleased with the thaw in su-perpower relations or the prospect of the Cold War's end. Hard-line neoconservatives would never forgive Powell for his contribution to making peace with the Soviet Union and ending the Cold War; nor were they pleased with Powell's role in steering Reagan in a more moderate direction after years of hard-line ideological saber rattling. Photo credit: Ronald Reagan Presidential Library.

to an end. The crowds in the streets were far ahead of the administration in this perception, but by calling the INF treaty 'historic,' Reagan made it so, and by playing his part in the buddy movie of Mikhail and Ron, he destroyed the caricature of the Soviets he himself had done so much to create over the past thirty years."[61]

The Reagan years are rich with such ironies. The administration was more confused, chaotic, and internally divided than was previously understood. Reagan and his administration will remain a vexing subject of controversy. Few administrations have been so image conscious, so focused on the shaping of perceptions—a subject of the most revealing of the memoirs to come out of the administration by Alexander Haig, David Stockman, Donald Regan, Michael Deaver, and Powell himself, as well as of accounts by the most perceptive observers of the period, such as Lou Cannon, Frances Fitzgerald, Richard Reeves, Michael Schaller, Sean Wilentz, and Gary Wills. Future historians will continue to face the challenge of distinguishing between perceptions of what happened and the reality.

Figure 3.6. Powell with Reagan on the president's last full day in the White House. January 19, 1989. Powell's feelings toward Reagan were complicated. He believed the president had achieved much in restoring America's position in the world and in improving Americans' feelings about their country. As a career military man, Powell was also pleased with the large defense buildup that occurred during the Reagan years. But during his two years in the White House, Powell at times became concerned about Reagan's erratic behavior. Powell was troubled by incidents such as Reagan's reliance on astrology, his belief in the possibility of alien invasions from outer space, and his inability to focus during important briefings. Such observations about Reagan's intellectual shortcomings were a departure from the veil of silence that usually surrounded discussions of the president, his mental state, and his health. Powell and the previous national security adviser, Frank Carlucci, were two of the highest-level administration officials to later speak openly about these challenges. But Powell and Carlucci also served at a point in Reagan's administration—its last two years—when the president was more likely to be showing signs of age and mental fatigue, and they thus experienced challenges that earlier staffers and aids may not have faced. Photo credit: Ronald Reagan Presidential Library.

As for Powell, the Reagan years had transformed him from a largely obscure mid-level Pentagon appointee in 1981 into the president's national security adviser by January 1989. From his experiences in the Reagan administration, Powell gained an understanding of the complexities and controversies surrounding the question of U.S. military intervention. For all of its rhetorical bluster, the Reagan administration had not come any closer than its predecessors to resolving the question of when to intervene. On the contrary, the debacle of Lebanon, placed alongside the seemingly effortless intervention in Grenada, made easy answers elusive. Moreover, the ambivalence about intervention in Central America (1981–1986), Libya (1986), and the Persian Gulf (1987–1989) demonstrated the deep divisions within the administration over questions of war and peace, as well as over the meaning of the Vietnam Syndrome and the Weinberger Doctrine. During the early years of the Reagan administration, when the debate over these issues burned brightest, Powell was a marginal figure, on the fringes of the discussion, serving as a staffer to the secretary of defense. During the next administration, that of George H. W. Bush, Powell, as chairman of the Joint Chiefs of Staff, was a major participant in the debates over such controversies, and his opinions and perceptions came into clearer focus.

Notes

1. Colin Powell, My American Journey (New York: Ballantine, 1995, 2003), 306, 362–63.

2. Raymond L. Garthoff, The Great Transition: American-Soviet Relations and the End of the Cold War (Washington, DC: Brookings Institution, 1994).

3. David Halberstam, War in a Time of Peace: Bush, Clinton, and the Generals (New York: Scribner, 2001), 13.

4. Perhaps the best account of Gorbachev's strategy is Garthoff, The Great Transition. See also Jack Matlock Jr., Reagan and Gorbachev: How the Cold War Ended (New York: Random House, 2004), 304–12.

5. James Mann, Rise of the Vulcans: The History of Bush's War Cabinet (New York: Viking Press, 2004), 159.

6. Quoted in Powell, My American Journey, 367.

7. Lou Cannon, "Powell Well-Regarded in Difficult Post," Washington Post, November 5, 1987.

8. Bernard Trainor, "Appointee to Security Post Is Praised," New York Times, November 6, 1987.

9. Interview with Clarke McCurdy Brintall, Foreign Affairs Oral History Collection, May 2, 1996, Library of Congress.

10. Interview with Robert S. Pastorino, Foreign Affairs Oral History Collection, March 6, 1998, Library of Congress.

11. Interview with George Shultz, Ronald Reagan Oral History Project, December 18, 2002, Miller Center for Public Affairs, University of Virginia.

12. Quoted in Lou Cannon, *President Reagan: The Role of a Lifetime* (New York: Public Affairs, 2000), 42.

13. Quoted in Powell, *My American Journey*, 356, 360.

14. John Tower, Edmund Muskie, and Brent Scowcroft, *The Tower Commission Report* (New York: Times Books, 1987), 62–100.

15. Quoted in Powell, *My American Journey*, 354.

16. William S. Cohen and George Mitchell, *Men of Zeal: A Candid Inside Story of the Iran-Contra Hearings* (New York: Penguin Books, 1989).

17. Richard Reeves, *President Reagan: The Triumph of Imagination* (New York: Simon and Schuster, 2005), 234.

18. Interview with Frank Carlucci, Ronald Reagan Oral History Project, August 28, 2001, Miller Center for Public Affairs, University of Virginia.

19. Powell, *My American Journey*, 350; Cannon, *President Reagan*, 42, 515–19.

20. Powell, *My American Journey*, 287, 349, 368.

21. Powell, *My American Journey*, 337; Alexander M. Haig Jr., *Caveat: Realism, Reagan, and Foreign Policy* (New York: MacMillan, 1984), 85.

22. Ethan Rarick, *California Rising* (Berkeley: University of California Press, 2005), 362–63; Cannon, *President Reagan*, 458.

23. Lou Cannon, *Governor Reagan: His Rise to Power* (New York: Public Affairs, 2003), 201; Jackson Putnam, "Governor Reagan: A Reappraisal," *California History* 83, no. 4 (2006); interview with Stuart Spencer, Ronald Reagan Oral History Project, November 15, 2001, Miller Center for Public Affairs, University of Virginia.

24. William Raspberry, "Reagan's Race Legacy," *Washington Post*, June 14, 2004.

25. Taylor Branch, *At Canaan's Edge: America in the King Years, 1965–1968* (New York: Simon and Schuster, 2006), 543–44, 770.

26. Henry Louis Gates Jr., "Powell and the Black Elite," *New Yorker*, September 25, 1995.

27. Quoted in Reeves, *President Reagan*, 295.

28. David J. Rothkopf, *Running the World: Inside the National Security Council and the Architects of American Power* (New York: Public Affairs, 2005), 210–12.

29. Interview with George Shultz, Ronald Reagan Oral History Project.

30. George Shultz, *Turmoil and Triumph: Diplomacy, Power, and the Victory of the American Ideal* (New York: Simon and Schuster, 1993), 991.

31. Interview with Frank Carlucci, Ronald Reagan Oral History Project.

32. Interview with George Shultz, Ronald Reagan Oral History Project.

33. Interview with Frank Carlucci, Ronald Reagan Oral History Project.

34. Powell, *My American Journey*, 355; interview with George Shultz, Ronald Reagan Oral History Project.

35. Powell, *My American Journey*, 359.

36. Reeves, *President Reagan*, 422.

37. Powell, *My American Journey*, 329, 402.

38. Powell to Lee Hamilton [on Nicaragua], February 1, 1988, folder 3, box 92476, Colin Powell files, Ronald Reagan Presidential Library.

39. Quoted in Powell, *My American Journey*, 328.

40. Interview with Frank Carlucci, Ronald Reagan Oral History Project.

41. Powell, *My American Journey*, 348–53.

42. Cannon, *President Reagan*, 515–19.

43. Interview with Frank Carlucci, Ronald Reagan Oral History Project.

44. Quoted in Cannon, *President Reagan*, 697.

45. Powell, *My American Journey*, 351; Cannon, *President Reagan*, 697.

46. Powell, *My American Journey*, 353.

47. Frances Fitzgerald, *Way Out There in the Blue: Reagan, Star Wars and the End of the Cold War* (New York: Touchstone, 2000), 433.

48. Powell, *My American Journey*, 356–61.

49. Powell, *My American Journey*, 361.

50. Quoted in Powell, *My American Journey*, 362, 531.

51. Quoted in Powell, *My American Journey*, 363.

52. Powell memorandum of conversation with Marshal Akhromeyev, May 31, 1988, Moscow, folder 9, box 92477, Powell files, Ronald Reagan Presidential Library.

53. Quoted in Powell, *My American Journey*, 377–81.

54. "Editorial: A Working National Security Team," *New York Times*, July 10, 1988.

55. Rothkopf, *Running the World*, 258.

56. Shultz, *Turmoil and Triumph*, 1138.

57. Quoted in Cannon, *President Reagan*, 42.

58. See Garthoff, *The Great Transition*, particularly chs. 5 through 8 on Gorbachev's strategy and intentions.

59. David Ignatius, "Reagan's Foreign Policy and the Rejection of Diplomacy," in *The Reagan Legacy*, ed. Sidney Blumenthal and Thomas Byrne Edsall (New York: Pantheon Books, 1988), 177.

60. Colin Powell, "Why History Will Honor Mr. Reagan," *New York Times*, January 15, 1989.

61. Fitzgerald, *Way Out There*, 438.

~

CHAPTER FOUR

Chairman of the Joint Chiefs, 1989–1993

Appointed in the fall of 1989 as chairman of the Joint Chiefs of Staff, Powell held that post throughout the remaining three years of the George H. W. Bush administration and into the first year of the Clinton administration. His timing again proved fortuitous. He became chairman, at the age of fifty-two, during a time of transformation for U.S. foreign and defense policy. Most importantly, he served as chairman during the Gulf War, where his steady and reassuring image was beamed into American homes nightly for the six o'clock briefing. The Gulf War transformed him into a national icon and ignited political aspirations he had never contemplated. In the following weeks and months, he further enhanced his public image, aided by *Washington Post* reporter Bob Woodward's revelation in his book *The Commanders* that Powell had worked strenuously against going to war. Although the war had gone remarkably well, the image of the chairman of the Joint Chiefs as a reluctant warrior, one who also happened to be a decorated Vietnam War veteran, appealed to millions of Americans.

From his encounters with Mikhail Gorbachev and other Soviet officials, Colin Powell understood that the Cold War was ending and that the Soviet Union had begun to focus largely on internal reforms. Change was expected in the U.S. military as well, change that would likely include both some reduction in defense spending and a radically restructured military establishment for a post–Cold War world. But these changes did not materialize during the Bush I years. Instead, the use of American military power was majorly reinvigorated as U.S. forces intervened in Panama, Iraq, and Somalia.

With the decline of the Soviet Union as a threat and the disappearance of Moscow's check on American power, the United States continued to engage in post-Vietnam interventions, and the Vietnam Syndrome continued to diminish. Although there had been a major reduction in threats, the end of the Cold War also removed America's remaining inhibitions. First, in Panama, the administration felt compelled to intervene against the regime of former ally Manuel Noriega on a scale that Washington had been reluctant to reach during the preceding struggle against the Sandinistas in Nicaragua. Then, in the Persian Gulf, freed from the restraints of the Cold War, the United States again intervened on a massive scale against another former ally, Saddam Hussein.

Powell believed the outcomes of both the Panama intervention and the Gulf War would serve to remind the American people of the importance of their military and reinforce the perception that, while the Cold War was ending, other threats could emerge. These interventions also eroded the restraints on the use of military force, the very restraints that Powell supported through the development of his "Powell Doctrine." The deceptive ease with which interventions like those in Panama and the Gulf were carried out obscured the real perils inherent in any military intervention. Many U.S. officials, although not Powell, became intoxicated with visions of what American military power might achieve. Many officials increasingly overlooked those incidents when the military had not prevailed or had suffered grievous defeats, such as in Vietnam or Beirut.

The growing support for military solutions to America's foreign policy dilemmas raised questions about the Vietnam Syndrome and the viability of the Powell Doctrine. President George H. W. Bush boasted that the 1991 war in the Persian Gulf had once and for all eradicated the Vietnam Syndrome. To Powell, this might have initially seemed something to celebrate, but in retrospect the restraints imposed on U.S. officials in the wake of Vietnam, along with the constraint posed by the USSR, had discouraged American officials from using military power as a one-size-fits-all solution to America's foreign policy challenges. Panama and the Gulf changed that. Moreover, the political benefits of being commander in chief during a popular war established a dangerous example for future presidents. The decline of the Cold War did not create the new world order Bush had predicted but instead left the United States confronting a host of new problems, such as the disintegration of states, ethnic conflicts, nation building, and terrorism.

Although Powell came to be identified with the administration of George H. W. Bush, their relations were often awkward. Bush wanted to put some distance between himself and his predecessor, Ronald Reagan, whom he had

Figure 4.1. Powell, as President Reagan's national security adviser, and Vice President George H. W. Bush confer at the last summit between Reagan and Gorbachev at Governor's Island, New York, December 7, 1988. Powell respected Bush, but his relations with the new president were complex. Powell would always be grateful to the president for appointing him the first black chairman of the Joint Chiefs of Staff, but Powell had reservations about Bush's commitment to racial harmony. Powell was dismayed by the racial politics of Bush's 1988 presidential campaign, when he frequently deployed the "race card" to drive a wedge between white voters and the Democratic candidate, Michael Dukakis. Such Republican tactics, and a general indifference to black Americans in general, exposed problems Powell would have with the Republican Party, problems that would present formidable obstacles to a possible Powell presidential run in 1996. Photo credit: Ronald Reagan Presidential Library.

served loyally—some said too loyally—over the previous eight years. He wanted to establish his own administration and subtly distinguish his foreign policy from Reagan's.

Powell had proven himself a capable national security adviser—no small achievement in a job known as Reagan's Bermuda Triangle. But he had also become identified with the last year of the Reagan administration, which presented Bush with a quandary. After Bush was elected in November 1988, he offered Powell the choice of a number of senior-level appointments in the new administration. "You're one of the few people in the White House I want to consider for the new team," Bush told him. "I have some options I hope you'll think about. Jim Baker would like you as deputy secretary of state.

Or you can have the CIA. Or you can stay on as National Security Adviser for a while, until you decide what you want to do."[1]

Powell found Bush's offers flattering and generous. As James Baker's deputy Powell might expect to become secretary of state one day, and the CIA job was certainly a compliment coming from Bush, who had briefly held that post in 1976 and 1977. But Powell had reservations about Bush's offers. He had already served as national security adviser and had seen his reputation enhanced further after he was mentioned several times as a potential vice presidential nominee. He was not interested in becoming Baker's deputy, which he saw as a demotion after having served as national security adviser. He did not want to go to the CIA, and he saw little point in staying on at NSC because it was widely known that Bush wanted Brent Scowcroft. Moreover, he may have been suspicious of Bush's motives. He later expressed to Woodward that several matters were troubling him. The president-elect may have seen the retention of Powell as a gesture aimed at overcoming the divisiveness of the recent campaign, which had featured less-than-subtle racial appeals to white voters. Something about Bush made Powell uneasy, although this was not uncommon among senior officials who had served with the vice president in the Reagan administration, a remarkably large number of whom had supported other candidates for president in 1988. Certain aspects of Bush's campaign had troubled Powell. The lurid nature of its partisan accusations and strident patriotic attacks dismayed him. Even Bush himself later confessed that he often indulged in "rhetorical overkill."[2]

The Bush campaign's Willie Horton strategy—by which Bush, hoping to stoke fears about race, made the crimes of a black convict on a weekend furlough a potent campaign theme—particularly distressed Powell. "Was the ad depicting this incident racist?" he asked. "Of course. Had it bothered me? Certainly."[3] Bush, like many Republican politicians during this era, had exploited racial fears and tensions to his advantage throughout his career. Dating back to his two terms as a congressman from Houston in the 1960s, Bush made outlandish claims about the civil rights movement and Lyndon Johnson's antipoverty programs. (As a congressman, Bush suggested in a speech that seven new microscopes, provided for schools in his district by federal antipoverty programs, could be retooled as riflescopes for use by black radicals.[4]) Powell's ambivalence about Bush and race once again raised the larger problem he faced serving in Republican administrations. It was an area where he found Bush "wanting."[5]

Shortly before Reagan departed Washington in January 1989, he rewarded Powell for his service in the White House with a promotion to four stars as commanding general of U.S. Forces Command (FORSCOM).[6] As commander of the national strategic reserve of one million troops, most of them National Guardsmen and reserves, Powell would be one of only ten four-star commanders in chief. Based at Fort McPherson, Georgia, he added his own personal touches to his headquarters, prominently displaying a framed poster of Dr. Martin Luther King Jr. given to him by King's widow, Coretta Scott King. It was, nevertheless, a difficult transition for Powell after serving as senior foreign policy adviser to the president. He had not been in a military assignment for more than two years. Much had happened in the world since his last command, and he had held a front-row seat throughout most of it. He had sat across a table from Gorbachev and listened to his vision of "New Thinking" and his unilateral declaration of the Cold War's end. Now, returning to the military, he discovered that while the United States had well-equipped and well-trained forces, senior commanders remained fixated on fighting the Soviet Union. He was concerned that the events of the past few years had not changed the military. He decided to use his command of FORSCOM as a "pulpit" to "deliver a dose of reality" about the Cold War and Soviet objectives. During a May 1989 speech at the Army War College in Carlisle, Pennsylvania, he could feel the resistance in the room as he praised Gorbachev and challenged the assumption that the Cold War would continue interminably.[7]

Powell knew that he could be taking a risk. The new Bush administration, particularly its national security team, which now included Scowcroft and the new secretary of defense, Dick Cheney, was dubious of Gorbachev's intentions and inclined to overstate Soviet objectives. The consensus at the time at the CIA, the Pentagon, and even the White House was that nothing would change and that the USSR would emerge from Gorbachev's reform movement sufficiently revitalized to carry on the Cold War.[8] Powell was particularly taking a chance in challenging Cheney, who, he observed, "was not a boss who enjoyed being contradicted."[9] But Powell went beyond pushing the idea that the changes Gorbachev had unleashed were real and lasting. He anticipated that NATO would be expanded and that the Atlantic alliance would serve as a cornerstone of the new, post–Cold War order. Powell accepted that, with the end of the Cold War, the military would have to retrench. He believed that Gorbachev had led the way toward deep and permanent reductions in the Soviet military, and the United States had been slow to react and adjust to these profound changes. Like many career officers, Powell viewed the prospect of a peace dividend with trepidation. But he believed the Pentagon could preempt many of the cuts with a retrenchment plan of its own, rather than waiting for orders to restructure.

Adm. William Crowe, the chairman of the Joint Chiefs, was nearing retirement, and many in the military assumed that the appointment would go to Powell, owing to his unparalleled political connections.[10] Former secretary of defense Frank Carlucci had been suggesting Powell as Crowe's replacement. In addition to Carlucci, Powell enjoyed the backing of the two previous secretaries of defense, Caspar Weinberger and Harold Brown, both of whom he had served as an aide. While lobbying Cheney, a persistent Carlucci described Powell as someone who held strong views but who would be loyal. "Dick, you're going to have one big decision during your tenure and that's who the chairman should be," Carlucci told Cheney. "There's only one person and that's Colin Powell."[11]

Cheney knew that Powell understood the workings and functions of the Pentagon and the White House but had reservations about him. After all, candidates for chairman did not normally have three former secretaries of defense lobbying on their behalf. Moreover, as a former national security adviser, Powell might be tempted to intrude into areas and responsibilities beyond those of the chairman of the Joint Chiefs. Cheney worried about the reaction to choosing someone who had served most of his senior postings in staff and political appointments. Perhaps Cheney's chief reservation was that Powell was the most junior of the fifteen eligible four-star generals and admirals.[12]

Cheney eventually agreed with Carlucci's idea of replacing Crowe with Powell, but he encountered reservations from Bush, who feared that elevating him over so many other qualified candidates could create tensions in the pool of senior officers. Powell would be the youngest ever to hold the position, and Bush thought Powell young enough to have an opportunity to serve as chairman later. Cheney pushed for Powell, and the president, also facing the campaign by the three previous secretaries of defense, made the appointment.[13] The Senate formally confirmed Powell in September 1989. He became the youngest officer ever to become chairman, the first African American, and the first ROTC graduate. He had been afforded a remarkable opportunity and saw his role as rethinking and reshaping America's defenses after the Cold War.[14]

Powell was developing a reputation as a political general par excellence. Even James Baker, one of the shrewder operators in Washington, respected Powell's political acumen. He was seen as the most politically deft chairman in decades.[15] Many believed he represented a new breed of post-Vietnam senior officer, one more skilled in dealing with the press and the Washington bureaucracy than more traditional combat-related roles. Recent structural changes in the chairman's job also made Powell the most powerful to date.

Figure 4.2. Powell, President George H. W. Bush, Secretary of Defense Dick Cheney, and outgoing Chairman of the Joint Chiefs of Staff Adm. William Crowe at the time of Powell's appointment as chairman. Although Cheney recommended Powell's appointment to Bush, he did so only after intense lobbying by three former secretaries of defense, George Brown, Caspar Weinberger, and Frank Carlucci. The relationship between the new secretary of defense and the new chairman of the Joint Chiefs would remain complex. During the George H. W. Bush presidency, few noticed the strains between Powell and Cheney. Years later, after the world learned of the intense infighting between Powell and Cheney in the George W. Bush administration, many would reexamine Powell's nuanced description of Cheney in his best-selling 1995 memoir. Photo credit: George H. W. Bush Presidential Library.

The Joint Chiefs, particularly the chairman's post, had been restructured by the 1986 Goldwater-Nichols Act. By freeing the chairman from having to reach consensus among the chiefs, these reforms allowed him more latitude than before, granting him authority to speak on his own to the president, giving him control over a large bureaucracy of fifteen hundred, and providing more power at the expense of the chiefs. A more independent chairman now had more power than in the past.[16] Powell also brought several stylistic changes to the office. He played calypso music and was amused when colleagues did not grasp the innuendo of the lyrics to tunes like "Come Water Me Garden" and "The Big Bamboo." The contrast with his white, sixty-four-year-old, Oklahoma-bred predecessor, Admiral Crowe, could not have been more pronounced.

Publicly, Powell's relations with Cheney and Bush appeared correct, but privately, things were more complicated. He had had ample opportunity to observe Bush up close during the Reagan years, particularly during his stints as deputy national security adviser and then national security adviser. Relations could be tricky with Bush, who often personalized differences so that the everyday rough-and-tumble of politics was perceived as a personal challenge. Reagan, more comfortable with himself, occasionally showed flashes of anger in public but rarely personal rancor. Unlike Reagan, who could be quite magnanimous and enjoyed engaging his critics, Bush often reacted viscerally, even emotionally, to challenges. Observers noted that despite decades in public life, Bush had a tendency to bear grudges. He had a long memory for those he believed had slighted him or stood in his way. Bush also had an unfortunate tendency to personalize conflicts, not only political ones but international ones, such as with Manuel Noriega or Saddam Hussein. There was an emotional element to his rhetoric, as if he took the very existence of such rogues as a personal affront. And yet, at one time, Bush considered both Noriega and Hussein to be suitable allies.[17]

Powell also observed that Bush ran things differently than Reagan. Reagan's style was detached, his administration conducted by remote control. The Reagan White House's structure of multiple layers around the president, with only a select few having coveted access, was not for Bush. Bush was hands-on and wanted details, whereas Reagan, more ideological and less pragmatic on matters of foreign policy, couldn't have cared less. The comparative pragmatism and moderation of Bush's advisers also differed from the Reagan years. The new team was collegial, having few of the ideological obsessions and less of the personal rancor and constant infighting of the Reagan administration.

As chairman of the Joint Chiefs, Powell's relationship with Secretary of Defense Dick Cheney was of particular importance. It was not always an easy fit. While Cheney may have shared with his predecessor, Carlucci, a talent for administration, he showed little concern for compromise and accommodation. Carlucci was a trusted conservative and cold warrior, but he also demonstrated an ability to adapt pragmatically to changed circumstances. Cheney was not known for his adaptability. Powell had experienced the Cheney style prior to becoming chairman. An uncompromising partisan of the Nicaraguan Contras, Cheney had served on the House intelligence committee during the Iran-Contra imbroglio. During the hearings over the scandal, Cheney staunchly advocated unfettered presidential power. Shortly thereafter, Powell, as Reagan's national security adviser, sought a deal with Congress over the Contras. The Contras had become unpopular in the wake of the Iran-Contra scandal, and Powell had invested long hours with members of Congress in early 1988 on a compromise Contra aid package, which required only that Republicans agree to a few minor concessions. Powell worked hard to find the Democratic swing votes he needed. "I had not reckoned, however, with the character of House Minority Whip Dick Cheney," Powell recalled. "He preferred losing on principle to winning through further compromise."[18] Years later, he revealed to *Washington Post* reporter Bob Woodward that Cheney "confounded" him. He had drafted and redrafted the sections on him in his 1995 memoir, but he never felt he captured the real Dick Cheney. He used circuitous descriptions, sometimes employing a telling anecdote to make his point.[19] Powell understood that Cheney knew little about the military prior to becoming secretary of defense. Moreover, during the Vietnam War, Cheney had received five deferments from the draft, loftily explaining that he had "other things to do" at the time, something the officers serving under him at the Pentagon did not overlook. Powell was puzzled by the choice: "This man, who had never spent a day in uniform, who, during the Vietnam War, had gotten a student deferment and later a parent deferment, had taken instant control of the Pentagon."[20] State Department official Arthur Hughes recalled, "Secretary Cheney never served in the military. He had a series of student deferments. I think that, plus the fact of who Colin Powell was . . . meant for a great amount of care and work on making sure that the relationship was a positive one that worked and was a collegial one."[21]

In his 1995 memoir, Powell revealed that during Cheney's first week on the job, while Powell was still commanding FORSCOM in Georgia, the secretary of defense provoked an incident with Air Force Chief of Staff Gen. Larry Welch. Cheney used a televised news conference to publicly rebuke

Welch for discussing MX missile deployment options with Congress. He charged that Welch had been insubordinate, but Welch's discussion with Congress had been approved by Cheney's own deputy and by National Security Adviser Scowcroft. Wisconsin congressman Les Aspin rose to General Welch's defense. "Jesus Christ, Dick," Aspin said to Cheney, "Welch wasn't doing anything like that, and he always made it clear it was your decision." Cheney responded that, although Aspin may have been correct, "It [the rebuke] was useful." Aspin understood that Cheney had his own agenda and that his public criticism of General Welch had more to do with Cheney's demonstrating that he was the alpha male at the Pentagon than with any transgression on Welch's part. Nonetheless, Cheney was harshly criticized by two former secretaries of defense, Harold Brown and James Schlesinger, both of whom thought his actions a breach of military protocol. Powell, too, knew that Welch had been set up and expressed satisfaction when Welch perhaps got the last word by implying that as a veteran of 137 combat missions in Vietnam, he had been in real combat, not just the bureaucratic kind.[22]

Powell described Cheney as "incisive, smart, no small talk, never showing any more surface than necessary." Powell also found Cheney difficult to work with. What some perceived as self-confidence, others saw as a detachment from the consequences of his decisions. Many saw Cheney as low-key, and this perception was certainly part of his appeal. But this may have been more about how Cheney presented himself. Powell once observed that Cheney was always "supremely self-confident," then added that perhaps he only "managed to give that impression."[23]

Having been national security adviser, Powell was in a strong position to assess the Soviet Union's capabilities and objectives. He, better than anyone else in the armed forces, understood the mounting problems Gorbachev faced. He believed Gorbachev's revolution would result in substantive changes, and he anticipated massive Soviet military budget cuts and the creation of a virtually new Soviet force strictly for defensive purposes. He predicted that soon there would be no Soviet forces in Eastern Europe, leading to the end of the Warsaw Pact. Borrowing from the question Gorbachev had posed to him in Moscow in the spring of 1988, Powell titled one of his speeches "When You Lose Your Best Enemy."[24]

Powell believed that the end of the Cold War also meant the end of the strategy of containment. He could foresee reductions in defense spending on the U.S. side, but perhaps not so much as those who anticipated a "peace dividend." He anticipated naval reductions from 550 ships to 450, as well as large reductions in U.S. troop strength in Europe and elsewhere in the active duty army from 760,000 to 525,000. Powell recognized the cuts would be hard to sell to Cheney and the civilians on Cheney's policy staff, which Powell saw as a refuge for Reagan-era hard-liners "from Paul Wolfowitz on down." Many of Cheney's people remained dubious of Gorbachev and his reforms, holding those who believed the Soviet Union would ever change in contempt. At one point, Cheney told Powell, "None of my civilian advisers supports you," to which Powell teasingly replied, "That's because they're all right-wing nuts like you."[25]

Powell began using the phrase "base force" to describe the minimum level of forces necessary for all the services. Military analyst Andrew Bacevich has argued that "the aim of the Base Force was less to get a head start on military reform than to preempt calls for a 'peace dividend'—suggesting the possibility of draconian cuts in defense spending." At the same time, Bacevich noted, concerns arose that the end of the Cold War might render obsolete the military machine so painstakingly rebuilt after Vietnam. Moreover, the subsequent triumphs in Panama and the Persian Gulf revived enthusiasm for increased military spending, and an opportunity may have been lost for meaningful reform at the end of the Cold War. Curiously, even after the Berlin Wall fell in November 1989 and many of Powell's assumptions about the inevitability of the end of the Cold War were confirmed, there was scant debate about the appropriate uses of military force or, more broadly, the role of the military in American life. "In the aftermath of the Cold War, the principle that the United States required great military strength commanded universal assent in Washington," Bacevich observed. "To dissent from that position was to place oneself beyond the bounds of respectable opinion."[26]

Indeed, crises continued to occur that ostensibly affirmed the need for more defense spending, not less. The first such crisis occurred in Panama. Panamanian strongman Manuel Noriega had gained power with American support in the early 1980s and had been an important part of the Reagan Doctrine in Central America. Powell was aware that Noriega had been on the CIA payroll for a quarter century. He had witnessed Noriega being feted as a savior of the Contras by Weinberger at the Pentagon. Support for Noriega had been so staunch that for a time the Reagan administration impeded investigations into allegations of his drug trafficking. The U.S. Drug Enforcement Agency had even awarded him with a commendation for his contributions to the "war on drugs." Powell observed that the Reagan and Bush administrations should have known that "you could not buy Manuel Noriega, but you could rent him."[27]

With the Cold War ending and the obsessive fear about Nicaragua dissipating, Noriega's usefulness to Washington evaporated. He also took the fateful step of endorsing the Contadora Peace Process for Central America, which the Reagan administration had strongly opposed. His special relation-ship with the United States having ended, Noriega was indicted by grand juries in Tampa and Miami for drug trafficking and suddenly was transformed from a valued ally into the target of public vilification by the Bush administration. Noriega's indictments came at a time when Bush was making the war against drugs a centerpiece of his stalled domestic agenda. The focus on Noriega fit nicely with the administration's charge that the drug problem had more to do with overseas supply than domestic demand, but the administration had al-lowed the indictments to go forward with Noriega still on the U.S. payroll.

Panama revealed some of the paradoxes and contradictions of American foreign policy. The Bush administration had prior notice of a coup plot against Noriega in October 1989 but, despite much rhetoric demonizing Noriega, had hesitated to act against him when the Panamanian leader faced down a coup attempt. Powell was appalled by the Bush team's disorganization and observed that "critical deliberations were taking place with no prepara-tion or follow-up planned."[28] The administration, particularly Powell as the new chairman of the Joint Chiefs, endured withering criticism in the press and Congress for the alleged missed opportunity. Thereafter, the administra-tion began planning Noriega's overthrow, citing his contempt for democracy as one of the chief reasons for his removal, but this had never been a serious consideration during the Cold War, when Noriega was providing assistance for America's campaign against Nicaragua. Noriega, like Ferdinand Marcos in the Philippines, Saddam Hussein in Iraq, and Mobutu Sese Seko in Zaire, discovered that with the Cold War waning, his usefulness to the United States had expired.

As the new chairman of the Joint Chiefs, Powell was involved in every aspect of planning the invasion of Panama. He was convinced that if Bush was determined to attack Panama, it must be done with overwhelming force. Panama was the largest U.S. military endeavor since Vietnam. Powell also moved to shore up his relationship with the news media. He felt abused by the way the disastrous coup had played out in the press. "So far, news stories recounting my role in the Panama coup had painted me as the fair-haired boy who had fallen flat on his face. Consequently, I was not averse to getting my version of events across in a newspaper of note." He began to cultivate a remarkable and even unorthodox relationship with *Washington Post* reporter Bob Woodward, a partnership that established the benchmark for mutual back scratching in the Beltway. "Woodward had the disarming voice and manner of a Boy Scout offering to help an old lady across the street," Powell recalled. "He assured me that anything I said would be on 'deep background.'"[29] Thus began an extraordinary relationship between the famous general and the famous reporter, which resulted in Powell's becoming Woodward's chief source—and a key character almost always depicted in a highly favorable light—for Woodward's best-selling book about the 1991 Gulf War, *The Commanders*, and later for Woodward's blockbuster accounts of the George W. Bush administration's wars in Afghanistan and Iraq, *Bush at War* (2002), *Plan of Attack* (2004), and *State of Denial* (2006).

The invasion of Panama began on December 20, 1989, when more than twelve thousand U.S. troops, joined by the ten thousand already in the Canal Zone, overran the tiny Central American country. The management of public opinion and the media had an Orwellian quality. A complete news blackout was maintained throughout, and the only images the American public saw depicted the operation as an effortless success. Moreover, the invasion was renamed from Operation Blue Spoons to Operation Just Cause, beginning the now-common process of giving military interventions names with propagandistic overtones. Powell recalled that "even our severest critics would have to utter 'Just Cause' while denouncing us."[30]

The power of news media imagery in shaping public perceptions was also on full display in Panama, as it would be, to an even greater extent, in the forthcoming Persian Gulf conflict. At one point, Powell had to order the destruction of a harmless commercial radio tower owing to the news media's obsession with the structure. Since Vietnam, the military had become more aware of the dangers of bad press. Powell thus devoted much attention to the media's depiction of the Panama offensive.[31] He had revealed the importance he placed on media management during an address to the National Defense University in Washington only a week before the invasion. He explained that he worked hard on relationships with reporters and that he aimed to earn their trust. "Once you've got all the forces moving and everything's being taken care of by the commanders, turn your attention to television because you can win the battle or lose the war if you don't handle the story right. . . . A great deal of my time is spent sensing that political environment. People sometimes say, well, Powell, he's a political general anyway. The fact of the matter is there isn't a general in Washington who isn't political, not if he's going to be successful, because that's the nature of our system. It's the way the Department of Defense works. It's the way in which we formulate foreign policy. It's the way in which we get approval for our policy."[32]

Many believed Panama the purest expression of the Weinberger Doctrine, which was being transformed into Powell's doctrine. Powell noted that "in the future, when it became my responsibility to advise the president on committing our forces to combat, Weinberger's rules turned out to be a practical guide." When he arrived in Panama on January 5, 1990, reporters asked why such a large force was used. Powell replied, "I'm always a great believer in making sure you get there with what you need to accomplish the mission and don't go in on the cheap side."[33]

Writing in his memoir nearly six years later, he claimed to have absorbed a number of lessons about the experience in Panama. It was imperative that the United States have clear objectives and that it use all the force necessary. "Do not apologize for going in big if that is what it takes. Decisive force ends wars quickly and in the long run saves lives. Whatever threats we faced in the future, I intended to make these rules the bedrock of my military counsel." He also saw Panama, as well as the positive media attention it attracted, as heaven-sent for the military. "I hope this has a great effect," he told reporters in Panama. "I hope it has enormous effect. . . . And as we start to go down in dollars and as we see the world changing, don't bust this apart. . . . Don't think that this is the time to demobilize the armed force of the United States, because it isn't. There are still dangers in the world."[34] By suggesting that the world remained a dangerous place for the foreseeable future, the Panama crisis made a strong statement against steep military force reductions.

The Panama experience also began the process of Powell's transformation. "When Powell appeared in public as Reagan's national security adviser," James Mann observed, "he had been a quiet, dark-suited, self-effacing staff aide. Now he took on a new role. Outspoken, assured, bedecked in green dress uniform, he was the symbol of and spokesman for the revived, newly triumphant American armed forces. Panama made him a nationally recognized figure."[35] Just as he had done during his emergence on the national scene after his appointment as national security adviser in 1987, Powell provided a reassuring presence with control over his ego. The positive public impression he left also enhanced his influence as chairman. Moreover, the proliferation and growing importance of television and cable television news, together with Powell's effective use of that medium, meant that he was emerging as the most powerful chairman in the history of that office.

Powell's stature continued to grow during the 1991 Gulf War, the first major war of the post–Cold War era, which ultimately transformed him into a national icon. And yet, ironically, he had been a reluctant warrior throughout. "Perhaps more than any of the president's other councilors," Rick Atkinson, the *Washington Post*'s military correspondent, noted, "Powell had resisted war with Iraq. From the moment Saddam invaded Kuwait, until Bush's decision in late October to double the force in Saudi Arabia, he subtly sought to steer the United States away from a military solution. He preferred 'strangling' Saddam with a United Nations blockade and economic sanctions."[36]

The war's origins were rooted in an often overlooked historical context. Iraq had endured eight exhausting years of struggle against neighboring Iran, receiving small amounts of support from the United States. Going back to Donald Rumsfeld's 1983 meeting with Hussein, which led to normalization in 1984 after sixteen years of no official relations, the Reagan administration saw the Iraqi leader as a key part of its Gulf strategy of containing Iran. The U.S. ambassador to Iraq had subsequently impressed upon Hussein that Bush desired better relations.[37]

The administration's muddled diplomacy contributed to the crisis, and it remained mired in confusion during the first few days after Iraq's August 1990 invasion of the small but oil-rich sheikdom of Kuwait. When Bush was asked if he was sending troops, he replied, "I am not contemplating any such action." He began reconsidering after discussions with Margaret Thatcher, who seems to have impugned Bush's manhood—a surefire way of goading him into action. Bush thereafter grew increasingly inclined toward a military solution. After a few days of hesitation, he began to steel himself for a military confrontation with Iraq, although Powell remained skeptical. "I don't see the senior leadership taking us into armed conflict for the events of the last twenty-four hours," he predicted. "The American people do not want their young dying for $1.50 gallon of oil, and the Arabs are not happy about cutting their lines off."[38]

Initially, the United States was concerned about defending Saudi Arabia, hence the name Operation Desert Shield. Powell moved to lay out options for the administration. He offered Bush two courses of action: build up forces to defend Saudi Arabia and possibly carry out offensive operations to drive Iraqi forces out of Kuwait and develop a containment policy. The first option, to deter further Iraqi aggression, required U.S. troops in Saudi Arabia. To strike against Iraq and liberate Kuwait required planning and logistics on a scale not seen since Vietnam. "Looking at this option," Powell said, "this is harder than Panama and Libya. This would be the NFL, not a scrimmage. It would mean a major confrontation." Powell supported containment, but he never directly offered containment as his personal recommendation. He explained that no one asked him, so he did not offer his views. But he did begin using the term "strangulation," deeming it more active than "containment" and thus more appealing to Bush, who Powell believed was itching for a fight.[39]

Initially, the administration's objectives were entirely defensive, aimed at deterring an Iraqi attack on Saudi Arabia. Throughout the early debates in the Pentagon with Cheney and Wolfowitz, Powell sought to keep the focus on the limited goal of defending Saudi Arabia. He supported the idea of communicating to Hussein that "Saudi Arabia is the line." But on August 5, he watched in astonishment as Bush, on television, began jabbing the air with his finger, saying "This will not stand. This will not stand . . . this aggression against Kuwait." Powell sprang upright in his chair. The United States had just gone, with the president's seemingly off-the-cuff remarks, from "we're not discussing intervention" to "this will not stand." Powell understood the implication of this change in policy. His mind racing, he began mulling the key question: had the president just committed the United States to liberating Kuwait? At the White House, Powell made several points to Bush. First, he warned that they needed to make Hussein think about the consequences of war. He suggested Iraq had to be warned of U.S. resolve so that any attack on Saudi Arabia would also be an attack on American forces. Second, they needed to ensure that sufficient force be sent to the region to make their threats credible and that, at the very least, a token force should be sent immediately. In keeping with the evolving Powell Doctrine, if the United States were going to commit forces to the region, it had to do so with all the resources necessary to achieve its goals.[40]

The dispatch of a large force to defend Saudi Arabia made a large-scale military intervention almost unavoidable. Powell discovered that the presence of forces many believed had to be used to maintain U.S. credibility undermined the case for sanctions. Such a large deployment made it too costly to continue that more patient policy. Moreover, as the months went by, Bush grew increasingly committed to a war to remove Iraqi forces from Kuwait. In hyperbolic public utterances about the crisis, Bush referred to Saddam Hussein as "Hitler" or "worse than Hitler."[41]

Powell complained in August to the commander of the U.S. Central Command, Gen. H. Norman Schwarzkopf, that the administration had left him to handle a number of diplomatic angles as well. In reality, Powell could not resist playing a larger role than that of chairman. Throughout the first months of the crisis, however, he remained concerned that the administration agree upon clear military and political objectives. He had been appalled by what he saw as the docility of the Joint Chiefs during Vietnam and was frustrated that Scowcroft was not posing the important questions. Bush had expressed impatience at the length of time it would take to make the sanctions work. Powell believed Scowcroft had failed to give Bush all the alternatives. He confronted Scowcroft and told him that he needed to be sure to offer all sides. Perhaps the administration's objectives could be achieved without resort to force.[42]

Powell felt frustrated that while he had wrestled with weighty matters of state for two years in the White House under Reagan and had participated as the president's national security adviser in three superpower summits, he was now expected to stay within the confines of his job, merely offering military advice. At one point, Powell was chastised for overreaching. "Colin," Cheney snapped, "you're Chairman of the Joint Chiefs. You're not Secretary of State. You're not the National Security Adviser anymore. And you're not Secretary of Defense. So stick to military matters." Nevertheless, Powell felt strongly that such questions had to be raised and was not sorry that he had spoken out. The support of the American people and the Congress was crucial at every step, and Powell harbored misgivings about the way Bush was proceeding. Powell urged that public opinion and diplomatic considerations should also help to shape the policy. "We can't make a case for losing lives for Kuwait," he told Cheney, "but Saudi Arabia is different. I am opposed to dramatic action without the President having popular support." Cheney, a staunch advocate of executive power, disagreed with Powell over the importance of going to Congress and urged Bush not to seek congressional approval before going to war.[43]

Further tensions developed between Cheney and Powell, who continued to counsel restraint and sanctions. Cheney grew frustrated with Powell's cautious approach, and their strained relationship surprised witnesses to their exchanges. Cheney wanted Powell to present a menu of military options, but Powell kept demanding that the civilian leadership define and clarify its political goals. Cheney also discussed troop increases on television without first consulting with Powell, then went behind his back and brought to the White House a war plan, cooked up by Cheney's neoconservative advisers, that Powell did not support. An angry Powell complained to Schwarzkopf, "I can't go out of town anymore. When I go out of town things get out of control."[44]

Powell's caution ran contrary to Bush's desire for action. Powell worried that the administration was going to war without considering other options. He remained committed to the importance of the deployment to protect Saudi Arabia—Operation Desert Shield—but he feared that the rush to launch the offensive—Operation Desert Storm—was being pursued without adequate exploration of other avenues, such as sanctions or an embargo. He was astonished that Bush had so little interest in a nonmilitary outcome to the crisis. In late November, he revealed to his predecessor, Admiral Crowe, that he was struggling to restrain the enthusiasm for war. "I've been for a containment strategy, but it hasn't been selling around here or over there," Powell told Crowe, gesturing across the Potomac in the direction of the White House. To Powell's distress, Bush continued to make decisions about escalating the U.S. commitment without consulting all of his inner circle, including Powell. The chairman of the Joint Chiefs often learned about changes in policy from the television coverage.[45]

Powell became increasingly apprehensive that the senior members of the administration did not have a comprehensive understanding of what was at stake and feared that the civilian leadership had not given sufficient consideration to the real consequences of a war. Reflecting the military's cautious estimate of Iraqi military capabilities, he remained skeptical that a war would be easy. He was distressed when certain phrases were tossed around, such as "surgical strike" and "limited war." He broached the question of whether it was worth going to war to liberate Kuwait. He daringly used an October address at the anniversary of Eisenhower's hundredth birthday in Abilene, Kansas, to lay out his reservations.[46] "I think, perhaps because he took a political path to the chairmanship," recalled U.S. Ambassador to Saudi Arabia Charles Freeman, "he continually evidenced great caution in his approach to the possibility of an attack on the Iraqi occupying forces, and was very much concerned about the domestic impact of failure."[47]

The decision to shift to an offensive strategy was not agreed upon until late October. Powell told Bush, "Mr. President, we have accomplished the mission assigned." The defense of Saudi Arabia had been achieved. "Now, if you, Mr. President, decide to build up—go for an offensive option—this is what we need," Powell said, revealing Schwarzkopf's plans for an attack. He warned Bush that air power alone would not achieve his goal of removing Iraqi forces from Kuwait. As Bush's rhetoric about Iraq became increasingly extreme, Powell, uncomfortable with hyperbole, worried about such demonization, fearing that just as he had with Noriega, Bush was building Hussein up to be a bigger threat than he really was, unwittingly making his removal a U.S. military objective. "We are dealing with Hitler revisited," Bush said on one occasion. To some, Bush was using such rhetoric to remove any doubt from his own mind and steel himself for the conflict to come. Powell recommended to Cheney that Bush tone down the rhetoric as he thought it "unwise to elevate public expectations by making the man out to be the devil incarnate and then leaving him in place." Powell preferred to talk about the "Iraqi regime" during his public appearances. He knew that the administration's war planning, as well as the writ of the coalition it was assembling, contemplated only ejecting Iraq from Kuwait. "It did not include toppling Saddam's dictatorship," Powell recalled. "Within these limits, we could not bring George Bush Saddam Hussein's scalp." He felt that Bush's demonization of Hussein would ultimately make it more difficult for the public to understand why the Iraqi leader was allowed to stay in power.[48]

By all accounts, Powell did a remarkable job of keeping the civilian and military officials from clashing. "In retrospect, the Persian Gulf operation benefited from military-civilian relationships that were better than those of other administrations," observes Pentagon historian Dale Herspring. "Powell played a critical, perhaps central role. He worked well not only with the politicians, but with Schwarzkopf who, given his confrontational personality, probably would not have survived had Powell not been JCS chairman. . . . Probably no officer in the U.S. military could have performed as well as Powell did in acting as a buffer between Cheney, the White House, and Gen. Norman Schwarzkopf during the Gulf War."[49]

Powell also played a role in ensuring that the administration avoided alienating key allies. At one point, between the launching of the air campaign and the beginning of the ground war, Gorbachev intervened with a peace plan. Senior administration officials discussed Gorbachev's proposal on the evening of February 21, and Powell could sense that Cheney, who distrusted Gorbachev, was strongly opposed. Powell publicly challenged Cheney: "We don't stiff Gorbachev," he said, suggesting a compromise where Bush would set a deadline for Gorbachev's proposal. Powell recalled that Cheney "looked as if he had been handed a dead rat."[50]

The air portion of Operation Desert Storm began on January 15, 1991. After more than a month of devastating air attacks, coalition forces launched their ground war against Iraqi positions on February 24. The ground campaign ended after only one hundred hours and 148 American deaths. In the process, Powell became an overnight sensation, but any assertion that the war was a watershed proved ephemeral. "Americans soon recognized," the *Washington Post*'s Rick Atkinson noted, "that expeditionary warfare offered no panacea for the nation's most profound challenges." Moreover, while there had been generally good relations among Bush's senior advisers, there had also been a number of serious disagreements. This had been hidden from public view by shrewd media management and a public facade of unity. The celebrations of victory obscured the differences the war had provoked, particularly between Cheney and Powell over matters of intervention and the Powell Doctrine. Moreover, Cheney resented Powell's efforts to extend his power into areas the secretary of defense believed were the proper province of the civilian leadership.[51] Leaving Saddam Hussein in power also provoked controversy. James Baker later explained that the administration wanted to avoid the "Lebanonization" of Iraq and that going on to Baghdad would have provoked a military and geopolitical nightmare.[52] Even the hawkish Cheney agreed with this in 1991. But Bush's penchant for personalizing the conflict left lasting consequences. He had unwittingly made the removal of Saddam Hussein a war aim, only to have the man who had been described in such lurid terms continue in power and in control of Iraq after the war.

Powell had pondered this dilemma as early as October 1990, a good three months before the war began. "Do we want to go beyond Kuwait to Baghdad? Do we try to force Saddam out of power? How weakened do we want to leave Iraq?" Powell doubted that the United States and the world would benefit from the removal of the regime. He feared it would leave the Persian Gulf dominated by Iran. In his 1995 memoir, he stressed that the UN resolution authorizing force against Iraq made clear that the mission was only to free Kuwait. "However much we despised Saddam and what he had done," he wrote, "the United States had little desire to shatter his country. For the ten previous years, Iran, not Iraq, had been our Persian Gulf nemesis. We wanted Iraq to continue as a threat and a counterweight to Iran."[53]

Furthermore, Powell understood that America's Arab allies in the region never wanted to remove the regime in Iraq. Saudi Arabia, for one, feared the possibility of a predominantly Shiite regime next door. The chairman could not recall a single meeting where dismembering Iraq, instituting regime change, or occupying Iraq was ever seriously considered. He recalled a persuasive cable sent by Charles Freeman, the U.S. ambassador to Saudi Arabia, elaborating the chief reasons why the United States should not seek to remove Hussein. For one, it was believed that Iraq had to remain intact to avoid creating a power vacuum in the region. The stability of the Middle East would be jeopardized if Iraq fragmented into Sunni, Shia, and Kurd identities. Powell thought these were persuasive suggestions. "It is naive," Powell wrote in 1995, "to think that if Saddam had fallen, he would necessarily have been replaced by a Jeffersonian in some sort of desert democracy where people read the Federalist Papers along with the Koran." Several years after the war, Powell explained that "our practical intention was to leave Baghdad enough power to survive as a threat to an Iran that remained bitterly hostile toward the United States."[54] One problem was that in the wake of Bush's call for Shiites, Kurds, and various opponents of the regime to rise up, this U.S. strategy of leaving Hussein with sufficient power to contain Iran also meant that he would be able to crush brutally all opposition to his rule. Moreover, the rhetoric used to describe Saddam Hussein had created problems, leading to an almost obsessive focus on him in the years between the two wars with Iraq, so much so that successive administrations were slow to recognize other changes occurring in the region. The vulnerability of America's ties to the Saudi royal family had been exposed, and the United States was now emerging as the dominant factor in the Persian Gulf region, with American power more visible and significant in the Middle East. Many in the region grew increasingly resentful of the growing U.S. presence. Sending U.S. forces to Saudi Arabia had been portrayed as a request by the Saudi royal family, but the Saudis actually had misgivings about the long-term consequences of such a deployment. It was Cheney, according to Brent Scowcroft, who demanded that Saudi misgivings be ignored.[55]

Another major consequence of the Iraq War was the transformation of Powell's public reputation. The war had been a major television event, and Powell became a national celebrity. Even the official welcome home celebration for the troops was scripted as a made-for-television prime-time special. "Wherever Powell went," Rick Atkinson observed, "he exuded self-confidence, as though he were gliding about the shoals that snagged lesser mortals."[56] David Halberstam later observed that the post–Gulf War mood resembled shades of the post–World War II climate. "Powell was the new Eisenhower, the thoughtful, careful, tough but benign overall planner."[57] Andrew Bacevich added, "Credited (rightly or not) with having performed brilliantly during the successive interventions in Panama and the Persian Gulf, Powell by 1992 had become easily the most powerful JCS chairman in the history of that office."[58]

Powell's close relationship with the journalist Bob Woodward provoked controversy. It would not be the last time his collaboration with the *Washington Post* reporter caused problems with Powell's colleagues. Woodward's book on the Gulf War, *The Commanders*, revealed that Powell had spent many hours with the reporter and that he was a chief source for the account. Featuring excerpts from the book, *Newsweek* magazine ran a cover story, featuring Powell's photo and titled, "The Reluctant Warrior: Doubts and Divisions on the Road to War." Powell refused to comment when asked about the book and the *Newsweek* article, but he never disavowed the stories. Powell heard nothing from Cheney about the Woodward revelations and assumed Cheney was only too happy to see him cut down to size. Just the opposite happened. The release of Woodward's book further boosted Powell. The public responded positively to the portrayal of Powell as steady and sober minded. Moreover, rather than jeopardizing Powell's hopes for a second term as chairman, Bush expedited the announcement of his reappointment in order to end speculation about his standing in the administration. Though the announcement was made in May rather than September, both Powell and Bush were embarrassed when the Washington press corps focused on the revelations from *Newsweek*.[59] Woodward's revelations confirmed some people's suspicions that Powell was a political general who only pressed his views if he was sure they would find favor.

In Bush's own account, cowritten with his national security adviser, Brent Scowcroft, he largely focused on Panama and Iraq. But there were numerous other crises that for the most part elicited only halfhearted American interest. On issues Bush found less interesting, such as the domestic agenda and the economy, there was often serious drift and disinterest. Bush's successor inherited, on his first day in office, troubling crises in Somalia, Haiti, and Bosnia—crises with the potential to draw an American military intervention.

The Cold War was ending. But the paradox remained that as the Soviet Union faded, the United States often pursued a foreign policy inclined to inflate potential threats. Cheney and the cadre of civilian hawks around him at the Pentagon began drafting a blueprint intended to preempt further calls for cuts in defense spending. Their chief document, known as the "Defense Planning Guidance Paper of 1992," called for a transformation of American foreign policy from the traditions of Cold War–era containment to hegemony or even dominance.

Although the Gulf War was perceived as a triumph for the Powell Doctrine, it also made future interventions more likely. The quick victory left the illusion that war could be antiseptic, without costs. It created a mythology that military power could achieve anything and, with the Soviet Union in decline, that there would be few restraints on the future use of military force. Powell did not succumb to this illusion, but others, such as Cheney and Wolfowitz, did.

Bush believed the triumph in the Gulf had vanquished the Vietnam Syndrome. What did this mean for America? For the American armed forces? Furthermore, the political benefits of war had been amply demonstrated. Unlike the damage that Vietnam inflicted upon Lyndon Johnson's political fortunes, wars—more specifically, successful, televised wars—were increasingly seen as good for politicians and their reputations, useful for reviving the sagging fortunes of any American politician. Powell had reservations about this. At the beginning of the Gulf War, he thought of Robert E. Lee's observation that "it is well that war is so terrible, or we should grow too fond of it." Powell feared that the public and the politicians had only seen sanitized versions of war, with combat framed to look like an entertaining video game.[60]

Despite the end of the Cold War, peace remained elusive. The United States had an uncanny ability to find threats or to transform former allies into new threats. Andrew Bacevich observed that "no sooner had the United States prevailed in the twentieth century's great ideological competition than a whole new set of obstacles to peace materialized."[61] Moreover, throughout the war, Powell seemed unconcerned about Congress's losing its war-making powers and much of its oversight authority over foreign and defense policy. And yet, this might have been one way to secure adherence to the Powell Doctrine, rather than concentrating so much power in the executive branch.

As for Powell, he never felt wholly at home in the Bush administration. He once observed that Bush "and I never, in nearly four years, spent a single purely social hour together." And, on the last day of the administration, he went up to Cheney's suite in the Pentagon to bid him farewell, only to discover that Cheney had already departed hours before without saying so much as goodbye. Powell recalled, "I was disappointed, even hurt, but not surprised."[62]

Powell may not have known it at the time, but the dramatic events of the Bush administration had seriously undermined his doctrine. The seeming ease with which the interventions in Panama and the Gulf (and even, initially, Somalia) had been carried off suggested that Powell's doctrine had always been overly cautious, even timid, and paralyzed by unrealistic images of "another Vietnam." Moreover, Powell's critics, particularly among the burgeoning neoconservative Right, charged that the Powell Doctrine remained blind to America's dynamic ability to wage small wars with perfection. Powell no doubt saw the remarkable success of the interventions in Panama and the Gulf, along with Bush's declaration of the end of the Vietnam Syndrome, as important moments for transforming the role of the American armed forces from the imperatives of the Cold War to the post–Cold War era. Powell may not have realized at the time, however, that without the check previously provided by the Cold War and the Soviet Union, and with a new spirit of national amnesia about the troubling lessons of Vietnam and, more recently, Lebanon, military intervention had come to be seen as a one-size-fits-all solution to America's foreign policy challenges. Although Powell would dominate debates over questions of intervention and the Powell Doctrine during the first year of the forthcoming Clinton administration, these problems, rooted as they were in perceptions of the Panama and Gulf interventions, would cast a long shadow over the next Republican administration, that of George W. Bush. "The ramifications of these Gulf War debates, and of the interactions among Powell, Cheney and Wolfowitz, lingered for years," observed James Mann. "This legacy of the Gulf War—an intellectual divide and a residue of mistrust between Cheney and Wolfowitz, on the one hand, and Powell on the other—still hung in the air, unacknowledged but undeniable, when the George W. Bush administration took office a decade later."[63]

Figure 4.3. George H. W. Bush, Powell, and Secretary of Defense Dick Cheney. The tension with Cheney would boil over during Powell's tenure as secretary of state (2001–2005) in the next Bush administration. But to observers who closely studied their relationship during the George H. W. Bush administration (1989–1993), there was ample evidence of the problems to come. Observers who knew Powell thought that Dick Cheney was the one official who consistently frustrated Powell throughout his career. Photo credit: George H. W. Bush Presidential Library.

Notes

1. Quoted in Colin Powell, *My American Journey* (New York: Ballantine, 1995, 2003), 375.

2. Quoted in George H. W. Bush and Brent Scowcroft, *A World Transformed* (New York: Vintage Books, 1999), 380.

3. Quoted in Powell, *My American Journey*, 388; Bob Woodward, *The Commanders* (New York: Touchstone, 1991), 47.

4. See Taylor Branch, *At Canaan's Edge: America in the King Years, 1965–1968* (New York: Simon and Schuster, 2006), 642.

5. Henry Louis Gates Jr., "Powell and the Black Elite," *New Yorker*, September 25, 1995.

6. Steven V. Roberts, "General Powell Getting Army's Top Command," *New York Times*, December 2, 1988.

7. Powell, *My American Journey*, 388–90.

8. Author interview with Col. Lawrence Wilkerson, September 20, 2007.

9. Quoted in Powell, *My American Journey*, 441.

10. Author interview with Lawrence Korb, March 17, 2006; H. Norman Schwarzkopf, *It Doesn't Take a Hero* (New York: Bantam, 1993), 314–15; Richard Halloran, "Scramble On to Succeed Chairman of Joint Chiefs," *New York Times*, August 7, 1989.

11. Interview with Frank Carlucci, Ronald Reagan Oral History Project, August 28, 2001, Miller Center for Public Affairs, University of Virginia.

12. Rick Atkinson, *Crusade: The Untold Story of the Persian Gulf War* (New York: Houghton Mifflin, 1993), 121.

13. Bush and Scowcroft, *A World Transformed*, 23; James Mann, *Rise of the Vulcans: The History of Bush's War Cabinet* (New York: Viking Press, 2004), 176–77.

14. Andrew Rosenthal, "Colin Luther Powell: A General Who Is Right for His Time," *New York Times*, August 10, 1989.

15. James Baker, *The Politics of Diplomacy: Revolution, War and Peace, 1989–1992* (New York: Putnam, 1995), 26; Atkinson, *Crusade*, 123.

16. Dale R. Herspring, *The Pentagon and the Presidency: Civil-Military Relations from FDR to George W. Bush* (Lawrence: University Press of Kansas, 2005), 292–303.

17. Woodward, *The Commanders*, 129; Alexander DeConde, *Presidential Machismo: Executive Authority, Military Intervention, and Foreign Relations* (Boston: Northeastern University Press, 1999), 246.

18. Powell, *My American Journey*, 355.

19. Bob Woodward, *Plan of Attack* (New York: Simon and Schuster, 2004), 176.

20. Powell, *My American Journey*, 393.

21. Interview with Arthur H. Hughes, Foreign Affairs Oral History Collection, January 27, 1998, Library of Congress.

22. Woodward, *The Commanders*, 75–80; Atkinson, *Crusade*, 94.

23. Powell, *My American Journey*, 412, 428.

24. Author interview with Col. Lawrence Wilkerson, September 20, 2007.

25. Powell, *My American Journey*, 525–26.

26. Andrew J. Bacevich, *American Empire: The Realities and Consequences of U.S. Diplomacy* (Cambridge, MA: Harvard University Press, 2002), 125–34.

27. Powell, *My American Journey*, 402.

28. Quoted in Powell, *My American Journey*, 405.

29. Powell, *My American Journey*, 407.

30. Quoted in Powell, *My American Journey*, 413.

31. Powell, *My American Journey*, 418, 515.

32. Woodward, *The Commanders*, 155.

33. Powell, *My American Journey*, 293; Woodward, *The Commanders*, 194.

34. Powell, *My American Journey*, 421; quoted in Woodward, *The Commanders*, 194.

35. Mann, *Rise of the Vulcans*, 182.

36. Atkinson, *Crusade*, 122.

37. Bruce W. Jentleson, *With Friends Like These: Reagan, Bush and Saddam, 1982–1990* (New York: Norton, 1994).

38. Powell, *My American Journey*, 448; quoted in Michael R. Gordon and Bernard E. Trainor, *The Generals' War* (Boston: Back Bay Books, 1995), 33.

39. Bush and Scowcroft, *A World Transformed*, 324; Woodward, *The Commanders*, 41–42.

40. Quoted in Powell, *My American Journey*, 453; Gordon and Trainor, *The Generals' War*, 33–34.

41. Powell, *My American Journey*, 478; Schwarzkopf, *It Doesn't Take a Hero*, 366; Bush and Scowcroft, *A World Transformed*, 375, 388.

42. Gordon and Trainor, *The Generals' War*, 65.

43. Powell, *My American Journey*, 451–52; Gordon and Trainor, *The Generals' War*, 33–34, 151–53.

44. Interview with Arthur H. Hughes, Foreign Affairs Oral History Collection, January 27, 1998, Library of Congress.

45. Woodward, *The Commanders*, 38; Powell, *My American Journey*, 453.

46. Woodward, *The Commanders*, 307–8.

47. Interview with Charles Freeman, Foreign Affairs Oral History Collection, April 14, 1995, Library of Congress.

48. Woodward, *The Commanders*, 319; Bush and Scowcroft, *A World Transformed*, 380–81; Powell, *My American Journey*, 478, 513.

49. Herspring, *The Pentagon and the Presidency*, 323, 330.

50. Quoted in Powell, *My American Journey*, 502.

51. Atkinson, *Crusade*, 500; Mann, *Rise of the Vulcans*, 196.

52. Baker, *The Politics of Diplomacy*, 435.

53. Quoted in Powell, *My American Journey*, 457, 477.

54. Interview with Charles Freeman, Foreign Affairs Oral History Collection, April 14, 1995, Library of Congress; Powell, *My American Journey*, 513, 516.

55. Bush and Scowcroft, *A World Transformed*, 323.

56. Atkinson, *Crusade*, 121.

57. David Halberstam, *War in a Time of Peace: Bush, Clinton, and the Generals* (New York: Scribner, 2001), 13.

58. Bacevich, *American Empire*, 174.

59. Patrick E. Tyler, "Bush Reappoints Gen. Powell to Top Military Post," *New York Times*, May 24, 1991.

60. Woodward, *The Commanders*, 375.

61. Bacevich, *American Empire*, 117.

62. Author interview with Col. Lawrence Wilkerson, September 20, 2007; quoted in Powell, *My American Journey*, 554.

63. Mann, *Rise of the Vulcans*, 184.

$\sim$

The Military and Diplomacy after the Cold War

Bill Clinton's defeat of George H. W. Bush in the 1992 elections brought substantial changes. Clinton desired to reorient U.S. foreign policy away from its emphasis on national security and military power and toward an emphasis on economics and international cooperation. He faced numerous obstacles, such as a well-organized and well-funded Republican opposition, an aggressive conservative media, and the growing power and influence of right-wing think tanks. Moreover, the military itself proved powerfully resistant to reform or change, and the new commander in chief proved ill equipped to face an entrenched uniformed military bureaucracy.[1] For Colin Powell, the Clinton years challenged his belief that the post–Cold War transition could be managed smoothly. Clinton was the first president to have come of age during the Vietnam era. His advisers, largely shaped by that tumultuous period and having internalized much of the Vietnam Syndrome, represented an abrupt shift from the personnel of the outgoing Bush administration. Powell's former associates, including Dick Cheney, James Baker, Brent Scowcroft, and Paul Wolfowitz, departed with Bush. Powell, as chairman of the Joint Chiefs, continued on in the new administration, at least until September 1993 when his second term as chairman concluded.

For the previous twelve years, Powell had served Republican presidents, and his three most important professional relationships—with Caspar Weinberger, Frank Carlucci, and even George Shultz—had all been with Republican appointees. He found it difficult adjusting to a Democratic administration. Even Clinton observed that "[h]aving risen to the highest ranks with the support of presidents Reagan and Bush, Powell would serve his last nine months as chairman under a very different Commander in Chief."[2]

The United States now stood as the lone superpower. What this meant in terms of American power, and the redefinition of American interests, was tested in the first years of the new administration. Questions of intervention arose sooner than anyone anticipated. When Clinton defeated Bush in November 1992, the Democrats had been out of the White House since Jimmy Carter's defeat twelve years before. Carter's administration had been the only Democratic administration in the previous twenty-four years. Clinton's team consisted of several familiar appointments from the Carter administration and several new figures.

Opinion is divided over Powell's performance under Clinton. Some credited him for having a moderating, realist influence and serving as a constructive force for continuity. Others saw him as playing an obstructionist role in terms of the new president's policies, particularly regarding both the controversial effort to allow gays and lesbians to serve openly in the military and debates over humanitarian intervention, especially in the Balkans. To one observer, by 1993 Powell had emerged as "a military spokesman restrained by little reluctance to challenge civilian leaders with whom he disagreed, but also that perhaps paradoxical figure, a soldier reluctant to employ military force."[3]

The many news stories speculating about his political ambitions rendered his relations with the new administration more awkward. Members of the new administration were aware that Powell had been discussed for the Republican vice presidential nomination in both 1988 and 1992 and that Clinton had even seriously considered him as his running mate in 1992. Some believed Powell had been Clinton's first choice.

Clinton and Powell had different approaches to foreign affairs. Clinton's chief political interests had been domestic in nature. The struggle for racial justice in the South was for Clinton a defining issue, not the struggles of the Cold War. Economic issues were his strong suit, and he believed in emphasizing these aspects of foreign policy, seeing America's place in the world through the framework of economic integration, trade, and globalization. He stressed the "soft power" approach to American foreign policy. A healthy U.S. economy would strengthen America's position in the world, and by restoring its competitive edge, the United States would best maintain itself as the sole superpower. He believed a strong economy could enhance other aspects of U.S. foreign policy. But he soon discovered that many of the challenges the United States confronted during his two terms could not be understood or resolved through an emphasis on trade and economics alone.

This proved true for the major foreign policy crises of these years, such as the breakup of the former Yugoslavia and the subsequent U.S.-led interventions in Bosnia and Kosovo, as well as the ongoing intervention in Somalia, the crisis in Haiti, and ethnic cleansing in the Congo and Rwanda.[4]

Although wary of Powell's popularity, Clinton admired much about him and believed they could work together. The new president was genuinely committed to racial progress and saw Powell as a strong role model and moral example for millions of Americans, white and black. Despite Powell's previous service to Republican administrations, Clinton had reached out to him several times, both during the campaign and after. Powell had been under serious consideration not only as Clinton's vice presidential nominee but also as a possible secretary of state or defense.[5] During their first meeting, at the Hay Adams Hotel across from the White House on November 19, 1992, Powell was impressed by Clinton's intellect and memory. To his surprise, he found the president-elect well informed on foreign policy questions. "Clinton was self-assured, smart, curious, likable, and passionate about his ideas," he recalled of their first meeting. "He also seemed to be a good listener." Without notes, Clinton discussed the challenges he had inherited in Bosnia, Somalia, Iraq, Russia, and the Middle East. Powell observed, "Bill Clinton had the background to put history, politics, and policy into perspective." They talked for more than an hour, finding a rapport that seemed to surprise Powell. After the meeting, Clinton told an aide, "He's very political." To Clinton, the ultimate political animal, this was the highest praise.[6]

Powell became uncomfortable when Clinton spoke highly of Congressman Les Aspin as a potential secretary of defense, and it was apparent early on that there would be problems between the two. Powell did not like Aspin. Their differences stemmed from the fact that, as chairman of the House Defense Committee, Aspin had frequently angered Powell, who described him as an "adversary" who conducted "policy by one-liners and occasional cheap shots." Warren Christopher recalled that Aspin "had a testy relationship with the man who knew everything about the Pentagon, Joint Chiefs chairman Colin Powell, having jousted with him about military intervention in the Balkans. So, although Aspin's appointment was widely praised in the press and on Capitol Hill, his welcome at the Pentagon was not warm. Given how much an incoming cabinet member depends on resident professionals, especially in the hierarchical and sometimes hidebound Pentagon, Aspin's stint at Defense may have been doomed from the start."[7]

Powell also seemed to disapprove of Aspin on aesthetic grounds. Image was always important to Powell. Among other things, he had admired Ronald Reagan's immaculate tailoring and starched white shirts. He disapproved of Aspin's disheveled image. "In a building full of neatly pressed uniforms," he observed, "the top man looked out of place in his dated rumpled tan suits and wrinkled shirts." He did not like the way Aspin spoke and disliked his lack of organization. He was even repelled by the way Aspin ate.[8] "It would be hard to find two people who were less alike," recalled Lawrence Korb, a Pentagon official during the Reagan administration. "Aspin had a reputation for being a rumpled intellectual. But we shouldn't overlook that Aspin truly knew and understood military issues."[9]

The problems with Aspin were part of a larger issue Powell had with the entire Clinton team. He acknowledged that, as a dedicated realist, he was not a good fit with a group of advisers largely made up of liberal internation-

Figure 5.1. Powell and Secretary of Defense Les Aspin enjoy a moment of mirth with President Bill Clinton, May 6, 1993. Powell had very strained relations with Secretary Aspin, who, with his rumpled attire and professorial manner, seemed to rub Powell, the quintessential military man, the wrong way. But it was much more than a mere contrast in styles that separated the two men. In his conflict with Powell, Aspin faced one of the most difficult personnel challenges a new secretary of defense has ever faced: a broadly popular chairman of the Joint Chiefs, fresh from a wildly popular war, who had also been a high-level foreign policy appointment in a recent Republican administration. Aspin never really established his footing at the Pentagon and was forced to resign shortly after the debacle of the Somalia intervention—a deployment initiated by Powell during the previous Bush administration. Photo credit: William J. Clinton Presidential Library.

alists. He feared they might not be sufficiently schooled in the ways of the Vietnam Syndrome. Powell "was starting to feel like the kid about to enter a new school full of strangers." Although he saw himself as a bridge spanning the Reagan and Clinton generations, he often made only a halfhearted effort with the new administration and admitted that he approached his duties with little enthusiasm. He told Clinton that he had served most of the last twelve years in Republican administrations and that his "fingerprints are all over their national security policies." He warned Clinton that "anytime I find that I cannot, in good conscience, fully support your administration's policies because of my past positions, I will let you know. And I'll retire quietly, without making a fuss." Clinton did not seem to take his remarks as a threat, but the exchange did underscore the problems of having a political general as chairman, particularly one with such strong ties to the opposition party.[10]

Lawrence Korb suggested to Aspin that Clinton should consider replacing Powell, predicting that the Clinton-Powell relationship would be troubled, particularly when the new president pursued foreign and defense policies that departed from his predecessors' approach. This would place Powell in a difficult position, Korb feared. Though intrigued by the suggestion, Clinton and Aspin feared the political consequences. Clinton's relationship with Powell underscored Powell's unique position as a chairman of the Joint Chiefs who had been a Republican political appointee. Some officials suspected that Powell viewed them as interlopers who had deposed his Republican benefactors.[11] Moreover, Powell preferred highly structured meetings. For a man who was even critical of Brent Scowcroft's informal style, Powell would find the new commander in chief's approach vexing. Powell often had difficultly adjusting to the contrasting styles of other national security advisers, whether it be Scowcroft's chummy style in the first Bush administration or the graduate-seminar messiness of Clinton's NSC.

To Powell's dismay, Clinton's White House turned out to be even more collegial than George H. W. Bush's. The new commander in chief enjoyed analyzing issues, valued informality, information, and input, and encouraged an open atmosphere of discussion and debate.[12] To Powell, coming from a military culture that prized hierarchy, deference, and paternalism, Clinton's style gave the impression of anarchy. He was shocked that subordinates spoke with the authority of cabinet officers. As Andrew Bacevich observed, Powell, like many professional soldiers, often valued the form and process of organizations as much as the substance of their work. Meetings that did not conclude with clear recommendations made Powell uncomfortable. He observed that the president "had an academic streak himself and seemed to enjoy these marathon debates."[13]

Clinton and his advisers liked to make use of meetings to learn more about the questions before the administration and, if possible, reach a consensus. Moreover, Clinton possessed a voracious appetite for information and was notoriously overscheduled, whereas Powell valued punctuality and hated to be kept waiting, seeing it as inconsiderate, even on the part of a busy commander in chief. Powell also had an unfortunate tendency to count the precise number of minutes the new president took to complete meetings, compounding his displeasure with the new administration. But the president's frequent tardiness was in no way intended to be disrespectful to the chairman. Powell himself observed that his own meetings with the president usually ran over and that others behind him on the schedule were often kept waiting while Clinton sought to address one more issue.[14]

Powell was a larger-than-life presence in a new administration that lacked foreign policy experience, the Democrats having been in the White House only four years in the previous quarter century. The administration's foreign policy personnel obviously lacked gravitas, with the colorless Anthony Lake as national security adviser and the reserved Warren Christopher at State. Some described Christopher as "Dean Rusk without the charisma." Clinton joked that Christopher was the only man in the world who ate M&Ms with a knife and fork. Christopher further confirmed his reputation for blandness when he marched into the airport bar in Shannon, Ireland—a watering hole popular with the traveling press for its Irish coffees, generously laced with whiskey—and proceeded to order an Irish coffee, decaf, hold the whiskey.[15]

Some officials were intimidated by the chairman. "Powell simply overwhelmed the administration," Richard Holbrooke recalled. "He regarded the new team as children. And the new team regarded him with awe."[16] Several of the president's top advisers seemed reluctant to challenge him. "Until his departure in September 1993, Powell dominated Clinton's foreign policy councils," recalled Clinton insider Sidney Blumenthal. "Neither Secretary of State Christopher nor Lake openly challenged his positions to his face."[17] One of the few who did, UN Ambassador Madeleine Albright, recalled that "Powell's good looks, humor, and obvious decency combined with his military bearing make him an immensely attractive figure." His power at the Pentagon and within the new administration was enhanced as the disorganized Aspin had difficulty gaining traction. Powell dominated meetings with his smooth PowerPoint presentations. "The sight of Powell walking into meetings with his charts and briefing papers was impressive," Albright recalled.[18]

The new president, a former governor of Arkansas without any national or federal experience, was uncertain on foreign affairs and uncomfortable with the military culture. It was no secret that relations between the Clinton administration and the military were strained.[19] It was more than Clinton's desire to avoid serving in the military during the Vietnam War. After all, other high-profile politicians had avoided Vietnam. George W. Bush and Dan Quayle used family connections to secure highly coveted places in the Texas and Indiana National Guards, and Dick Cheney requested and received five deferments from the draft. So, it was not merely about what Clinton was doing during Vietnam. It also had to do with the perception of President Clinton's incompatibility with the military culture. To many in the military, he represented a cultural affront to the military's way of doing things. Clinton was perceived, even before the gays-in-the-military imbroglio and perhaps owing to Bush's searing attacks on his character during the 1992 campaign, as alien to the culture of the armed forces. To some of their harshest critics, Bill and Hillary Clinton represented some of the more distressing aspects of the 1960s, of which Clinton's desire to avoid the draft was emblematic and a focal point of the displeasure some had with him as the first baby boomer president. But the new commander in chief also faced the challenge with an entrenched uniformed bureaucracy. The president sought to reorient U.S. foreign policy away from its focus on national security and military power and toward economics and international cooperation. The military proved resistant to change. "Since the end of the Vietnam War," Andrew Bacevich wrote, "the officer corps had become increasingly conservative in its outlook and Republican in its political sympathies." Following the Cold War, military aspects of U.S. policy were paradoxically becoming more, not less, relevant, and as Bacevich has observed, "[A]lmost without anyone's noticing, military power became a central element in what little remained of an American national identity."[20]

Clinton's difficulties with the Pentagon began early when a story circulated around Washington that a female staffer in the West Wing had snubbed one of Powell's assistants, Lt. Gen. Barry McCaffrey. What soon became more important than the veracity of the story was the perception that the new administration was antimilitary. The inevitable overreactions and media frenzies followed. Powell mentioned the incident in his 1995 memoir, but he was always generous in his comments about the president and his difficulties with the military. In Powell's view, Clinton was the commander in chief, and signs of disrespect toward him were genuinely dismaying. Powell took criticism for standing up for the president when veterans booed the commander in chief during his 1993 Memorial Day address at the Vietnam Memorial.[21] President Clinton later praised Powell's defense of him that day as demonstrating his "conviction and class."[22]

Figure 5.2. President Clinton and Powell at the Vietnam Veterans Memorial, May 31, 1993. Clinton appreciated Powell's class and grace while standing up for the new commander in chief when he was resoundingly booed at the Vietnam Veterans Memorial in May 1993 during his first Memorial Day in the White House. During Powell's final year as chairman of the Joint Chiefs, which coincided with Clinton's first year in office, the president and Powell clashed over controversies such as gays in the military and whether to intervene militarily in Bosnia. Clinton seemed reluctant to challenge Powell directly, and while Powell remained chairman for the first eight months of the administration, he usually got his way. Powell was a large presence (and, in many ways, a holdover from the previous Republican administrations) in a new Democratic administration that had difficulty establishing itself in the areas of foreign and defense policy. Powell's influence was reinforced by the fact that he overshadowed Clinton's primary foreign and defense policy team, which comprised the less-than-inspiring lineup of Secretary of State William Christopher, National Security Adviser Anthony Lake, and Secretary of Defense Les Aspin. Photo credit: William J. Clinton Presidential Library.

Recalling that incident two years later, Powell pointed out that many people, not just Clinton, had avoided service in Vietnam. He noted that he had worked with many officials who did not flinch at sending other people's children into harm's way in Kuwait, Panama, Lebanon, and Grenada. "I had worked in the Reagan-Bush era with many hard-nosed men—guys ready to get tough with Soviets, Iranians, Iraqis, Nicaraguans, or Panamanians—all of whom were the right age, but most of whom had managed to avoid serving during the Vietnam War. Bill Clinton, in my judgment, had not behaved much differently from these men." After a year of working together, Powell acknowledged that there was much mutual respect between him and Clinton and that they had not only gotten along well but grown increasingly close.[23]

In the wake of the good publicity from the Gulf War, the services had been reeling from a succession of high-profile sex scandals in 1991 and 1992, which drew unwanted attention to the military's perceived attitudes toward gender. The president's proposal to allow openly gay people to serve was guaranteed to provoke controversy. He first raised the issue with Powell during their meeting at the Hay-Adams in mid-November 1992. "Most military people don't want [the ban] lifted," Powell advised. He warned the president-elect that doing so would be a tough issue and a "culture shock for the armed forces." He shrewdly recommended that Clinton order his new secretary of defense to investigate the issue and report back to him in six months. "Give yourself some breathing space," he urged the president-elect. "Get it out of the Oval Office. Don't make the gay issue the first horse out of the gate with the armed forces."[24]

Powell passionately opposed the proposed policy. Such strong feelings provoked him to go one step further. He sought to preempt president-elect Clinton by giving a controversial speech at the Naval Academy nine days before the inauguration. Uncharacteristically, he urged the midshipmen to resign in protest if they felt strongly about the new commander in chief's views on gays in the military, although this advice clearly contradicted much of what Powell himself professed to believe about the efficacy of resignations.

When Congresswoman Patricia Schroeder, a Democrat from Colorado, raised the matter, she provoked Powell's anger. She produced a 1942 U.S. government report justifying continued racial segregation of the armed forces and pointed out that similar arguments made in support of racial segregation were now being used against gays. "Your reasoning," Schroeder told him, "would have kept you from the mess hall, a few decades ago." Powell disputed Schroeder's logic. "I need no reminders," he replied to Schroeder, "concerning the history of African-Americans in the defense of their nation. . . . Skin color is a benign, nonbehavioral characteristic," he argued. "Sexual orientation is perhaps the most profound of human characteristics. Comparison of the two is a convenient but invalid argument."[25] The Congressional Black Caucus agreed with Schroeder's interpretation and reasoning and endorsed the removal of the ban on homosexuals.

At a White House meeting between the Joint Chiefs and the new president in late January 1993, Powell and the other officers argued against the proposal for nearly two hours. Rumors spread that the chiefs would resign in protest if they did not get their way, and some officers began arguing that if the president didn't demonstrate more loyalty to the military, he faced the possibility of mutiny. The new commander in chief began to doubt his ability to control the Pentagon. He later complained that Powell opposed "my policy to allow gays to serve in the military, even though during the Gulf War, which made him a popular hero, the Pentagon had knowingly allowed more than one hundred gays to serve, dismissing them only after the conflict, when they were no longer needed."[26]

When Powell spoke out openly and often against the president on the issue, he and the chiefs came under withering criticism. A *New York Times* editorial accused Powell and the chiefs of being "defiantly opposed, almost to the point of insubordination." *Times* op-ed columnist Abe Rosenthal, echoing Congresswoman Schroeder, pointed out that Powell could never have risen to chairman had it not been for Harry Truman's integration of the armed forces in 1948, an act he compared to Clinton's effort to allow gays to serve openly in the military.[27]

To those who knew him well, Powell could be a much more emotional and even sensitive man than his public appearances conveyed. Accustomed to largely positive, even fawning press coverage, he was stung by the criticism. He had lost control of the media. "Over the next couple of weeks, I took the most scathing public criticism of my career," Powell recalled in his 1995 memoir. "It hurt." He felt deeply conflicted about his role in the controversy, in part because he acknowledged that "some of those who wanted to keep the ban on gays did, in fact, spout arguments similar to those used to resist racial integration in the armed forces forty years before." Eventually, Powell and Clinton worked toward a compromise. "We could stop asking about sexual orientation when people enlist," Powell suggested. Thus was born the "don't ask, don't tell" policy, although the outcome satisfied few on either side of this bitter controversy.[28]

Defending his position several years later, Powell acknowledged that, just as with the racial issue, public attitudes might change with time. He rationalized his opposition by arguing that "requiring people of different color to live together in intimate situations is far different from requiring people of different sexual orientation to do so."[29] He blamed others for injecting politics into the controversy, but he himself had taken an openly political role—something quite unexpected from a chairman of the Joint Chiefs. Some Clinton insiders began to resent Powell's activities, which they saw as insubordinate. "On the issue of gays in the armed forces, he had wrong-footed the President from the start," recalled Sidney Blumenthal. "Clinton had little room for maneuver."[30] Andrew Bacevich concluded that "civilian control of the military, the bedrock of civil-military relations in a democracy, was badly eroded," and respected military historian Russell Weigley observed that Powell had badly undercut the new commander in chief's authority in the very first days of his presidency.[31]

The Use of Force after the Cold War

The George H. W. Bush administration had left a number of other unresolved problems for the new Clinton team. In fact, few could remember another transition in which so many foreign policy crises required the new commander in chief's immediate action. The administration inherited foreign policy challenges in Somalia, where American troops, nominally under the United Nations, remained deployed; ethnic cleansing and state disintegration in the former Yugoslavia; political upheaval and a refugee

Figure 5.3. President George H. W. Bush and Powell participate in an Oval Office briefing on the situation in Somalia, examining maps and briefing papers, December 3, 1992. Participants include Vice President Dan Quayle, Powell, Secretary of Defense Dick Cheney, CIA director Robert Gates, and National Security Adviser Brent Scowcroft. The December 1992 decision to intervene in Somalia remains a mystery, coming from one of the most realist administrations in recent years. The Somalia intervention in 1992 and the later Iraq intervention in 2003 became the two outstanding examples in which the Powell Doctrine was never applied as a criterion for the deployment of troops, despite, in each case, Powell's playing an important role in the administration. In both Somalia and Iraq, the consequences were disastrous. Photo credit: George H. W. Bush Presidential Library.

crisis in Haiti; and military strikes against Iraq occurring at the very moment Clinton was being inaugurated. Moreover, the Bush administration, for all of its much-touted foreign policy prowess, had not resolved the most essential questions about the uses of American power in a post–Cold War era. The invasion of Panama and the Gulf War had been perceived as unmitigated successes. But in other areas where the issues were not so clear cut—such as Somalia, the Balkans, and Haiti—and the probability of success uncertain, the questions remained as complicated as ever.

Somalia was the major foreign policy challenge the new administration had to contend with during its first year in office. The origins of America's tragic involvement in Somalia were rooted in the final months of the Bush administration, when, several weeks after Bush's November 1992 defeat, he called a meeting to discuss Americans' growing discomfort over televised images of Somalia, where several years of civil war and warlordism had rendered the county incapable of feeding itself. Discussions in the Bush administration about the crisis ultimately led to a humanitarian intervention called Operation Restore Hope.[32]

Powell's support for the deployment to Somalia remains puzzling. On the question of intervention in Somalia, Powell dropped much of his usual caution.[33] Oddly enough, his support for humanitarian intervention in Somalia did not extend to Bosnia. The many points he had made during the first year of the Clinton administration in opposing Bosnia, he had avoided making previously with regard to Somalia in the final weeks of the Bush administration. Perhaps, in the afterglow of the Gulf War and the presence of trusted colleagues, he felt a degree of confidence that Operation Restore Hope's objectives could be fulfilled. Perhaps, as America's most prominent black official, he felt a moral obligation to induce the administration to focus on Somalia.

Powell laid out the details for Bush. A substantial number of U.S. troops would be put on the ground in Somalia "to take charge of the place" and oversee the distribution of food. Bush was enthusiastic, but Scowcroft remained uneasy. "Sure we can get in," Scowcroft warned. "But how do we get out?" Bush responded, "We'll do it, and try to be out by January 19. I don't want to stick Clinton with an ongoing military operation." Powell made little effort to challenge illusions about the efficacy of military intervention with regard to Somalia, even though after January 20, 1993, he would be the most senior official with responsibility for the deployment still serving in the new administration.[34]

Powell had facilitated an enormous miscalculation. His role in the Bush I administration during debates over Somalia anticipated his later reticence in the administration of Bush II over Iraq. When the commanders in Somalia requested helicopter gunships and strike planes to go after Somali warlords, Powell, in accordance with the Powell Doctrine, supported the request. But in many other respects, the Somalia deployment contradicted his doctrine. For example, the mission was allowed to change and "creep" into political objectives without adequate discussion and examination, and the national objectives being pursued were never effectively articulated. Moreover, Congress and the American people never received an adequate explanation of the reasons for the deployment, beyond vague statements about humanitarian need. Powell supported the deployment throughout, and even requested that more troops be sent after the deaths of four servicemen in August 1993. When eighteen Americans were killed in downtown Mogadishu during a deadly day of fighting in October 1993, overwhelming calls for an immediate withdrawal ensued.[35]

Powell understood that dramatic and moving televised images of suffering had drawn America into the Somalia crisis, and when things went badly, the American people were equally repelled by the resulting images of the conflict. Perceptions mattered. Powell saw small triumphs such as Grenada and Panama as hugely important in enhancing the American military's reputation. Interventions in small, almost undefended nations like Grenada and Panama allowed the U.S. military to flex its muscles on the cheap. He feared that debacles such as Vietnam, the 1980 Desert One rescue mission to Iran, Lebanon, and Somalia would undermine public support for the military.[36]

During the 1992 campaign, as it became increasingly clear that Clinton might defeat Bush, Powell sought to draw renewed attention to the Vietnam Syndrome and the Powell Doctrine. Despite his previous support for the Somalia deployment, he made it known that he opposed humanitarian interventions, particularly in places such as Bosnia. This was an unorthodox move for a sitting chairman of the Joint Chiefs. After the inauguration, when the new commander in chief inquired about military options, Powell turned away questions about Bosnia by drawing on Vietnam analogies, responding that the president first had to give him more precise political reasons for considering intervention.[37] Not everyone agreed that the Vietnam analogy applied to Bosnia, and some, such as UN Ambassador Madeleine Albright, argued that it differed from Vietnam in a number of significant ways.[38] For one, unlike the North Vietnamese, the Serbs were internationally isolated, and the conflict was not entangled in the politics of the Cold War. Moreover, unlike in Vietnam, where the United States essentially fought a unilateral war without major allies and contrary to UN priorities, the United States had significant allies in Europe willing to form a genuine coalition, and institutions like

NATO, the European Union, the United Nations, and the Organization for Security and Cooperation in Europe were involved in meaningful ways. The very multilateral nature of the enterprise ensured that the kinds of questions Powell liked to ask—the very kinds of questions not asked in Vietnam (or Somalia in 1992 or Iraq in 2003)—would be addressed.

Powell also compared the crisis in Bosnia to the situation in Lebanon in the 1980s. He feared an intervention in Bosnia would, like that in Lebanon in 1982 and 1983, lack focus and clear goals. In a 1992 *New York Times* op-ed piece, he wrote that whenever the military had been given a clear set of objectives, as with Panama (1989) and the Gulf War (1991), the result had been a success, whereas when goals and objectives remained murky—such as during the Bay of Pigs invasion of Cuba (1961), Vietnam, or Lebanon—the results had been disastrous. He implied that Bosnia resembled these confused and murky fiascos.[39] Such reasoning dismayed Albright, who argued that the relief of the long siege of Sarajevo, the opening of its airport, and strikes against Serbian militia positions surrounding the city represented clear and achievable goals. Powell saw Bosnia as a "baffling conflict" and argued that the United States would be "dealing with an ethnic tangle with roots reaching back a thousand years." He believed that he had "learned the proper lessons of history even if some journalists [had] not." But the recent successful deployments of military forces in Panama and the Persian Gulf undermined Powell's position. These interventions had given officials like Albright more confidence about what a military force might achieve.[40]

Throughout most of his career, Powell had usually taken the position that when a president asks you to do something, you have to sit down and figure out ways to get it done. This was not always his response to President Clinton.[41] Former air force chief of staff Gen. Merrill McPeak observed that Powell "did not frame the issue in a way that made it possible for the president to do what he wanted. Instead, he said, 'Here's Option A, it is really stupid. Here's Option B, it is dumber than dirt.'"[42]

"During our meetings in the White House Situation Room," Albright recalled, "Powell used a red laser pointer and maps of the difficult Balkans terrain to show where bombing could take place and troops could move if we pursued a military option. When we asked what it would take to free Sarajevo airport from the surrounding Serb artillery, he replied consistently with his commitment to the doctrine of overwhelming force, saying it would take tens of thousands of troops, cost billions of dollars, probably result in numerous casualties, and require a long and open-ended commitment of U.S. forces. Time and again he led us up the hill of possibility and dropped us off on the other side with the practical equivalent of 'No can do.'"[43]

Clinton and Lake remained reluctant to challenge Powell. Only Albright summoned the courage to question his views. The debate over Bosnia exploded at one session when Albright asked him in frustration, "What's the point of having this superb military that you're always talking about if we can't use it?" Although the Albright-Powell exchange echoed the divide between Shultz and Weinberger in the Reagan administration, with Powell clearly taking Weinberger's more cautious approach, Powell later recalled, "I thought I would have an aneurysm." He observed that "American G.I.s were not toy soldiers to be moved around on some sort of global game board." Albright recalled, "In the face of all his medals and prestige, I found it hard to argue with Powell about the proper way to employ American force. Even though I was a member of the Principals Committee, I was still a mere female civilian. I did, however, think then as now that the lessons of Vietnam could be learned too well."[44]

Powell described himself as the skunk at the picnic. Clinton's people saw him as trying to set policy through the adroit use of seemingly neutral military recommendations. He argued that neither air support for Sarajevo nor bombing of Serb positions would change Serb behavior. He believed the Serbs would successfully conceal tanks and artillery in the Bosnian woods and fog. He believed that only troops on the ground could deter the Serbs and proceeded to argue against such a deployment.[45] Others disagreed. Some later pointed out that the 1995 Dayton accords, which eventually achieved a settlement in Bosnia after limited military pressure, revealed the fallacy of Powell's caution. "It was understandable that Powell would want clarity about mission and certainty about success before committing our forces, but 'no more quagmires' was not a sufficient strategy in a messy and complex world," Albright concluded. "With careful planning, limited force could be used effectively to achieve limited objectives. There was an urgent need to do that in Bosnia, but Powell did not want the American military to take on that job."[46]

Powell's perception of the political and historical context in the Balkans, as well as the Vietnam Syndrome, influenced his views and the advice he offered. He was inclined to see the conflict as age-old and insoluble, just as he had believed that the problem in Lebanon was a "thousand-year-old hornet's nest." This hardly reflected the complex realities of either. Likewise, he saw Bosnia as a land of "ancient ethnic hatreds."[47] Few with knowledge of, or experience in, Bosnia found this description useful, and Powell's remarks during this time and afterward revealed a startling ignorance of what was actually happening in the area, where Serb militias systematically slaughtered perhaps as many as two hundred thousand civilians, most of them Muslims, in the worst acts of violence in Europe since World War II.

Powell later shared with Henry Louis Gates Jr. his opinion that "[t]he biggest mistake was recognizing all these little countries when they started to decide they were independent." More curiously, he added that the "Serbs had very good reason to be worried about being in a Muslim-dominated country. It wasn't just paranoia. . . . I think you ought to send a clear signal: that we're not going to get involved in this war, and it's not going to end until people are tired of fighting one another. . . . I believe in the bully's way of going to war. I'm on the street corner, I got my gun, I got my blade, I'ma kick yo' ass."[48] Yet, this contrasted with his support for the 1992 humanitarian intervention in Somalia.

Clinton also inherited the crisis in Haiti, which had been an ongoing U.S. foreign policy challenge in the early 1990s, with thousands of Haitians risking their lives to flee their troubled island for the United States. Powell faced the problem during the Bush administration, when newly elected, reformist Haitian leader Rev. Jean-Bertrand Aristide, whom many of Haiti's most desperately poor supported, ran afoul of the Haitian ruling elite and military and was overthrown by a coup in September 1991. During the Bush administration's discussions on Haiti, Powell warned Cheney that while the United States could take over Haiti with a company or two of Marines, the problem would be getting out. Powell understood that the United States had intervened in Haiti in 1915 for similar reasons and remained for fifteen years.

Clinton had criticized Bush's inaction on Haiti but had difficulty becoming the master of his own policy. The CIA preferred to continue collaborating with the ruling elite and military. The CIA and the Pentagon favored the coup leader Raul Cedras and opposed the president's policy of restoring the democratically elected Aristide. The CIA's bitterly anti-Aristide sources in Haiti were on the agency payroll; thus, intelligence on Haiti was selective and dependent upon self-interested Haitians. The CIA also collaborated with President Clinton's opponents on Capitol Hill to undermine the policy.[49]

By the time Haiti exploded as a full-blown foreign policy crisis, Powell had already retired as chairman. Though he could have served a third two-year term, he let it be known that he was not interested in continuing. Throughout the summer of 1993, the Clinton administration, in seeking a replacement for Powell as chairman, purportedly had one priority: it did not want "another Powell."[50]

A year after Powell's retirement, Clinton declared in September 1994 that he would invade Haiti unless Cedras stepped down and Aristide was restored to power. At Clinton's request, Powell went to Haiti, along with former senator Sam Nunn, as part of a mission headed by former president Jimmy Carter. Powell came away from the experience with admiration for

Carter's "imagination and dogged determination to find peaceful solutions to crises."[51] The delegation succeeded in getting Cedras and the other members of the junta to step aside at the eleventh hour, averting the U.S. invasion as troops were en route to Haiti. Clinton later recalled that through their dogged diplomacy, Powell, along with Nunn and Carter, "had done a courageous job under difficult and potentially dangerous circumstances."[52]

Powell and the Republican Party: An Ambivalent Relationship

After the success of the Haiti mission, Powell received a phone call from President Clinton. Despite their differences, Clinton had always respected

Figure 5.4. Powell presents President Clinton with a "Report on the Nation" to commemorate the second anniversary of the President's Summit for America's Future, May 13, 1999. After Powell retired as chairman of the Joint Chiefs in September 1993, he rebuffed Clinton's efforts to name him secretary of state. Powell later welcomed the same appointment, in December 2000, when offered by George W. Bush, but Powell was never a comfortable fit with the Bush II administration, due in part to the fact that his innate realism and support for the Powell Doctrine were completely antithetical to the administration's unilateral and neoconservative ideological coloration. This was compounded by the fact that the Bush Doctrine of preemptive, unilateral wars and the Rumsfeld Doctrine of fighting with the lightest and smallest force possible contradicted the Powell Doctrine in every way. In retrospect, Powell might have been much more successful as secretary of state had he served in a moderate Democratic administration rather than the intensely ideological, even radical, neoconservative Republican administration of George W. Bush. Photo credit: William J. Clinton Presidential Library.

Powell and wanted to reach out to him. Powell joked to the president that he hoped he was not being recalled for another Carter mission, but he knew from Clinton's friend Vernon Jordan that the president was calling to offer him the secretary of state position held by Warren Christopher, who wanted to leave the administration. Powell and Clinton met at the White House the following day, where Powell expressed his desire to enjoy his retirement.

Why did Powell turn down the offer to be Clinton's secretary of state and yet accept the offer, under much less favorable circumstances, six years later? No doubt he still had misgivings about the disorganization of the Clinton White House, as well as philosophical disagreements over matters such as gays in the military and humanitarian intervention. Moreover, Powell remained a staunch realist in the Weinberger and Shultz tradition, while the Clinton administration was moving increasingly in the direction of liberal internationalism. As Clinton might have suspected, however, Powell may also have been saving himself for a run for the presidency. In the years immediately after Powell's retirement as chairman, a national movement arose to draft him for president. His political stardom had come with surprising ease. By his fifty-fourth birthday, in March 1991, people were talking about him as a national political figure. This was based on only a year as national security adviser and a few years as chairman of the Joint Chiefs. Normally, this would have been a slender resume for a potential presidential candidate, but perceptions had become increasingly important in American politics, and the Gulf War had been an unprecedented media spectacle. Powell had emerged as perhaps its most compelling figure, spawning a "Powell phenomenon" with "Powell for president" clubs sprouting up across the country.

Powell's was one of the more unconventional presidential boomlets, beginning in January 1988, only two months after he became Reagan's national security adviser. Senator Ted Stevens of Alaska wrote to Vice President George H. W. Bush to suggest that he put Powell on his short list for vice president. White House Chief of Staff Howard Baker also mentioned Powell as a potential vice presidential prospect, and Washington pundits increasingly listed him in their speculations until the August 1988 Republican National Convention.[53] Writing in the New York Times, columnist Tom Wicker observed "that he is black but a military man, not a politician, might even be an asset, and his selection surely would be a 'bold stroke.'"[54] In 1990, Parade magazine raised the prospect of a Bush-Powell ticket in 1992, and such rumors became so frequent that Powell felt compelled to call Vice President Quayle to reassure him that he had done nothing to encourage them. Vernon Jordan had even approached Powell to gauge his interest in being Clinton's running mate.[55] Polls in the fall of 1995 showed him running ahead of

President Clinton, and a poll of New Hampshire Republicans placed Powell ahead of the front-runner, Republican senator Bob Dole of Kansas.

Much of Powell's appeal derived from his success in concealing just how ambitious he really was. Close friends and associates understood that his charm often obscured his ambition. He also appeared to be nonpartisan. In his 1995 memoir, he declared, "I am not ideologically liberal or conservative." He acknowledged that neither political party fit him perfectly, but therein lay the crux of the problem. Powell had only two options: run as a Republican or run as an independent. No one had ever run successfully as an independent. Even Ross Perot, who had spent an estimated $100 million, received only 19 percent of the popular vote and no electoral votes. Running as a Republican, Powell would face major problems with the Republican Party. Predicting that his Republican rivals would exploit his views on social issues, Stu Spencer, Ronald Reagan's longtime political adviser, warned Powell that his positions would alienate much of the GOP and that he should run as a Democrat. "You were raised in an old-fashioned Democratic home," Spencer observed. "You're too socially conscious."[56] Spencer had identified one of the essential dilemmas of the boomlet. Powell's background and experiences made him an odd fit with the GOP of the 1990s. He was a former member of the International Brotherhood of Teamsters (Local 812), his mother was a staunch union supporter and "diehard Democrat" and a member of the International Ladies Garment Workers Union, and both parents had been New Deal Democrats. Powell had voted for Lyndon Johnson in 1964 and for Carter in 1976.

Moreover, the public enthusiasm for a presidential run was only partly about Powell himself. The public reception to his 1995 memoir, My American Journey, made the point starkly. The book spoke effectively to American assumptions about themselves and their country. His story seemed to reaffirm long-held beliefs in America's special character and destiny, particularly with regard to racial progress and Vietnam. His was a different face of the Vietnam generation. In the decades after that war, Vietnam veterans began to play a steadily larger role in public life. But Vietnam had also been revived as a divisive political issue when Vietnam veterans began seeking political office. In 1988, Quayle's service in the Indiana National Guard became a subject of some controversy, and in 1992 the Republicans branded Bill Clinton a "draft dodger." The fallout from Vietnam seemed to effect different politicians in different ways, once again demonstrating that perceptions about Vietnam trumped realities. For example, Quayle and Clinton faced harsh scrutiny and criticism about their choices during the Vietnam era, whereas George W. Bush and Dick Cheney largely escaped such consequences.

GOP political operatives frequently resorted to crude appeals to patriotic symbolism in order to slander those who had served in Vietnam. George W. Bush and Karl Rove's attack strategy used the service of Vietnam veterans like John McCain and John Kerry against them. The experiences of McCain in 2000 and Kerry in 2004 would demonstrate what might have happened had Powell run in 1996. Such attacks began even before he had made up his mind about running, revealing that his opponents in a Republican primary wouldn't have hesitated to "redefine" his military career. His very compelling life story might well have been turned against him. One could anticipate politically motivated "veterans groups" materializing to cast doubt on his service record. His memoir would have proven especially problematic and been parsed to provide incendiary political fodder. Powell would have reinforced the trend that a compelling personal narrative can, in this media-driven age of spin, often be transformed into political baggage.

Many commentators pointed to Powell's obvious political strengths. His public persona was never about resentment but optimism, more in line with the political appeal of Reagan, Clinton, and Eisenhower. Perhaps sensing that Reagan remained a polarizing figure in 1995 and strongly identifying with Ike's military background, Powell most frequently encouraged comparisons with Eisenhower. He said he had a "special affinity for Dwight Eisenhower" and that Ike "did not have to bark or rattle sabers to gain respect and exercise command." He admired Eisenhower because "he did not stampede his nation into every trouble spot" and "understood both the use of power and the value of restraint." Powell described Ike as possessing "the secure character" to exercise caution. "It was Ike," Powell wrote, "who resisted pressure to intervene in Vietnam when the French went under at Dienbienphu."[57]

There were additional obstacles to a potential presidential candidacy. Powell would have had difficulty in the South, which was becoming the one geographic region in the country upon which the Republicans could consistently rely. Southern politics had been polarizing over race since the civil rights era, and Richard Nixon's "Southern strategy" of appealing to resentful white voters revealed the shrewd exploitation of racial anxieties in the region, an approach effectively emulated by Reagan and George H. W. Bush.

Race was an issue that loomed large over a potential Powell campaign. While the army may have grown increasingly color-blind, not so the GOP. While some, like former Republican congressman Jack Kemp, wanted a more inclusive party, many more wanted to continue to exploit the "race card" to political advantage. Powell revealed genuine discomfort with such Republican "wedge" tactics, whether on race, affirmative action, or immigration.

He was frequently asked how he felt about the GOP's use of racially charged rhetoric and symbols. The Republican Party's exploitation of racial politics, as well as the "troubling mix of politics and religion," disturbed him. Referring to the notorious Willie Horton strategy, he asked, "Was the ad depicting this incident racist? Of course. Had it bothered me? Certainly. . . . Republican strategists had made a cold political calculation: no amount of money or effort could make a dent in the Democratic hold on the black vote, so don't try. Some had gone even further—if the racial card could be played to appeal to certain constituencies, play it. The Horton ad served that purpose. It was a political cheap shot."[58]

Powell believed Bush "seemed unmindful of the racial polarization being caused by the far right wing of his party." While he refused to believe that either Reagan or Bush was personally racist, he did allow that both "led a party . . . whose principal message to black Americans seemed to be: lift yourself by your bootstraps. All did not have bootstraps; some did not have boots. I wish Reagan and Bush had shown more sensitivity on this point." Bush's remarks at the time of the 1992 Los Angeles riots were also distressing. The president implied that the violence had no connection to the severe social and economic problems of America's inner cities. Powell concluded that Bush, fearing the right wing of his own party, emphasized law and order but omitted references to the social, economic, and political oppression of African Americans. Fearing that Bush's law-and-order rhetoric would only fan the flames of racial polarization, Powell had preferred that Bush talk more about reconciliation and less about polarization. Problems such as the Los Angeles riots, he later wrote, had "deep social roots." These views were guaranteed to raise a red flag to the Republican Right.[59]

Moreover, the racial issue cut both ways, and support from black voters could not be taken for granted. One poll showed Powell receiving favorable ratings from 73 percent of white voters but only 57 percent of blacks, while another revealed that 75 percent of the black electorate would have supported Clinton in a Powell-Clinton matchup. "Historically, there's been this search—whites always want to create the black of their choice as their leader," observed Jesse Jackson, who had himself been a candidate for president in 1984 and 1988. "So for the white people this nice, clean-cut black military guy becomes something really worth selling and promoting. But have we ever seen him on a picket line? Is he for unions? Or for civil rights? Or for *anything*?" Clifford Alexander, whose efforts, as Carter's secretary of the army, tripled the number of black generals, resulting in Powell becoming the youngest general in the army at forty-one, was also ambivalent. "You see, this has been pulled on us many times," Alexander said in an interview with

Henry Louis Gates. "White America says, 'This is your new leader, and you ought to feel good about it.'"[60]

Powell was understandably defensive regarding the role of race in his remarkable career. He bristled at the suggestion that he had benefited from "tokenism"; yet Republican administrations desperately needed black appointees, and race had been a factor at numerous points in his rapid ascent. "I am also aware that, over the years, my career may have given some bigots a safe black to hide behind," Powell allowed. "I nevertheless tried to keep matters in perspective. I had been given responsibility at the highest level in a Republican administration. National Security Advisers to presidents are not chosen as tokens." More controversially, he came out in support of affirmative action and wrote, enigmatically, that he had "benefited from equal opportunity and affirmative action in the Army, but I was not shown preference."[61]

Even the title of Powell's memoir, My American Journey, seemed intended to reaffirm national myths and the sense of mission that some believe to be at the center of American identity. At the time, reviewers tended to focus obsessively on whether Powell would run. The book was seen more as a personal story, with Powell at the center, rather than as an account of the broader events of the Reagan, Bush, and Clinton administrations. Parts of the book read like standard political memoir boilerplate. While he acknowledged that his political philosophy was still evolving, he embraced safe issues, such as support for the free enterprise system and lower taxes. He summarized his political philosophy as "a fiscal conservative with a social conscience," but this could just as easily have been a description of the incumbent at the time, Bill Clinton.

Part of Powell's appeal was that he had never been a politician, but that perception would have changed the moment he began to take more specific positions on the issues. Since the end of the Gulf War, he had maintained the facade that he could be all things to all people. His comments on politics in his speeches and in his memoir were guarded and vague enough to elicit support, but he could not have retained this stance in the heat of a real campaign. This underscored the problem that, as Powell actually took positions on the controversies of the day, his support would inevitably have eroded. "Once the ugly attacks and assaults really begin, Colin Powell will be forced, to some degree, to come out swinging," observed the prominent African American intellectual Cornel West. "Then they'll say, 'Oh, my God, he *is* a black man. Look at him. He's full of rage. He's been that all the time.'"[62]

At one point in the frenzy came the shrewd assessment, from beyond the grave, of former president Richard Nixon. Although the thirty-seventh president had died more than a year before, his opinion of the Powell phenomenon appeared in the *New Yorker* in October 1995. Shortly before he died, Nixon had confided to his political director, Roger Stone, his assessment of Powell, who had been a White House fellow during the Nixon administration. "He's not Eisenhower," Nixon offered. "People don't understand how tough and ruthless Eisenhower was in the struggle to get to the top. Powell may be a great soldier, but he is not a politician. And I don't think he would survive in this realm. . . . Maybe for Vice-President, in a controlled environment. But the top spot? There's not going to be another Eisenhower."[63]

In the fall of 1995, Powell embarked on a remarkable book tour organized like a political campaign: five weeks, twenty-five cities, beginning on September 16, 1995. The memoir was a phenomenon unto itself. Sales exceeded all expectations, reaching an astonishing 1.4 million volumes. To put this into perspective, President George H. W. Bush's memoir, *A World Transformed*, sold just fifty thousand copies.[64] During this "mother of all book tours," several problems emerged. Powell began to hear the siren call to run, but he also became aware that most diehard Republicans were not enthusiastic about his candidacy. Powell's many speeches and media appearances revealed that he was out of step with the Republican Party on its most cherished issues. The 1995 Republican Party, fresh from sweeping the 1994 midterm elections, was in the process of transforming from a party led by comparatively moderate, Midwestern Republicans like Bob Michael and Bob Dole into one led by more ideological, right-wing, Southern Republicans like Tom Delay, Newt Gingrich, and Trent Lott. "They're trying to make him the political Antichrist," said Patrick H. Caddell, a former Democratic strategist. "If he runs as a Republican, it's the biggest mistake in his life. This party doesn't want him."[65] Moreover, the Republican Party had cultivated a political alliance with fundamentalist religious groups, and Powell admitted that he was "troubled by the political passion of those on the extreme right who seem to claim divine wisdom on political as well as spiritual matters."[66] He believed that faith should provide people with private inspiration and guidance, not a political agenda, and found the rhetorical undertones of class and race alarming.[67]

Many Americans seemed desperate to convince themselves, often against all available evidence, that Powell agreed with them on the issues. But the end of this quixotic effort came on November 8, 1995, when Powell held a press conference in Alexandria, Virginia, to announce that he would not be a candidate for president in 1996. His cousin and business partner, Bruce Llewellyn, whom Powell proudly described as one of America's wealthiest African Americans, put Powell's problem succinctly. When asked by Henry

Louis Gates if Powell would run, Llewellyn replied, "No. Because he can't win. He can't get the Democratic nomination, he's not going to get the Republican nomination, and nobody can win as an independent. Second, the Republican Party is in the hands of the conservatives, the right-wing zealots, the religious zealots, and they're not about to give him the nomination. I think it's very interesting. Everybody loves Colin Powell, but that's because nobody knows what he stands for."[68]

Although Powell's flirtation with a presidential campaign simulated a news media frenzy, in retrospect, Powell's service as chairman during the first year of Clinton's presidency left a larger legacy. Powell exercised great influence over the deliberations of the early Clinton administration and cast a lingering shadow over questions of intervention and war. Although Powell only served as chairman during the first eight months of Clinton's presidency, his impact was profound and lasting. Throughout the first year of the Clinton administration, he successfully checked the administration's desire to mount a more active liberal internationalist foreign policy, and his influence would continue to be felt long after his departure in the fall of 1993. Powell dominated discussions over war and peace during a crucial year in the Clinton administration. After the Somalia debacle in the fall of 1993 and after the Democrats lost both houses of Congress in the midterm elections of 1994, Clinton felt compelled to cooperate more closely with Republicans on Capitol Hill, while simultaneously moving his administration in the direction of a foreign and defense policy consensus. The president's overtures to Powell at this time revealed his desire to create a perception of a bipartisan foreign policy, as did his efforts to appoint more Republicans to important posts in the Pentagon and CIA.

Crises in places such as Bosnia, Somalia, and Haiti raised difficult questions about post–Cold War interventions. Increasingly, many senior officials, both military and civilian, were coming to understand that foreign policy problems could not be resolved adequately if insufficient attention was paid to postconflict challenges. Clinton and many of the people around him believed that nation building was a necessary evil. Afghanistan, where the Taliban regime ultimately came to power after a civil war, stood as a tragic reminder of what could happen when insufficient attention was given to postconflict challenges. Clinton's critics derided nation building, but it was often necessitated by crises that Clinton himself had inherited, as in Bosnia, Somalia, and Haiti. The United States might not want to get involved, but what choice did it have when the alternative was the chaos of Afghanistan? Powell, too, was critical of nation building. He thought it sounded idealistic and inspirational and saw it as yet another way for the military to get bogged down in quagmires. He remained dubious of most humanitarian endeavors.

Notes

1. Author interview with Andrew Bacevich, September 21, 2007. See also, Andrew J. Bacevich, *American Empire: The Realities and Consequences of U.S. Diplomacy* (Cambridge, MA: Harvard University Press, 2002), and *The New American Militarism: How Americans Are Seduced by War* (Oxford: Oxford University Press, 2005).

2. Quoted in Bill Clinton, *My Life* (New York: Vintage, 2004), 450.

3. Russell Weigley, "The American Civil-Military Cultural Gap," in *Soldiers and Civilians: The Civil-Military Gap and American National Security*, ed. Peter D. Feaver and Richard H. Kohn (Cambridge, MA: MIT Press, 2001), 242.

4. David Halberstam, *War in a Time of Peace: Bush, Clinton, and the Generals* (New York: Scribner, 2001), 167.

5. John F. Harris, *The Survivor: Bill Clinton in the White House* (New York: Random House, 2005), 48; Warren Christopher, *Chances of a Lifetime: A Memoir* (New York: Scribner, 2001), 149, 176.

6. Colin Powell, *My American Journey* (New York: Ballantine, 1995, 2003), 548–62; Harris, *The Survivor*, 49.

7. Powell, *My American Journey*, 549–51; Christopher, *Chances of a Lifetime*, 174; author interview with Lawrence Korb, March 17, 2006.

8. Powell, *My American Journey*, 563.

9. Author interview with Lawrence Korb, March 17, 2006.

10. Quoted in Powell, *My American Journey*, 549–55; Bacevich, *American Empire*, 171.

11. Author interview with Lawrence Korb, March 17, 2006; James Mann, *Rise of the Vulcans: The History of Bush's War Cabinet* (New York: Viking Press, 2004), 220; Sidney Blumenthal, *The Clinton Wars* (New York: Farrar, Straus and Giroux, 2003), 60.

12. Richard A. Clarke, *Against All Enemies: Inside America's War on Terror* (New York: Free Press, 2004), 243–44.

13. Bacevich, *American Empire*, 136–37; Powell, *My American Journey*, 560–62.

14. Powell, *My American Journey*, 432, 549.

15. Halberstam, *War in a Time of Peace*, 175; Madeleine Albright, *Madam Secretary* (New York: Miramax Books, 2003), 165–66.

16. Quoted in Harris, *The Survivor*, 49.

17. Blumenthal, *The Clinton Wars*, 63–64.

18. Albright, *Madam Secretary*, 229–30.

19. Eric Schmitt, "Clinton, in Gesture of Peace, Pops in on Pentagon," *New York Times*, April 9, 1993.

20. Bacevich, *American Empire*, 122, 171.

21. Thomas Friedman, "Clinton, Saluting Vietnam Dead, Finds Old Wound Is Slow to Heal," *New York Times*, June 1, 1993.

22. Quoted in Clinton, *My Life*, 522.

23. Powell, *My American Journey*, 566, 573; Eric Schmitt, "Clinton and Powell Discover That They Need Each Other," *New York Times*, June 4, 1993.

24. Powell, *My American Journey*, 549–50.

25. Quoted in Powell, *My American Journey*, 533.

26. Blumenthal, *The Clinton Wars*, 53; Clinton, *My Life*, 450.

27. Powell, *My American Journey*, 557.

28. Bob Woodward, *The Choice: How Bill Clinton Won* (New York: Simon and Schuster, 1996), 289; Powell, *My American Journey*, 557–59.

29. Quoted in Powell, *My American Journey*, 558.

30. Blumenthal, *The Clinton Wars*, 53, 64.

31. Weigley, "The American Civil-Military Cultural Gap," 242.

32. Michael R. Gordon, "Somali Aid Plan Is Called Most Ambitious Option," *New York Times*, November 28. 1992.

33. Author interview with Andrew Bacevich, September 21, 2007.

34. Powell, *My American Journey*, 550; Lester H. Brune, *The United States and Post–Cold War Interventions: Bush and Clinton in Somalia, Haiti, and Bosnia, 1992–1998* (Claremont, CA: Regina Books, 1998), 19–23.

35. Brune, *The United States and Post–Cold War Interventions*, 30–33.

36. Powell, *My American Journey*, 304, 568–73.

37. Powell, *My American Journey*, 543–44.

38. Blumenthal, *The Clinton Wars*, 62; Albright, *Madam Secretary*, 230.

39. Colin Powell, "Why Generals Get Nervous," *New York Times*, October 8, 1992.

40. Quoted in Powell, *My American Journey*, 544–45, 562.

41. Michael R. Gordon, "Report by Powell Challenges Calls to Revise Military," *New York Times*, December 31, 1992.

42. Michael Steinberger, "Misoverestimated," *American Prospect*, April 1, 2004, www.prospect.org/cs/articles?articleId=8853.

43. Albright, *Madam Secretary*, 230.

44. Powell, *My American Journey*, 561; Albright, *Madam Secretary*, 230.

45. Harris, *The Survivor*, 49.

46. Albright, *Madam Secretary*, 231.

47. Powell, *My American Journey*, 281.

48. Henry Louis Gates Jr., "Powell and the Black Elite," *New Yorker*, September 25, 1995.

49. Halberstam, *War in a Time of Peace*, 270.

50. Peter J. Roman and David W. Tarr, "Military Professionalism and Policymaking," in *Soldiers and Civilians: The Civil-Military Gap and American National Security*, ed. Peter D. Feaver and Richard H. Kohn (Cambridge, MA: MIT Press, 2001), 242.

51. Quoted in Powell, *My American Journey*, 586.

52. Clinton, *My Life*, 618.

53. Gerald Boyd, "Bush Is Lining Up Prospects for No. 2 Spot on the Ticket," *New York Times*, July 28, 1988.

54. Tom Wicker, "A Balance for Bush," *New York Times*, July 29, 1988.

55. Powell, *My American Journey*, 355, 371, 539.

56. Quoted in Powell, *My American Journey*, 540.

57. Powell, *My American Journey*, 301.

58. Powell, *My American Journey*, 388, 545.

59. Quoted in Powell, *My American Journey*, 388, 538, 553.

60. Gates, "Powell and the Black Elite."

61. Powell, *My American Journey*, 341, 388, 592.

62. Gates, "Powell and the Black Elite."

63. Sidney Blumenthal, "Ghost in the Machine," *New Yorker*, October 2, 1995.

64. Halberstam, *War in a Time of Peace*, 238.

65. Richard L. Berke, "Right Tries to Mobilize against Powell Candidacy," *New York Times*, November 2, 1995.

66. Powell, *My American Journey*, 592.

67. Woodward, *The Choice*, 292.

68. Gates, "Powell and the Black Elite."

CHAPTER SIX

~

Secretary of State

Colin Powell saw himself as a potential bridge between the new administration of George W. Bush and those of the previous three presidents. But his time at the State Department paralleled a radical departure from many of the traditions of American diplomacy. Because of the tumultuous and polarizing events of these years, the policies of the Bush II administration completely contradicted the Powell Doctrine. Instead of bringing Powell's doctrine, as well perhaps as the realist foreign policy he envisioned, to fruition, a new "Bush Doctrine" of unilateral preventive war failed its first test in Iraq, and a "Rumsfeld Doctrine" of using smaller, lighter units undermined almost all of what remained of the Weinberger/Powell Doctrine. "In essence, the Powell Doctrine looked at what the military needed and sought to double it," observed former Pentagon official Lawrence Korb, "whereas the Rumsfeld Doctrine looked at what the military needed and then cut it in half." Bush and his senior advisers were determined to vanquish, once and for all, the so-called Vietnam Syndrome; instead, a new "Iraq Syndrome" emerged with equally profound consequences for the military and foreign policy.[1]

The new administration oversaw other troubling developments. It frequently resorted to crudely exploiting foreign policy and military crises for domestic political advantage. Efforts to use the events of 9/11 and the Iraq War as political wedge issues proved increasingly polarizing. The administration also greatly expanded the powers of the presidency at the expense of the other branches of government. The kind of congressional involvement and oversight in foreign policy common during the Reagan and Clinton eras became unimaginable. Moreover, Bush and his legal advisers promoted increased secrecy and sought to roll back three decades of trends toward more openness and transparency in government.

George W. Bush entered office assuming domestic matters would be the focus of his presidency. He confidently pledged during the 2000 campaign that he would reduce the highest rates of income taxes, appoint federal judges opposed to abortion rights, and seek to reverse much of Clinton's social and economic record. On the subject of foreign policy, Bush was less self-assured. His answers to foreign policy questions were often uncertain and incoherent. He demonstrated scant interest in the world beyond poll-tested phrases about the need for "humility" in foreign policy and a hostility to "nation building." Much of what he said about foreign and defense matters merely criticized the previous administration, for example, by charging that Clinton had weakened the military by overexpanding its commitments abroad.[2] Bush appeared only dimly aware of world affairs. He often exhibited prickliness and not only a lack of basic knowledge about but also a disdain for the crucial details of world affairs.[3] "I don't do nuance," Bush once boasted. This proved to be his undoing. "Bush had come into office with less knowledge of the outside world, and less interest in it, than any other modern American president," observed former New York Times diplomatic correspondent Stephen Kinzer. "He had traveled little outside the United States and had not read widely or thought seriously about world history."[4]

When Bush announced Powell's nomination for secretary of state, some saw it as an immediate effort to establish his legitimacy after the most troubling and controversial presidential election in modern times. In the disputed election of 2000, Bush received 550,000 fewer popular votes than his opponent, Vice President Al Gore. For a month after the election, Bush remained stalled with only 246 electoral votes to Gore's 267, the outcome awaiting a resolution of the electoral debacle in his brother Jeb's state of Florida. The "Sunshine State" had twenty-five electoral votes, just enough to tip the presidency to Bush. After more than a month of political and legal wrangling, the U.S. Supreme Court decided, after producing nine separate and bitterly partisan opinions, to award the presidency to Bush by the narrowest of margins, 5–4. Bush's announcement of Powell as his secretary of state–designate was his first major personnel decision after the Court handed him the presidency.

Powell seemed enthusiastic about accepting the appointment, despite his reservations six years before when President Bill Clinton had offered him the same post on much more attractive terms. Under Clinton, Powell would have dominated a weak cabinet and a president who remained unsteady on foreign affairs. Moreover, his acceptance of the post in December 2000 contradicted his stated reasons for remaining out of public life when he refused to run for president in late 1995, as well as the excuses he gave Bob Dole about preferring retirement in 1996 when declining to serve as Dole's running mate. Perhaps even more curiously, Powell readily accepted the appointment without first extracting any sort of agreement or even understanding from Bush (or Vice President Dick Cheney) about his role. In light of Bush's uncertain legitimacy in December 2000, Powell certainly had the upper hand and could have sought the kind of guarantees that previous high-profile appointees had often requested. At the very least, Powell should have sought to obtain some sense of how the administration would function, what its lines of authority would be, and with whom the de facto power would reside. By overlooking such crucial details, Powell guaranteed that, while he would serve in *office* for the next four years, he would not necessarily be in *power*. Perhaps, having long avoided the kind of scrutiny and challenges other officials had faced, Powell overestimated his own abilities. Or, he may have perceived no reason to secure his role in the administration given Bush's foreign policy inexperience.

Powell's relationship with Bush was never strong. Powell had many obvious assets, such as his smooth style, command of the facts, and ready sense of humor. At sixty-three, he seemed more vigorous and at ease with himself than Bush. In answering questions from the press about his appointment, his old sense of command returned immediately. A large man, with an ease of speaking and fluid style, Powell stood in sharp contrast with the physically smaller Bush and his inventive speech patterns and halting public performances. Powell came across as commanding whereas Bush did not. Powell's answers were more detailed than Bush's. Observers believed that Powell had upstaged Bush that December day during their press conference for his nomination, something that did not go unnoticed. Cheney, who had been running the transition, was reportedly incensed. Reporter James Mann later observed that Powell's influence may have peaked on that day and declined soon afterward.[5]

In the shortened period between the Supreme Court's intervention in the presidential contest and Inauguration Day, Powell sought to shape the staffing of the Bush administration in ways that complemented his objectives. He suffered some of his earliest setbacks in a long string of defeats that ultimately led to his departure from the administration at the end of the first term.[6] Powell had closely observed several secretaries of state and wanted to establish himself as a relevant force in the administration. He had noted how James Baker, like George Shultz, strode into meetings and acted as the steward of U.S. foreign policy. Baker had certainly benefited from his close relationship with George H. W. Bush, something Powell did not enjoy with George W. Bush. But, from his observations of Baker, Powell took to heart the need for bipartisan consensus and backing from Capitol Hill. A bipartisan approach would also aid him in framing policies that recognized the complexity of the world, rather than the more rigidly ideological policies favored by other senior figures in the administration.

Powell shared with several officials with whom he had served, such as Baker, Frank Carlucci, Caspar Weinberger, and George H. W. Bush, an innate caution and small "c" conservatism. He was not an administrative force of nature like Donald Rumsfeld but rather the consummate staff officer. Shultz was the most obvious model for what he sought to achieve. Following Shultz's example, Powell wanted to build a team, both inside the State Department and outside, in the larger cabinet and administration. He did not seek to dominate the administration. On the contrary, he merely believed that, as the president's chief foreign policy appointment, it made sense to build the kind of team Shultz eventually had in place by 1987. Powell respected Shultz not only for his demonstrated abilities but also for the way he "determinedly managed to put substance into Ronald Reagan's vision." With another new president unsteady in foreign affairs, Powell may have seen his chance to provide Bush with a similar service. He also noted how Shultz fought to become the Reagan administration's "single minister of foreign policy." This, Powell knew, was the key to Shultz's triumphs in 1987 and 1988, when he successfully steered Reagan toward rapprochement with Mikhail Gorbachev.[7]

Powell's cautionary example was Alexander Haig, who sought to be the "vicar" of Reagan's foreign policy but was instead undermined by other advisers and resigned after little more than a year. Powell's career bore similarities to the Haig precedent. Haig rose from colonel to four-star general owing mostly to his political service to Henry Kissinger and Richard Nixon. Like Powell, Haig had flirted with the notion of running for president in 1980 (he unsuccessfully took the plunge in 1987 and 1988). Although Haig's brief flirtation with the campaign in late 1979 went nowhere, it was sufficient to plant seeds of doubt about his loyalty in an administration where he, like Powell in 2001, was an outsider in his relations with the new president.

Even under the best of conditions, Powell was an awkward fit in the Bush administration. With an extraordinarily powerful vice president in Cheney and secretary of defense in Rumsfeld, Powell confronted challenges that Shultz and Baker never faced. Still, Powell may initially have been optimistic. Rather than having to vanquish his adversaries, as Shultz had through a patient bureaucratic war of attrition, he had an opportunity to influence the selection of personnel from the very beginning. Powell thus pushed for former congressman and Pennsylvania governor Tom Ridge to become secretary of defense. Ridge, a Vietnam veteran like Powell, arrived in Congress in 1982 as the first enlisted Vietnam combat veteran elected to the House. He had a reputation as a moderate and pragmatic problem solver in Pennsylvania and had been seriously considered as a running mate for Bush prior to Cheney's penciling himself in for the job. While in Congress, Ridge's voting record had also often been at variance with Cheney's, particularly on such right-wing obsessions as the Contras and Reagan's Strategic Defense Initiative. Powell also fought for his close friend Richard Armitage to become deputy secretary of defense. Armitage, another Vietnam veteran, was regarded as a nonideological straight shooter. Powell may not have realized it at the time, but he had a kind of reverse Midas touch. The fact that he was known to be supporting Ridge and Armitage for the two top Pentagon posts hurt their chances. Rumsfeld bluntly rejected Armitage as his number two at the Pentagon, leaving him to become Powell's deputy at the State Department.

Even if his efforts to secure Ridge's and Armitage's appointments failed, Powell had occupied three of the seats in the White House situation room—national security adviser, chairman of the Joint Chiefs, and secretary of state. The media hailed him for his skills and popularity and duly noted that he entered office in the strongest position of any modern secretary of state. In reality, he held a weak hand. Unlike Shultz, whom Reagan desperately needed after Haig's tempestuous resignation, Powell was never, contrary to what the media asserted, an indispensable part of Bush's team. Cheney, on the other hand, proved indispensable. As vice president, he, constitutionally, unlike everyone else in the administration, could not be fired or easily swept aside. Moreover, Cheney's machinations were largely removed from public scrutiny and transparency, further enhancing his power while at the same time shielding him from accountability.

Because Bush had relatively little knowledge of, or interest in, foreign affairs, advisers played an immense role in his foreign policy. For Powell, this was both an opportunity and a peril. He might have gained some influence over Bush, just as Shultz eventually did over Reagan, but Bush's lack of engagement and interest allowed Cheney and Rumsfeld to exercise exaggerated influence. Moreover, whereas Shultz had key allies in the Reagan White House like James Baker, Michael Deaver, and Ed Meese, Powell had none in the Bush White House. In fact, both Cheney and Karl Rove, Bush's chief political adviser who had been dubbed "Bush's Brain," eyed him with suspicion and plotted to check his influence.

Powell also faced an unusually fierce challenge from the Pentagon. Shultz had poor relations with Weinberger, but as a bureaucratic battler, Weinberger was never in the same league as Rumsfeld. Shultz also had control of the State Department, whereas it was less clear that Powell did, particularly since several of the key appointments below him had been imposed by Cheney and Rove and were known to be more loyal to the White House than to Powell. Although Powell and Armitage had an excellent relationship and were about as close as two senior officials could possibly be, Powell had little power over other appointees in the department. On Cheney's orders, the right-wing ideologue John Bolton was named undersecretary of state for arms control and international security, presumably to keep Cheney informed about Powell's thinking and actions. "In order to be allowed to get Armitage, Powell had to accept Bolton," Powell's former chief of staff, Col. Lawrence Wilkerson, recalled. "But it soon became apparent that Bolton was working for Cheney, not Powell." Powell sought to thwart this move and took the extraordinary step of urging members of the Senate Foreign Relations Committee to reject Bolton's nomination.[8] As Powell feared, Bolton became a major source of his misery at State, openly defying him and pursuing vastly different foreign policy objectives, presumably at the behest of the vice president. "I think Powell underestimated how difficult Rumsfeld and Cheney would make things for him," recalled Lawrence Korb.[9]

Powell believed that the only way he could prevail in such an environment was to keep the administration's deliberations inclusive and transparent. He wanted foreign policy made in a systematic way, following a formal process. This was not to be. Unlike the collegiality of National Security Council meetings under Bush I or even the messiness of Clinton and Anthony Lake's NSC, the Bush II NSC meetings had a rehearsed quality, as if they were being held only as a formality, concealing from the participants where the real decisions were being made. The new administration's foreign policy was run behind the scenes, dominated by Cheney and Rumsfeld with Condoleezza Rice orchestrating matters for the consumption of the NSC, the cabinet, and the press. Powell soon discovered that most meetings were irrelevant. He might appear to have won the first round of a policy debate, only to lose the second or third rounds. He was allowed to prevail occasionally, but rarely on matters important to Cheney or Rumsfeld.[10] A back channel existed by which Cheney and Rumsfeld, with Rice's complicity, made most of the important decisions. "In many cases, policies weren't debated at all," noted James Risen, the national security correspondent of the New York Times. "The absence of effective management has been the defining characteristic of the Bush administration's foreign policy and has allowed radical decisions to take effect rapidly with minimal review."[11]

Powell and Cheney embodied the deepest divisions in the administration. To rise within it, one had to have and maintain the confidence of the vice president, who proved to be the most relevant source of power. Treasury Secretary Paul O'Neill, a witness to previous Beltway power struggles, thought it remarkable to have such open combat in the first month of a new administration.[12] Powell's feelings toward Cheney had grown more complex since their last service together in the Bush I administration. He told *Washington Post* reporter Bob Woodward that he remained "confounded" by Cheney. It soon became apparent to Powell that Cheney played by his own rules. To some observers, it was not clear that Cheney was accountable to the president. His low-key manner, facilitated his accumulation of power. NSC official Richard Clarke, for example, confessed to being "fascinated at how complex a person he was. On the surface, he was quiet and soft-spoken. Below that surface calm ran strong, almost extreme beliefs. He had been one of the five most radical conservatives in the Congress. The quiet often hid views that would seem out of place if aired more broadly."[13]

From the beginning, Cheney's role in the administration provoked speculation. Was he head of government to Bush's head of state? Was he the CEO in Bush's corporate-structured presidency? Was he the prime minister, a holdover from the reign of King George I, now serving the dauphin, King George II? He had accumulated immense power. Even prior to Inauguration Day, he ran Bush's transition, a process thrown into upheaval when Cheney was hospitalized with heart problems. Therefore, he was a major power with whom to contend. Unlike his father, who largely marginalized the much-maligned Dan Quayle, George W. Bush frequently had Cheney present when meeting with official visitors. Visitors to the White House might appear with Bush for a photo opportunity but then sit down to talk business with Cheney. Some officials left the White House with the impression that Bush only knew what Cheney allowed him to know. In one of the more extraordinary moments of the first term, when Bush had to testify before the commission investigating 9/11, Cheney sat alongside him, responding to questions that otherwise would have been directed at Bush.[14]

Cheney had immense power over staffing and personnel decisions. The vice president succeeded in gaining the appointment of his friend Paul O'Neill as Treasury secretary. It had been Cheney who wanted Rumsfeld at the Pentagon to block Powell. Even the key deputies, such as Stephen Hadley as Rice's and Paul Wolfowitz as Rumsfeld's, were from Cheney's 1989–1993 Pentagon staff. The vice president intervened in matters that, under normal circumstances, were the domain of the secretary of state. Powell suspected that Cheney had established his own separate government consisting of Rumsfeld, Deputy Secretary of Defense Wolfowitz, and Assistant Secretary of Defense Douglas Feith.

Powell's confidante, Bob Woodward, speculated that the secretary of state harbored a "deep-seated anger" toward the vice president. According to Woodward's well-informed analysis, Powell "had always been just one level beneath Cheney in the pecking order. Over three decades he had worked his way up to become the top uniformed military man, chairman of the JCS, and had wound up reporting to Cheney, who had been an improbable pick as Bush senior's defense secretary when the nomination of Senator John Tower was rejected by his Senate colleagues. Then as secretary of state, the senior cabinet post, Powell was again outranked by Cheney, this time the unexpected pick as vice president. At NSC meetings, Cheney sat at Bush's right hand, Powell at his left." Each had a fundamentally different view of the world and idea of what American foreign policy should be. Making matters even more difficult for Powell, the conflict between them intensified as the administration faced growing difficulties. The relationship between the two was so bad that they could not even discuss their differences.[15]

Throughout his tenure as secretary of state, Powell also worried about his relationship with Bush. He did not have close relations with the president and enjoyed nothing remotely like the comfort level Bush's father had with Baker. Bush and Powell had little personal chemistry and never achieved any genuine rapport. He revealed to Woodward that he and Bush were often uncomfortable around one another. The British ambassador to Washington, Christopher Meyer, observed that "during Blair's visits to the U.S., we saw Bush and Powell together, it was the impression of all in the British team that this was not a relationship made in heaven."[16] Bush remained wary of Powell. Not only had Powell consistently proven more popular than the new president in public opinion polls over the previous five years, but he was not seen as a true loyalist in an administration that so highly prized loyalty above all else. Powell had not needed to be unnecessarily obsequious. Rove sensed that Powell might be out of his reach, and perhaps most damning, he had not been as ready as others to offer himself in the service of Rove's and Bush's political objectives.[17]

Based on their temperaments, interests, and life experiences, Powell and Bush could not have been less alike. Powell had served at senior levels in the previous three administrations. Their worldviews were vastly different. Powell's nuanced approach often tended to see much of life in shades of gray, whereas Bush seemed driven by his strong sense of certainty, perhaps fueled by his intense religious beliefs, and convinced that his instincts were always right. This left little room for complexity. To some, Bush's sense of what his partisans liked to call "moral clarity" was the essence of his strength as a leader. To others, it came across as arrogance and hubris. Bush did not like to linger over subjects, and those around him knew he had difficulty sitting still for briefings. Moreover, a fiercely protective bubble existed around the president, reinforcing the dilemma that he did not like to hear things that conflicted with his own beliefs. He acknowledged that he rarely read newspapers or magazines. What he did know was provided for him by a small coterie of select advisers, particularly Condoleezza Rice. Powell feared that Bush was hostage to the information this chosen few conveyed. Observers recognized that Bush lacked curiosity about matters of importance to the nation and, even more troubling, had little interest in what he did not already know. His White House was airtight, not unlike Reagan's, with his schedule rigidly guarded by gatekeepers such as Chief of Staff Andrew Card. Only a few people, such as Rice and Cheney, had the right of unfettered access. Powell knew Rumsfeld also had access through Cheney, but he recognized that he enjoyed no such influence.[18]

The structure of the administration presented further challenges for Powell, who had developed his own distinctive sense of how to approach foreign policy questions. Powell's style had evolved over the years. Through working with various presidents, he had a reputation as a shrewd briefer, laying out for each president the available options but also sometimes shading the briefings in ways that favored his own point of view. He may have assumed this would be his approach in the new administration, but he soon discovered that Bush did not like debate or discussions about policy. Richard Clarke and Paul O'Neill concurred with this assessment. Clarke, who, like Powell, had served the three previous presidents, lamented that Bush always "looked for the simple solution, the bumper sticker description of the problem. The problem was that many of the important issues, like terrorism, like Iraq, were laced with important subtlety and nuance. These issues needed analysis and Bush and his inner circle had no real interest in complicated analyses; on the issues they cared about, they already knew the answers, it was received wisdom."[19]

Powell was not particularly ideological. Like Shultz, he had developed a reputation as a moderate who could navigate around hard-liners. Unlike many of his rivals in the administration, such as Cheney, Rice, Bolton, or Rumsfeld, he did not appear overly obsessed with the accumulation of power. Many suspected that if matters got beyond his control and he felt he could no longer make a difference, he would simply walk away. He never established a reputation as someone ready to fight to the end for something he believed in deeply. Rather, he was known as a servant of power, someone happy to serve at the behest of the president but not particularly driven by core convictions. This perception made him an easy target for others in the administration.

Cheney and Bush were not Powell's only challenges. Cheney's former mentor and longtime associate, Donald Rumsfeld, proved more than a match for Powell's political skills.[20] Powell had watched Weinberger and Shultz struggle for power between 1982 and 1987 and may initially have assumed he could prevail by following Shultz's patient example. But Rumsfeld was not Weinberger. In fact, one could argue that Rumsfeld was unrivaled in the history of modern Beltway bureaucratic wrangling. Although Rumsfeld had been out of government for many years—he had not held a senior post since January 1977—he still had a reputation as a bruiser. Back in the Ford administration he had, at age forty-three, been the youngest secretary of defense, battling with Kissinger, Vice President Nelson Rockefeller, and CIA director George H. W. Bush. He had been Kissinger's only rival in bureaucratic infighting. He was known to wear down his opponents through tenacity, energy, and ruthlessness. "Rumsfeld is as bold and as relentless as any modern ministerial figure," observed diplomatic correspondent John Newhouse.[21] His appointment as secretary of defense–designate came as a surprise to many, Powell included. Not only had Rumsfeld held the job a quarter century before, but many assumed it more likely that he would be made director of the CIA. George W. Bush had no prior relationship with Rumsfeld, who had a history of bad blood with Bush's father. The appointment was an early demonstration of Cheney's extraordinary power.

Rumsfeld entered the Pentagon in early 2001 with the objective of dominating the military chiefs. He wanted to be the administration's public face to the world, not only on defense matters, but also on foreign policy. This caused Powell much grief. Even before 9/11, he had difficulty keeping Rumsfeld out of his province. As a result, for the first time in history, the Pentagon, not the State Department, emerged as the locus of U.S. foreign policy. Rumsfeld invaded State's turf with impunity and staked out positions opposing Powell. In previous administrations, this might not have mattered. Secretaries of state have often warred with secretaries of defense. But in this administration, with its emphasis on military power, compounded by the dynamic personality of Rumsfeld himself, this proved a fatal problem for Powell. When the two appeared at a press conference in Australia one month before 9/11, they faced questions about the rift between them. One reporter asked, "Do you agree on everything?" Rumsfeld, taking the lead, tellingly replied, "Everything except those few cases where Colin is still learning."[22]

The new national security adviser, Condoleezza Rice, caused Powell further difficulty. Bush valued Rice because of her uncompromising loyalty. During the campaign, she had served as Bush's principal foreign policy adviser. Rice had never spent much time on post–Cold War issues, was not known as a particularly sophisticated or original thinker along the lines of a Henry Kissinger or Zbigniew Brzezinski, and rarely revealed much interest in matters beyond her area of expertise in Soviet affairs. She was known to possess knowledge of the former Soviet Union, but much less about the Middle East, Asia, or Latin America. Rice had difficultly moving outside the old Cold War framework and at times demonstrated astonishing naiveté. For example, skeptical of the seriousness of the threat of terrorism prior to 9/11, she downgraded the national coordinator for counterterrorism. Her most astute biographer, Glenn Kessler of the *Washington Post*, has noted that "while Rice was Bush's teacher, she was remarkably inexperienced for the job of national security advisor. . . . Even today, these deficiencies in her background are apparent. Rice, aides and associates say, is not good at either execution or following up on problems"[23] Powell soon discovered that Rice, perhaps intimidated by Cheney and Rumsfeld, was rarely willing to challenge their views. Observers described Rice's National Security Council as weak and dysfunctional. Foreign policy was often forged far from her office, and she found herself struggling to keep pace with Cheney and Rumsfeld. Many believed Cheney to be the real national security adviser. "I think Rice didn't really manage anything, and will go down as probably the worst national security advisor in history," one top CIA official told the *New York Times*. "I think the real national security adviser was Cheney, and so Cheney and Rumsfeld could do what they wanted."[24]

Powell had an awkward relationship with Rice and came to see her as a factor in his marginalization in the administration. Having been national security adviser himself, Powell felt she was too eager to tell the president what she believed he wanted to hear. Rice, who saw her duty as looking after Bush, had a close personal relationship with him but lacked the power and political skills to get things done. On many occasions, after Powell assumed he had gotten his point across to Bush and Rice at the White House, he would return to the State Department only to discover that he had had no influence.

Powell's State Department

After eight years of Clinton, many Republicans anticipated massive increases in the defense budget, confrontation with China, closer ties to Taiwan, immediate withdrawal from Bosnia and Kosovo, abandonment of the Antiballistic Missile Treaty, and the launching of a new Manhattan Project for national missile defense. Powell shared no passion for any of these issues. In fact, many of his goals and aims, as expressed in the first weeks of the administration, were more a modified continuation of the Clinton agenda than the clear break with the past that many of the more ideological figures in the administration desired.

Powell proved the least doctrinaire senior member of the administration. Despite his new surroundings, he retained his essential pragmatism, which was more pronounced from 2001 to 2004 owing to the ideological mindsets of his colleagues. Still, Powell had reason to believe he could succeed. There was the example of Shultz to consider. Through tenacity, bureaucratic skill, timely threats to resign, and adroit handling of the press, Shultz eventually built his team with Carlucci at the Pentagon and Powell ensconced at the NSC. Powell hoped to avoid the debilitating bureaucratic warfare between State and the Pentagon and between State and the NSC that had plagued the Reagan administration. Like Shultz, he also hoped to gain the president's trust and, ultimately, backing. Both Kissinger, as national security adviser in 1969, and Haig at State in 1981 had made bold moves to dominate American foreign policy. Kissinger succeeded in reorganizing the foreign policy bureaucracy, placing all power in his hands at the NSC and marginalizing Secretary of State William Rogers and the entire State Department. Haig, on the other hand, never recovered from his early, faltering effort to achieve mastery over Reagan's foreign policy.

Powell never made such a move, perhaps fearing the consequences. For one, it was not in his character and temperament to make a Kissingerian grab for power. He appeared content to play a more traditional role, more in the Shultz mode, of patiently gaining the president's confidence and allowing events to unfold in ways favorable to him. The danger was that events and relationships could not be managed so easily. What if, rather than emerging as another Shultz, Powell was instead reduced to the status of a Haig or Rogers? He knew that for every secretary with the trust of the president, such as Shultz or Baker, for every example of Kissingerian bureaucratic dominance, there were just as many examples of irrelevance.

Powell wanted to be the champion of the State Department and its bureaucracy, and he saw no reason why the department should be hostile to Bush's policies. He believed he could successfully mediate the more extreme elements of Bush's administration. "Colin is mindful of his popularity being greater than the President's," a colleague observed, "and he feels he does have a veto capacity that can be used to hold in check the administration's worst instincts. He thinks he has a voice."[25] But he never succeeded in establishing himself as master of his own domain. While he had complete confidence in Armitage, he struggled with Rove, whose office vetted all administration appointees, selecting people loyal to Rove for every department, appointees who, like political commissars, reported directly to him. Rove used this patronage as his means of infiltrating departments and agencies, giving him immense power in the administration.[26]

Given this personal and bureaucratic context, what kind of secretary of state would Colin Powell be? His long record of public service, going back to 1987, when he became Reagan's sixth national security adviser, provided insight. He had evolved into a Republican internationalist. He came out of the "qualified" realist tradition of internationalism, believing that America should pursue its interests, but not without regarding human rights, liberal values, and respect for allies and alliances. He believed American interests could be best realized working in concert with allies in the pursuit of shared goals. While he believed in the selective use of American military power, he was skeptical that military power alone could ever provide the basis for global leadership.

His outlook drew from both Shultz and Weinberger. He shared Shultz's internationalism and worldliness, his willingness to accept international realities and work with them. But Powell, in part owing to his Vietnam experiences, had never been as inclined as Shultz to use military force. Thus, from Weinberger, he inherited caution about its use. These views set him apart from the more hawkish faction in the administration represented by Cheney, Rumsfeld, and the neoconservatives. Powell believed the new administration should marshal all of the elements of American power—political, military, economic, diplomatic—and place them at the disposal of U.S. foreign policy. He believed that sound statecraft complemented military power and often made military interventions unnecessary. He was thus a firm believer in putting "soft power" to work in the pursuit of American objectives. Unlike other members of the administration, he truly believed in diplomacy. Unlike Cheney, Rumsfeld, and the neoconservatives, he did not believe that raw military power alone was sufficient to achieve American aims.

What would be the fate of the administration's chief diplomatic official in an administration that disdained diplomacy and statecraft? It soon became apparent that Powell and Rumsfeld disagreed on just about every major issue. Moreover, a cadre of neoconservatives at the Pentagon and in the vice president's office supported Rumsfeld. Therefore, Powell's relations with the neoconservatives require examination. Powell certainly had no love for the neoconservatives or their views. Once, when talking to British foreign secretary Jack Straw, Powell derisively referred to them as "fucking crazies."[27] Powell shared with other realists a concern about the neoconservative hold on the administration. Former national security advisers Zbigniew Brzezinski and Brent Scowcroft, both respected realists, aired similar concerns, earning Powell's gratitude. But the reaction to such candor demonstrated the degree of rancor within the administration. As punishment for questioning neoconservative orthodoxy, Scowcroft was removed from the chairmanship of the Foreign Intelligence Advisory Board. Even the president's own father, George H. W. Bush, was alarmed over the degree of influence the neoconservatives wielded in his son's administration. At one point in 2003, he told his son on the telephone that he was disturbed that he had allowed Rumsfeld and a cabal of neoconservatives to dominate American foreign policy, particularly toward Iraq, and that more moderate voices, such as Powell's, had been ignored. The younger Bush slammed down the telephone.[28]

Defining who is and who is not a neoconservative is a difficult and often perilous endeavor. Few subjects provoke as much anger, hyperbole, and emotion, with doctrinaire commentators demanding that others adhere to precise definitions of who is, and who is not, a neoconservative. Without seeking to reignite these arcane ideological disputes, I use terms such as "neoconservative" or "vulcan" here not for theological precision but as a broad description to classify those appointees, particularly in the Pentagon, the White House, and the vice president's office, as well as their fellow travelers in the media and right-wing think tanks, who battled with Powell during his tenure as secretary of state.

The neoconservatives "became excessively distrustful of anyone who did not share their views," observed neoconservative polemicist Francis Fukuyama, "a distrust that extended to Secretary of State Powell and much of the intelligence community."[29] They believed America had entered a postmodern, postdiplomatic age, where raw military power created radically new realities. This belief created problems for Powell on two fronts: First, as the administration's chief diplomatic officer and the presumed steward of its foreign policy, he could hardly have been encouraged by the many officials who embraced the illusion that American military power had rendered diplomacy irrelevant. Second, as the father of the eponymous Powell Doctrine, he looked on with alarm at an administration staffed with so many officials with a penchant for overemphasizing the uses and potential of American military power. Perhaps Paul Wolfowitz was the most troublesome for Powell. The two had long clashed, and Powell believed Wolfowitz lacked flexibility. Soon after his nomination as secretary of state, he had tried but failed to get Wolfowitz out of Washington by offering him the ambassadorship to the United

Nations. Wolfowitz saw the offer as an attempt to marginalize him and instead went to the Pentagon as Rumsfeld's deputy, taking the post Powell had hoped would go to Armitage. When Wolfowitz was asked why he became Rumsfeld's deputy secretary, he gave a one-word answer: "Powell."[30]

The disagreements between the neoconservatives and Powell's State Department, particularly over Iraq, were legendary. Gen. Tommy Franks observed that "these advisers' deep and inflexible commitment to their own ideas was disruptive, as they sought to influence their bosses—and ultimately George W. Bush—with respect to Iraq policy. On far too many occasions they . . . fought like cats in a sack."[31] Journalist George Packer asserted, "[T]he Iraq War will always be linked with the term 'neoconservative,'"[32] and neoconservative Francis Fukuyama has lamented that "the very word neoconservative has become a term of abuse."[33] But the neoconservatives alone were not wholly responsible for the most controversial aspects of the administration's foreign policy. Their influence required support at the senior levels, from Bush, Rumsfeld, and Cheney. Cheney and Rumsfeld themselves were known previously not as neoconservatives but as unilateral hawks, less interested in the internal composition of regimes and less interested than the neoconservatives in the exportation of American values.

Powell had observed that the ideological nature of the neoconservative worldview led its proponents to shape facts to conform to their deeply personal versions of reality. There was an almost theological edge to their beliefs, with esoteric doctrinal disputes becoming emotional slugfests.[34] They made no allowance for those who did not agree with them about the purity of America's motives, where good triumphed over evil and the United States was always on the side of right. They simply ignored inconvenient facts that conflicted with their objectives. Such absolutist mindsets promoted the use of invective. In their use of bombastic rhetoric, and owing to their polemical style, they were, unlike Powell, prone to hyperbole and shared a fondness for incendiary terms like "cowardice," "appeasement," "humiliation," and "weak-willed."[35]

Unlike Powell, the neoconservatives possessed a fundamentalist faith in the indispensability of American military power. They passionately embraced the illusion of America's unchallenged military dominance and thus turned their backs on a half century of diplomatic collaboration and alliances. They deemed it more important to be feared than admired. Those seeking to maximize their power through military strength alone, Powell believed, were misguided. He thought they overemphasized what military force could achieve. He saw military power as only one of the many assets the United States possessed and emphasized the "soft" elements of American strength, such as economic and political power. Powell's background and experience taught him that the neoconservatives failed to see the paradox at the heart of their emphasis on military might: as American military power rose, and as the unilateral impulse grew with it, American influence would actually decline.[36] Contrary to the Powell Doctrine, neoconservative members of the administration demonstrated a fondness for grand conceptualizing and a disdain for detailed planning and follow-through. They demonstrated a proclivity for absolutes and ideologically arranged facts that fit comfortably into an uncomplicated worldview.[37]

Powell was frequently undermined by their resort to leaks and attacks against him, often in concert with their allies in the media and right-wing think tanks. They saw Powell as an adversary, a multilateralist, marking him as "soft," an "appeaser," someone ready to throw away America's military advantages through the pursuit of needless diplomacy. Their hostility toward the United Nations and traditional allies, particularly the Europeans, inevitably put them at odds with Powell, who had a long-held suspicion of defense intellectuals and civilian hawks without military experience. He often thought neoconservative views unrealistic, having a kind of dreamlike quality, untroubled by firsthand experience. Powell observed that their arguments were almost always at odds with the history and realities of Iraq and the Middle East. To Powell, the neoconservatives revealed a naiveté about how the world and power really worked. They rejected Powell's realism. His military career and experience in Vietnam made him an exception in the administration. He had expressed concern about officials who were too often prone to separate their abstract ideas from the consequences. "The intellectual community is apt to say we have to 'do something,'" Powell wrote in his 1995 memoir. "But in the end, it is the armed forces that bring back the body bags and have to explain why to parents."[38] The neoconservatives were obsessed with promoting American "manliness" and "manhood," yet most of them had never served in the military and had instead scrambled to secure safe havens for themselves during times of war. The cultural and social trends in American society dating from the 1960s—the changes in politics, music, sex, and gender roles—had alarmed many neoconservatives, leading to hostility toward multiculturalism, a curious fixation on the supposed perils to American manhood, and a deep distrust of modernity. These frustrations with the modern world produced passionate attachments to authority figures. Journalist George Packer concluded that they "were closer to Dostoyevsky's religious authoritarianism than to John Stuart Mill's secular liberalism. They advocated democracy, but at bottom they were anti-Enlightenment."[39]

The Struggle over Foreign Policy

These fundamental philosophical differences rendered Powell's clashes with Cheney, Rumsfeld, and the neoconservatives inevitable. Essentially an Atlanticist in orientation, Powell assumed Europe would be at the center of American foreign policy, just as it had been since 1945. He understood that leaders around the world needed to sustain political support at home and that American policymakers should be mindful of the political environments in other nations. He recognized that other leaders had their own political problems, whereas many in the administration seemed to believe that the primary responsibility of foreign leaders was to make their policies correlate with American objectives. "Colin Powell is a marvelously reassuring figure, knowledgeable, articulate and charming," recalled Chris Patten, the European commissioner for external relations. "Powell was as calming an influence on Europeans as other members of the administration and some of its hangers-on were irritants. If America wanted to look like Gary Cooper in *High Noon*, send in Colin Powell; if it wanted to appear like Charles Bronson in *Death Wish*, then deploy the public talents of vice president Cheney, Donald Rumsfeld or one of the neocons like Richard Perle."[40]

The Bush administration deemphasized relationships and alliances that had emerged from World War II. The president and his advisers were convinced that America's massive military power would render diplomacy and international relations unimportant. Its contempt for treaties was seen abroad as emblematic of its disdain for other countries. The administration opposed no less than five major international agreements, including the 1972 Antiballistic Missile Treaty and the 1997 Kyoto Protocol on climate change. The desire to scrap so many international accords and treaties created headaches for Powell, who preferred to improve, repair, or amend agreements rather than abandon them.

The administration's disregard for diplomacy after 9/11 compounded Powell's problems, particularly with the Europeans. Europe had long shared America's values, even when specific European nations disagreed with Washington on certain points. But the administration's "with us or against us" approach left little room for honest disagreement. Moreover, on Europe, Rumsfeld meddled in Powell's areas of responsibility with impunity, particularly after 9/11 when he began talking about "Old Europe" versus "New Europe." This designation apparently turned on the extent to which various European countries were willing to follow the American lead in Iraq. It was a bizarre distinction. Britain, Poland, Spain, and Italy ended up in Rumsfeld's "New Europe," while France, Germany, and the Scandinavian nations (with the lone exception of Denmark) ended up in "Old Europe." To most Europeans, Rumsfeld appeared eager to divide them. He warned the Europeans that NATO was headed for the scrap heap if it did not fall in line behind the United States on Iraq. Bush's behavior hardened the polarization. By March 2003, he had further alienated the Europeans with rhetoric about other countries either being on the side of the United States or with the terrorists.[41]

At the beginning of his tenure, Powell was widely regarded as the one member of the administration with credibility in Europe. But Powell's efforts to connect Iraq to al Qaeda at the United Nations in February 2003 damaged his standing with the Europeans. His reputation in Europe, once quite high, plummeted. Washington's relations with Europe, particularly Britain, France, and Germany, had been at the center of American foreign policy since Harry Truman. Powell's 1995 memoir said little regarding U.S. relations with Europe, Africa, or Asia, so it was something of a mystery as to how he would approach these regions.

The Bush administration was the first in recent U.S. history not to value the Atlantic Alliance as a cornerstone of its foreign policy. Many in the administration had a visceral dislike of Europe and Europeans. Powell's earliest remarks as secretary reveal his belief that the traditional European focus had not changed, but the other principals in this administration instead emphasized the Middle East, in ways not congenial to Powell's worldview.[42] For example, relations with British prime minister Tony Blair, French president Jacques Chirac, and German chancellor Gerhard Schröder were subordinated to relations with Israel's hard-line Likud prime minister Ariel Sharon. The administration's closeness to Likud and passionate interest in Israel's strategic objectives limited Powell's maneuverability on Middle East policy. He confronted the novel problem of serving in an administration staffed with officials who were not only sympathetic to Israel but, as staunch supporters of the Likud party, had actively opposed the stated objectives of the U.S. government, particularly efforts to promote an accord between the Israelis and Palestinians.[43]

A rift developed between the State Department, which wanted to restart the Middle East peace process, and the Pentagon, led by Rumsfeld, Wolfowitz, Feith, and what Powell called Feith's "Gestapo office." Powell thought the latter had redefined U.S. Middle East policy as unconditional support for Sharon.[44] Francis Fukuyama has observed that "certain neoconservatives had internalized a hard-line Israeli strategic doctrine" and vehemently opposed the peace process.[45] Assuming that raw military power, not diplomacy or a political solution, would ultimately prevail, they promoted Israel's strategic and military objectives rather than peacemaking and pushed a radical agenda of Middle Eastern transformation through regime change, starting with Iraq, but possibly including other nations, such as Iran, Syria, and perhaps, ultimately, Lebanon, Saudi Arabia, and the Palestinian-occupied territories.[46]

When Powell arrived at the State Department in January 2001, President Clinton had just spent his final months in office seeking an eleventh-hour Middle East peace accord, only to see it unravel in escalating violence and Sharon's rise to power. Powell understood that the Middle East had been a major area of concern for every administration at least since the Nixon era and that every secretary of state since William Rogers (1969–1973) had been immersed in the question of peace between Israel and the Arabs. Powell sought to lower expectations about the Middle East, but he did not share Bush's view that the United States should withdraw from the peace process altogether.

Regardless of Powell's views, the Bush White House abandoned the peace process, refusing to send an envoy to the emergency peace talks and abolishing the post of special Middle East envoy. Eight months into the administration, the National Security Council still did not have a senior director for the Middle East.[47] In January 2001, Bush told an NSC meeting that in 1998 Sharon had taken him on a helicopter ride over the Palestinian refugee camps. "It looked real bad down there," Bush said. "I don't see much we can do over there at this point. I think it's time to pull out of that situation." Apparently, and without input from the secretary of state or the State Department, Bush had already decided to cast aside the peace process. The United States adopted a "wait and see" attitude toward the Middle East crisis but offered unquestioning support for Sharon. "We're going to tilt it back toward Israel," Bush curiously announced. Powell warned that such a radical move would leave the Palestinians at Sharon's mercy. "The consequences of that could be dire," Powell said, "especially for the Palestinians." Bush merely shrugged. "Maybe that's the best way to get things back in balance. . . . Sometimes a show of strength by one side can really clarify things."[48] Powell was appalled. He had not been privy to this decision, which marked a major shift in what had been U.S. policy since Kissinger's dramatic shuttle diplomacy after the 1973 Arab-Israeli war.

Powell wanted to use the events of 9/11 as momentum for restarting the peace process. The United States needed Arab support to build a broad coalition. Addressing the Israeli-Palestinian question would reduce the impact of a major grievance in the region. The Bush administration had been determined to let matters drift, but developments in the Middle East forced the administration's hand as violence between Israel and the Palestinians escalated, and Jordan, Egypt, and Saudi Arabia publicly called for American reengagement. Powell wanted to achieve a cease-fire between Israeli and Palestinian forces and a withdrawal of Israeli forces from the West Bank. He also wanted to promote the administration's ill-fated "road map" to peace in the Middle East, which aimed to establish a Palestinian state by 2005. While the Palestinian leadership accepted the road map, Bush's allowing Sharon a veto over U.S. policy guaranteed its ultimate failure.[49]

As matters deteriorated, Bush turned to Powell and said, "You're going to have to spend some political capital. You have plenty. I need you to do it." Telling Powell that he "could afford it," Bush dispatched him on a spring 2002 mission to the Middle East, vaguely encouraging Powell's support for a regional peace conference. Former national security adviser Brent Scowcroft publicly hinted that Bush was doing Sharon's bidding. Powell, too, doubted that Bush had the courage to stand up to the Israeli premier. Sharon avoided Powell by going directly to Cheney. The secretary of state's efforts in the Middle East were increasingly micromanaged from the White House, and Cheney insisted that Powell not meet with Palestinian leader Yasser Arafat. Though he thought it absurd to meet with only one of the parties to the conflict, he faced mounting pressure from the administration to demonstrate support for Sharon. Unlike Bush and Cheney, Powell held a low opinion of both Arafat and Sharon. At one point, after days of taking orders from Rice, Powell exploded. He felt he had been set up. Once again he was little more than window dressing for a policy that was really about backing Sharon, not about seeking peace through an acceptable compromise. Powell, an observer of some of the fiercest bureaucratic fights of the previous three administrations, described the effort to undermine him as "unbelievable."[50]

The persistent backbiting and infighting exacerbated the confusion in the administration's approach to the Middle East. Powell supported a two-state plan and sought to restrain Sharon from pursuing Israel's military objectives in the occupied territories. But Powell did not have the backing of his own administration, whose unconditional support for Sharon undercut Powell at every turn. Rumsfeld also strongly supported Sharon and tried to scuttle Powell's efforts. When Powell met with a delegation of Palestinian cabinet members in August 2002, Rumsfeld used the occasion to deliver a staunch defense of Sharon and his policies.[51]

Previous administrations had achieved some success in the Middle East when their secretaries of state enjoyed the full backing of the White House, as during Kissinger's "shuttle diplomacy" (1973–1974), or when the president himself became personally engaged in the quest for peace, such as Jimmy Carter's efforts at Camp David (1978–1979), George H. W. Bush's efforts to bring about the Madrid conference on the Middle East after the first Gulf War (1991), or Clinton's efforts after Oslo (1993–1999) and his return to Camp David (2000–2001). Bush's continued indifference to achieving the mastery of detail that the Middle East required compounded Powell's trials. "He does not have the knowledge or the patience to learn this issue enough to have an end destination in mind," an administration official told the *Washington Post*.[52] Moreover, the administration's embrace of the hard-line Likud ideology left it unable or unwilling to comprehend the Palestinian position. Thus, the administration assumed that Arafat was the problem and that he could be isolated or bypassed. The administration appeared to have included Arafat in its strategy of regime change, its one-size-fits-all solution to the region.

To Powell's frustration, other members of the administration consistently undercut him, and his Middle East pronouncements received no support. He suffered a further public humiliation in the spring of 2002 when, in the midst of his discussions with the Palestinians, Bush declared Sharon, who was in the process of launching a new military offensive into the occupied territories, a "man of peace." At one particularly frustrating moment, Powell lashed out at Douglas Feith, calling him a "card-carrying member of the Likud Party."[53] He returned to Washington without the cease-fire and without Sharon's withdrawal of Israeli forces from the West Bank. He learned that Cheney and Rumsfeld had been planting stories in the press, claiming that he had become a dupe of Arafat and that his mission had departed from the administration's foreign policy. Some observed that, in the post-9/11 atmosphere, many in the administration saw Powell's views on the Middle East "as tantamount to appeasement," and Cheney and Rumsfeld cited the mission's failure to further undermine Powell and urge that Sharon be allowed to deal with the Palestinians however he saw fit.[54]

At this point, having been publicly humiliated by Cheney, Rumsfeld, and even Bush, George Shultz might have confronted the president with a threat of resignation, forcing him to acknowledge the shabby treatment of his own secretary of state. "Shultz frequently used the threat of resignation very effectively to get what he wanted from Reagan," recalled former Reagan administration official Lawrence Korb. "Powell never did this." Instead, Powell took his lumps, which only emboldened his adversaries. "I won't let the bastards drive me from office," he said. But the ease and impunity with which they attacked him certainly hastened that outcome.[55]

Eventually, Iraq devoured everything, and the administration lost interest in its own Middle East policy. The decision to back Sharon yielded little.

During Powell's tenure at State, the violence escalated, and the Israeli settlements on the West Bank continued to grow. Nothing Powell did during his tenure stemmed either tide. Perhaps most striking was that so little was achieved on the diplomatic front. "Not a single negotiated agreement between the parties to the Arab-Israeli conflict was reached in the four-year period," observed former NSC Middle East specialist William Quandt. "Instead, American policy . . . had shifted to an unprecedented degree of support for a Likud-led Israeli government."[56] Sharon took center stage as the closest U.S. ally, and unconditional U.S. support for Sharon strained relationships not only with Arab allies but also with traditional European partners, who took a more balanced approach to Israel's conflict with the Palestinians.

There was also much anticipation about how policy toward China would change with the new administration. In the late 1990s, the Republicans in Congress and the right-wing think tanks had mounted a campaign of scaremongering, complete with references to the Rosenbergs and hysteria about an impending Chinese takeover of the Panama Canal. One alarmist congressional report declared that "essentially all Chinese visitors to the United States are potential spies."[57] Cheney and Rumsfeld saw China as a threat, while Rice possessed few known opinions on China. Thus, Powell's views might prove decisive. With the disappearance of the Soviet Union, some observers believed that China had been designated the administration's chief adversary. The Cheney-Rumsfeld worldview required the inflation of threats and adversaries to mobilize public opinion in support of their defense and foreign policies. Early on, administration rhetoric painted China as a serious challenge to American objectives in Asia, and Rice conceded that the administration might welcome a confrontation with China in 2001 or 2002. During the 2000 campaign, Wolfowitz described China as "the single most serious foreign policy challenge of the coming decades." Of course, this was before 9/11.[58]

Many of these anxieties over China came to a head in the first months of the administration when, on April 1, 2001, a Chinese fighter jet intercepted an American reconnaissance plane over the South China Sea and forced it to land on China's Hainan Island. The Bush administration initially responded to the crisis with bombastic rhetoric, but owing largely to Powell, cooler heads soon prevailed, and a more modulated tone emerged.[59] Powell won the crew's release. The resolution of the Hainan Island incident was a rare victory for him over administration hard-liners who desired a confrontation with China. Some thought the resolution of the Hainan Island incident the high point of Powell's tenure. Powell himself may have concluded from the incident that, despite the administration's reflexive impulse toward saber rattling and bombastic rhetoric, it needed his skills at conciliation and problem solving.[60]

The White House reacted with alarm, however, and preferred to keep him, as Powell and Armitage frequently joked, in the "icebox" or "refrigerator."[61] The reaction of neoconservative polemicists, who leveled charges of "appeasement" and "betrayal" at Powell and called his resolution of the crisis a "national humiliation," may have further damaged him. They predicted that Powell's achievement would have catastrophic consequences and that Bush, by following his secretary of state's instincts, was on the road to "surrender." Had 9/11 never occurred, the administration might have directed its energies toward inflating the perception of China and Russia as threats to the United States. In a way, 9/11 inadvertently opened the possibility for some degree of stability in relations with Beijing and Moscow.[62]

Policy toward North Korea further exposed the tensions within the administration over Powell's role. North Korea had gradually been coming in from the cold since 1994 after Clinton engaged Pyongyang and supported South Korea's "Sunshine Policy" of better North-South relations. Diplomats around the world welcomed North Korea's growing engagement with the nations of Europe, as well as Australia and Japan, and North and South Korean athletes marched together in the Olympic ceremonies in Sydney in 2000. Clinton had come close to a deal freezing the North Korean missile program, and Secretary of State Madeleine Albright met with North Korean leader Kim Jung Il in Pyongyang in October 2000, the culmination of several years of growing engagement between North and South Korea. Kim offered to end production, testing, and deployment of medium- and long-range missiles—a remarkable achievement. Bush needed merely to conclude the deal.[63]

Powell called such continuity a "no brainer,"[64] and South Korean president Kim Dae Jung, fresh from having won the 2000 Nobel Peace Prize, came to Washington seeking administration support for continuing the momentum. "We do plan to engage with North Korea," Powell said publicly, "to pick up where President Clinton and his administration left off."[65] But others in the administration sought to undermine Kim's Sunshine Policy and opposed the Koreans' taking their own initiative on matters related to the peninsula. Bush met with Cheney and Rice, and the decision was made to announce publicly that Powell did not speak for the administration on Korea.

It was a stunning rebuke for the new secretary of state, and Bush further astonished the world, particularly South Korean president Kim, by publicly rejecting the Clinton deal and shutting the door on further discussions. South Korean officials were dismayed, and Powell was forced to eat his own words publicly. "It was an early signal that the president was not going to allow the secretary of state to say whatever he wanted," one senior administration official observed. "It was a useful signal to other cabinet members, too."[66]

The administration's confrontational approach, as well as the inclusion of Pyongyang in Bush's January 2002 "axis of evil" speech, exacerbated the nuclear crisis and halted the efforts at opening up North Korea. The proclamation of an "axis of evil" complicated matters for both Powell and South Korea. Suddenly, and without warning, North Korea had been relegated to the status of international pariah, along with Iraq and Iran, putting South Korean president Kim in an almost impossible position. The Bush administration's abrupt change of course, revealing Washington's disregard of its South Korean allies, provoked a serious rupture in relations with Seoul. Around the world, there was increasing dismay over another missed opportunity.

Just as Washington's disdain for diplomacy brought Germany and France closer together, it inadvertently had the same effect on the two Koreas as growing numbers of South Koreans saw the United States as a greater threat to peace than their neighbors to the north. To many South Koreans, the United States was looking less like a protector and more like a menace with an interest in perpetuating tensions. As a result, North Korea accelerated its effort to build nuclear weapons. The regime restarted its reactor, unsealed its nuclear facilities, test-fired missiles, and began reprocessing plutonium. Pyongyang told the Bush administration, in no uncertain terms, that it was entitled to have nuclear weapons.[67]

Powell remained undeterred. In June 2002, four months after Bush's proclamation of an "axis of evil," Powell set out a four-point agenda for talks, requiring Pyongyang to commit to ending sales of weapons and halting long-range missile programs, in compliance with the efforts of the International Atomic Energy Agency.[68] North Korea accepted his four-point proposal, but an alarmed Pentagon sprang into action against the initiative. Cheney backed Rumsfeld and, eventually, so did Rice. Powell had once again lost control of the administration's Korea policy as well as of his own State Department. Two months later, Assistant Secretary of State John Bolton appeared in Seoul, acting without Powell's authorization and seeking to undo Powell's efforts by publicly castigating North Korea as an "evil regime." Speculation was rife that Bolton's speech aimed to derail Powell's initiative, demonstrating that the secretary had no control over his own department or its policies. Later, Armitage, speaking before Congress, committed the further transgression of praising Clinton's North Korea policy. Powell was called to the White House and put back in the "ice box."

On September 11, 2001, the day of the attacks on New York and Washington, *Time* magazine still had on its racks a cover story with the title, "Where Have You Gone, Colin Powell?" The article criticized him for losing so many battles to the neoconservatives and allowing himself to be marginalized. An angry Powell saw it as a hit piece orchestrated by the White House. But Richard Haas, Powell's head of policy planning, told him that, in this administration, the "only thing that would have been worse would have been if it had showed you were in charge. Then you would have been totally fucked."[69]

Powell was in Peru, attending a meeting of the Organization of American States, when the planes struck the Pentagon and the World Trade Center towers. The attacks reinforced the problems he had faced thus far. The Bush administration, because of its domination by Rumsfeld and Cheney, had a very Cold War–era mindset, what Richard Clarke described as an obsession with "vestigial Cold War concerns." September 11, as Clarke has argued, represented an intelligence failure of immense proportions. Clarke revealed that Bush had been briefed on al Qaeda—including one August 2001 briefing paper titled, "Bin Laden Determined to Strike in U.S."—and the threat al Qaeda posed to Americans and American interests prior to the events of 9/11. Still, the administration had done nothing, despite the fact that it had been warned when the attacks might occur and who might launch them. It would not be the last time that Bush's inattention to detail had profound consequences.[70] Only Powell had demonstrated any prior interest in terrorism, and he had been more interested in it before 9/11 than any other senior official, certainly more so than Bush, Rice, Cheney, or Rumsfeld. He had met with the Counterterrorism Security Group during the transition between the Clinton and Bush administrations. Powell was surprised at the unanimity of their concern about al Qaeda, and he took their warnings seriously.[71]

Powell saw 9/11 as an opportunity not only to wage a diplomatic offensive but also to recast administration policy after a rocky eight-month beginning. The tragedy could be used to rebuild damaged relationships. Only hours after learning of the attacks, he was already thinking about involving the United Nations and NATO. Nations all over the world offered their support, and in a demonstration of solidarity unprecedented in its fifty-two-year existence, NATO invoked Article V, declaring that an attack on the United States constituted an attack on all NATO members. "We are engaging the world," Powell told the cabinet on September 14. "We want to make this a long-standing coalition."[72]

In his initial reaction to 9/11, Powell was at his best: inclusive, multilateral, cognizant of the concerns of allies. He worked the phones constantly, making scores of calls to world leaders and seeking to assuage their concerns. His media appearances were measured, assured, controlled, and informed. His performances in the days after 9/11 were perhaps the high point of his tenure at State. But it was not to last. Dangers loomed over the inclusive approach. The day after 9/11, Rumsfeld began talking of "getting Iraq." He had complained that there were no easy targets in Afghanistan and that instead the United States should consider bombing Iraq, which, he added, had better targets. Powell pushed back, arguing that they should maintain the focus on al Qaeda. After the meeting, Richard Clarke vented to Powell, "I thought I was missing something here. Having been attacked by al Qaeda, for us now to go bombing Iraq in response would be like our invading Mexico after the Japanese attacked us at Pearl Harbor." Powell merely shook his head and warned, "It's not over yet." At a Camp David meeting on September 15, Rumsfeld and Wolfowitz both made a strong case for going after Iraq.[73] Powell grew increasingly troubled by the direction of these cabinet-level discussions. "Colin thinks we're obsessed with Iraq," a colleague of Powell's told diplomatic correspondent John Newhouse. "He thought that five or six years ago. He thinks Iraq should not be a major factor in foreign policy. He thinks Saddam is a problem and that we may have to deal with him. But he thinks we have many more urgent problems."[74]

Powell's other problem was Bush. The attacks brought out the president's unilateral and chauvinistic instincts. A cult of personality began to grow up around him. Bush embraced a politically popular, but astonishingly simplistic, interpretation of the event, arguing publicly that America was engaged in a biblical struggle of "good" versus "evil," that others hated America for its freedoms.[75] The attacks also brought to the fore some of the more unpleasant aspects of American life, of which Bush became something of a maestro, unleashing a strident form of messianic nationalism and victimization that justified almost anything in foreign and defense policy. Bush portrayed the coming conflict in apocalyptic terms, leaving little room for rational analysis. If Powell thought he could pursue a patient strategy with Bush, as Shultz had done with Reagan, and thereby wean him away from unilateralism, 9/11 doomed that strategy.

In another administration, Powell could have been cast as part of the public face of its policy. But the emphasis on a military response to the attacks, at the expense of diplomatic and political efforts, meant that the Pentagon became the primary instrument of the administration's response. The attacks and their aftermath transformed Rumsfeld into the darling of the Washington press corps. The intense media coverage focused on matters of style. "Rummy's" use of language and gestures became the toast of the

Beltway. Neoconservative commentators, as well as Thomas Friedman from the pages of the *New York Times*, celebrated Rumsfeld as the greatest military genius since Hannibal. His personal habits were scrutinized for evidence of his genius. *People* magazine placed him on their sexiest-men list, and Bush started calling him "Rumstud," which was certainly sexier than the peculiar nickname Bush had bestowed upon Powell, "Balloonfoot," presumably referring to his wound from stepping on a Punji stick during Vietnam.[76]

As Rumsfeld dominated the news coverage, Powell disappeared. Unlike during the 1990–1991 Gulf War, Powell's official briefings at the State Department went almost unnoticed. As Rumsfeld emerged as the administration spokesman during the war in Afghanistan, Powell shrank further in the public eye. Powell was alleged to have favored an approach that allowed for examining the "root causes" of terrorism. If so, he never shared this with the American public. He eschewed the role public diplomacy could play and appeared uninterested in using the enhanced public focus to educate the public about global realities following the attacks.

The effort to pull together international support for the U.S. invasion of Afghanistan fell to Powell. Not only was he the administration's most skilled coalition and alliance builder, but he was its most, perhaps its only, popular figure abroad. He also had some familiarity with the situation in Afghanistan, having been national security adviser during the effort to negotiate a withdrawal of Soviet forces in 1988. At an NSC meeting immediately following the attacks, he urged Bush to focus narrowly on the threat posed by Osama Bin Laden and al Qaeda. He believed that emphasizing Bin Laden would generate more international support and sensed that Bush's notoriously short attention span would lead him in other directions. His fears proved well founded. Rumsfeld wanted to move against Iraq and cared little about how other countries might react. Powell feared that Iraq would be a distraction. "Any action needs public support," he urged the day after the attacks. "It's not just what the international coalition supports; it's what the American people want to support. The American people want us to do something about al Qaeda."[77]

Pakistan caused Powell particular concern. Immediately after the 9/11 attacks, he began laying out a strategy for persuading Pakistan to assist U.S. efforts in neighboring Afghanistan. Washington needed Pakistan's support. Powell and Armitage drafted a list of concessions the United States required of Pakistan, such as overflight and landing rights and intelligence sharing. Powell knew the effort to go after al Qaeda would be impossible without Pakistan's assistance. Pakistan had been the strongest supporter of the Taliban regime, and it was no sure thing that President Pervez Musharraf would cooperate. "As one general to another," he said to Musharraf, "we need someone on our flank fighting with us. Speaking candidly, the American people would not understand if Pakistan was not in this fight with the United States." Musharraf agreed. It was another major accomplishment for Powell, perhaps not sufficiently appreciated at the time.[78]

Powell's success with Musharraf created resistance in Washington. Rumsfeld charged Powell and Armitage with being too concerned with diplomacy. The defense secretary focused on Iraq.[79] This underscored Powell's difficulties in pursuing the diplomatic offensive. For example, Powell wanted to avoid going it alone, but Bush said, "[W]e may be the only ones left. That's okay with me. We are America." Powell considered this approach simplistic, even counterproductive. However satisfying rhetorically, he understood that simply "standing alone" because "we are America" was not a workable policy. He believed the United States needed allies, even in Afghanistan. As with the 1991 Gulf War, he understood that tough posturing should not be a substitute for a coherent policy. He confided to Bob Woodward that such "Texas" and "Alamo" bravado made him uncomfortable. In public, Powell denied such sharp disagreements. Even over Afghanistan, however, they existed. He often found himself blocked from doing what he thought needed to be done on the diplomatic front. The administration decided that the response to 9/11 would be politicized, and Rove worried that Powell had become too visible following the attacks. The White House was unhappy that he was playing such a prominent role. One month after 9/11, his media appearances trailed off, and Powell again found himself relegated to the "ice box."[80]

The fateful decision to shift the focus to an invasion of Iraq, before completing work in Afghanistan, left most of al Qaeda intact and Bin Laden at large. As a four-star general and a former chairman of the Joint Chiefs, Powell had more than a passing interest in the planning for the Afghanistan operation; he had genuine concerns about the campaign. He recalled that back in December 1989, Noriega had eluded U.S. forces and knew that Afghanistan was eight times larger than Panama. Some of its border regions were largely unknown. When he heard Rumsfeld suggest that Bin Laden would be "bottled up," Powell replied, "Bottled up? They can get out in a Land Rover."[81]

Conclusion: The "Axis of Evil"

The events of 9/11 and their aftermath presented the Bush administration with an extraordinary diplomatic opportunity. The world stood with the

United States, looking to Washington for leadership. Even Iran had signaled its willingness to assist. Few secretaries of state have been presented with such an opportunity. The moment could have been seized to revive the peace process in the Middle East and might have given the United States remarkable leverage over North Korea. At the United Nations, the United States could have taken advantage of the events of 9/11 to change the political climate that had developed since Bush's first months in office. Powell was ideally suited to undertake such an initiative. But an administration already hostile to diplomacy became even more so in the wake of 9/11.

Powell had once written that terrorism should not be allowed to drive foreign policy decision making. He had counseled focus on al Qaeda and going after its sanctuary in Afghanistan. Cheney and Rumsfeld never had much interest in rebuilding projects; in any event, they were beginning to turn their attention to Iraq. The reconstruction of post-Taliban Afghanistan was thus left largely to Powell and State, but Powell worried that the administration was ignoring realities in that formidable land. He feared the consequences of a strategy of declaring war on everybody. The proclamation of an "axis of evil" in January 2002 compounded Powell's difficulties, marking the official beginning of the run-up to the Iraq War. Powell deemed Bush's axis-of-evil speech far too bleak. It demonized three vastly different nations, massively inflated threats, and exploited vague fears. Many of its claims were unsupportable. Powell questioned whether sowing fear and national hysteria could provide an effective basis for global leadership. The notion of a war against terror as the obsessive focus of the administration had little to do with the actual threat posed by al Qaeda and everything to do with the administration's political strategy of rallying the public behind its polarizing policies, both foreign and domestic. Five months had passed since 9/11, and Bin Laden had not been found.[82] In an interview five years later, Powell decried the inflation of the threat for political purposes. "What is the greatest threat facing us now?" Powell asked. "People will say it's terrorism. But are there any terrorists in the world who can change the American way of life or our political system? No. Can they knock down a building? Yes. Can they kill somebody? Yes. But can they change us? No. Only we can change ourselves. So what is the great threat we are facing? . . . These are dangerous criminals, and we must deal with them. But come on, this is not a threat to our survival! The only thing that can really destroy us is *us*. We shouldn't do it ourselves, and we shouldn't use fear for political purposes—scaring people to death so they will vote for you, or scaring people to death so that we create a terror-industrial complex."[83]

Bush's axis-of-evil speech provoked other nations to distance themselves from the United States. The overwhelming focus on Iraq underscored a failure to understand deeper forces reshaping the world. The decision to invade Iraq proved a turning point, not only for Powell but also for the nation. As Richard Clarke observed, "[W]hat was unique about George Bush's reaction to terrorism was his selection as an object lesson for potential state sponsors of terrorism, not a country that had been engaging in anti-U.S. terrorism but one that had not been, Iraq. It is hard to imagine another president making that choice."[84]

The administration had made its choice, and Powell would be one of its casualties. He was developing a reputation in Washington as an uncomplaining loser. This meant that Rumsfeld, Cheney, and even Rice could ignore him with impunity. Cheney no longer feared Powell's reaction to indignities while his attitude appeared to be, if Powell threatens to resign, let him. Powell increasingly rationalized that his presence was needed in the administration. "Powell seemed to have concluded *après nous le deluge*," observed former Pentagon official Lawrence Korb. "But when he had an opportunity to dissent—he didn't."[85]

When the White House or Pentagon gave Powell trouble, he shrank from provoking a confrontation. Instead, he appeared content to soldier on. He continued to see his role as softening the unilateralism and arrogance of the administration, but his decision to go along had its costs. Powell seemed to have been unaware that, rather than providing a moderating influence, he was merely providing cover, or window dressing, for the administration's actions. Powell's allies told the press that he was taking the high road, playing the long game. To where, and to what end, was never clear.

Notes

1. Author interview with Lawrence Korb, March 17, 2006.

2. Ivo Daalder and James Lindsay, *America Unbound: The Bush Revolution in Foreign Policy* (Hoboken, NJ: Wiley and Sons, 2005), 17–19.

3. Stefan Halper and Jonathan Clarke, *America Alone: The Neo-Conservatives and the Global Order* (Cambridge: Cambridge University Press, 2004), 131–34.

4. Stephen Kinzer, *Overthrow: America's Century of Regime Change from Hawaii to Iraq* (New York: Times Books, 2006), 276.

5. James Mann, *Rise of the Vulcans: The History of Bush's War Cabinet* (New York: Viking Press, 2004), 264.

6. Author interview with Col. Lawrence Wilkerson, September 20, 2007.

7. Colin Powell, *My American Journey* (New York: Ballantine, 1995, 2003), 355.

8. Michael Steinberger, "Misoverestimated," *American Prospect*, April 1, 2004, www.prospect.org/cs/articles?articleId=8853.

9. Author interview with Lawrence Korb, March 17, 2006.

10. John Newhouse, *Imperial America: The Bush Assault on the World Order* (New York: Alfred A. Knopf, 2003), 26.

11. James Risen, *State of War: The Secret History of the CIA and the Bush Administration* (New York: Free Press, 2006), 3, 64, 162; Ron Suskind, *The Price of Loyalty: George W. Bush, the White House, and the Education of Paul O'Neill* (New York: Simon and Schuster, 2004), 83.

12. Suskind, *The Price of Loyalty*, 97.

13. Bob Woodward, *Plan of Attack* (New York: Simon and Schuster, 2004), 176; Richard A. Clarke, *Against All Enemies: Inside America's War on Terror* (New York: Free Press, 2004), 19.

14. George Packer, *The Assassins' Gate: America in Iraq* (New York: Farrar, Straus and Giroux, 2005), 146; Nicholas Lemann, "The Quiet Man: Dick Cheney's Discrete Rise to Unprecedented Power," *New Yorker*, May 7, 2001, 56–71.

15. Woodward, *Plan of Attack*, 175–76, 292, 415.

16. Christopher Meyer, *DC Confidential: The Controversial Memoirs of Britain's Ambassador to the U.S. at the Time of 9/11 and the Iraq War* (London: Weidenfeld and Nicolson, 2005), 219.

17. Bob Woodward, *Bush at War* (New York: Simon and Schuster, 2002), 12.

18. Clarke, *Against All Enemies*, 243; Woodward, *Plan of Attack*, 79, 149.

19. Quoted in Clarke, *Against All Enemies*, 243.

20. Author interview with Col. Lawrence Wilkerson, September 20, 2007.

21. Newhouse, *Imperial America*, 32.

22. Risen, *State of War*, 64; Colin Powell, "Press Conference with Secretary of Defense Donald Rumsfeld, Admiral Dennis C. Blair, Foreign Minister Alexander Downer, Minister of Defense Peter Reith, and Admiral Chris Barrie," July 30, 2001, www.state.gov/secretary/former/powell/remarks/2001/4350.htm.

23. Glenn Kessler, *The Confidante: Condoleezza Rice and the Creation of the Bush Legacy* (New York: St. Martin's Press, 2007), 6–7.

24. Clarke, *Against All Enemies*, 229–30; Risen, *State of War*, 3, 64.

25. Quoted in Newhouse, *Imperial America*, 25.

26. Woodward, *Plan of Attack*, 127.

27. James Naughtie, *The Accidental American: Tony Blair and the Presidency* (London: Macmillan, 2004), 127.

28. Risen, *State of War*, 1, 222.

29. Francis Fukuyama, *America at the Crossroads: Democracy, Power, and the Neoconservative Legacy* (New Haven, CT: Yale University Press, 2006), 61.

30. Halper and Clarke, *America Alone*, 118; Daalder and Lindsay, *America Unbound*, 46.

31. Tommy Franks, *American Soldier* (New York: Regan Books, 2004), 376.

32. Packer, *The Assassins' Gate*, 15, 38.

33. Fukuyama, *America at the Crossroads*, 47.

34. Powell, *My American Journey*, 98; Woodward, *Plan of Attack*, 22.

35. A good example of the use of such rhetoric can be found in Richard Perle and David Frum, *An End to Evil* (New York: Random House, 2003).

36. Halper and Clarke, *America Alone*, 297; Powell, *My American Journey*, 588.

37. Fukuyama, *America at the Crossroads*, 5.

38. Powell, *My American Journey*, 403.

39. Murray Friedman, *The Neoconservative Revolution: Jewish Intellectuals and the Shaping of Public Policy* (Cambridge: Cambridge University Press, 2006), 185–204; Packer, *The Assassins' Gate*, 31.

40. Chris Patten, *Not Quite the Diplomat* (London: Penguin Books, 2005), 239.

41. Philip H. Gordon and Jeremy Shapiro, *Allies at War: America, Europe, and the Crisis over Iraq* (New York: McGraw-Hill, 2004), 120.

42. Mann, *Rise of the Vulcans*, 305–6.

43. See, for example, Richard Perle et al., "A Clean Break: A New Strategy for Securing the Realm," Study Group on a New Israeli Strategy, Institute for Advanced Strategic and Political Studies, www.iasps.org/strat1.htm.

44. Woodward, *Plan of Attack*, 292.

45. Fukuyama, *America at the Crossroads*, xii.

46. William Quandt, *Peace Process: American Diplomacy and the Arab-Israeli Conflict Since 1967* (Berkeley: University of California Press, 2005), 387.

47. Daalder and Lindsay, *America Unbound*, 65.

48. Suskind, *The Price of Loyalty*, 71–72.

49. Tanya Reinhart, *The Road Map to Nowhere: Israel/Palestine Since 2003* (London: Verso, 2006), 26–40.

50. Woodward, *Bush at War*, 323–26; Colin Powell, "Remarks at David Citadel Hotel," April 17, 2002, www.state.gov/secretary/former/powell/remarks/2002/9478.htm; "Interview by Tim Russert on NBC's Meet the Press," April 7, 2002, www.state.gov/secretary/former/powell/remarks/2002/9196.htm.

51. Newhouse, *Imperial America*, 31.

52. Quoted in Quandt, *Peace Process*, 403.

53. Packer, *The Assassins' Gate*, 444–45.

54. Quandt, *Peace Process*, 394.

55. Author interview with Lawrence Korb, March 17, 2006; Newhouse, *Imperial America*, 29.

56. Quandt, *Peace Process*, 408–9.

57. Anatol Lieven, *America Right or Wrong* (New York: Harper Collins, 2004), 163.

58. Mann, *Rise of the Vulcans*, 281–86.

59. For Powell's comments on the spy plane incident, see "Press Conference at Truman Little White House," April 3, 2001, www.state.gov/secretary/former/powell/remarks/2001/1910.htm; "Briefing for the Press Aboard Aircraft En Route to An-

drews Air Force Base," April 3, 2001, www.state.gov/secretary/former/powell/remarks/ 2001/1932.htm; "On-the-Record Press Briefing (China)," April 6, 2001, www.state .gov/secretary/former/powell/remarks/2001/2092.htm.

60. Author interview with Lawrence Korb, March 17, 2006; Daalder and Lindsay, *America Unbound*, 66–69.

61. Woodward, *Bush at War*, 13.

62. Lieven, *America Right or Wrong*, 163–64.

63. Chae-Jin Lee, *A Troubled Peace: U.S. Policy and the Two Koreas* (Baltimore: Johns Hopkins University Press, 2006), 208–11.

64. Newhouse, *Imperial America*, 4.

65. For Powell's comments on Korea, see "Press Availability with Her Excellency Anna Lindh, Minister of Foreign Affairs of Sweden," March 6, 2001, www.state .gov/secretary/former/powell/remarks/2001/1116.htm.

66. Quoted in Mann, *Rise of the Vulcans*, 279.

67. Mann, *Rise of the Vulcans*, 277–81, 344–47.

68. Colin Powell, "Remarks at Asia Society Annual Dinner," June 10, 2002, www.state.gov/secretary/former/powell/remarks/2002/10983.htm.

69. Woodward, *Bush at War*, 14; Woodward, *Plan of Attack*, 79.

70. Clarke, *Against All Enemies*, 228–34.

71. Risen, *State of War*, 19; Woodward, *Plan of Attack*, 24.

72. Quoted in Woodward, *Bush at War*, 65.

73. Clarke, *Against All Enemies*, 30–31.

74. Newhouse, *Imperial America*, 42.

75. Kinzer, *Overthrow*, 278.

76. Mann, *Rise of the Vulcans*, 307.

77. Quoted in Woodward, *Bush at War*, 48–49.

78. Woodward, *Bush at War*, 58–59.

79. Clarke, *Against All Enemies*, 237.

80. Woodward, *Bush at War*, 81, 322, 190.

81. Woodward, *Bush at War*, 224.

82. Woodward, *Plan of Attack*, 91.

83. See Powell's interview with Walter Issacson at www.despardes.com/FEATURES/ 20070911-colin-powell.htm.

84. Quoted in Clarke, *Against All Enemies*, 244.

85. Author interview with Lawrence Korb, March 17, 2006.

~

CHAPTER SEVEN

Powell, Iraq, and the "Fog of War"

The first war against Iraq in 1991 transformed Colin Powell into a national icon. At the end of that conflict, his standing was at an all-time high. To many he embodied the new professionalism of the post-Vietnam armed forces. The second war against Iraq, beginning in 2003, did much to damage his reputation. Memories of his speech before the United Nations in February 2003, together with subsequent investigations that cast doubt on most of his claims, complicated his legacy. Revelations such as the Downing Street Memo demonstrated that the administration was committed to war as early as July 2002, raising questions not only about Powell's actions in the months leading up to the U.S. invasion but also about his motivations for portraying himself to Bob Woodward as an internal dissenter toward the war. Rather than a campaign of dissent, Powell's actions between August 2002 and March 2003 seemed more geared toward seeking international legitimation for an inevitable war with Iraq. He may have seen his comments to Woodward as providing personal cover in the event that the war went badly. Yet, the fact remains that he had mounted a much more aggressive and persuasive case against possible U.S. intervention in Bosnia during the first year of the Clinton administration, in 1993, than he did with Iraq in 2002 and 2003. As Powell had feared, Iraq eventually sucked the oxygen out of everything else he had hoped to achieve as secretary of state.

Why did the United States go to war with Iraq? Most people, even those on the inside, could not answer that question with certainty. George Packer, one of the most eloquent chroniclers of the conflict, saw Iraq as the

Rashomon of wars. Richard Haas, the head of policy planning in Powell's State Department, conceded he would never know the real reasons why the administration went to war in Iraq.[1] "Who knows why we went to war," said Powell's former chief of staff Col. Lawrence Wilkerson. "In fact, I can't tell you when the decision to go to war was made. Worse, I can't tell you who made the ultimate decision."[2] There are nearly as many rationales for the war as there are supporters. One problem the administration faced in the months leading up to the invasion of Iraq was that it had decided to go to war before developing clear reasons for doing so. Thus, in the months between the decision to go to war sometime during the summer of 2002 and the actual invasion in March 2003, the rationales put forward often seemed dubious.

Powell had been at odds with much of the conventional wisdom in the administration on Iraq, beginning with the first discussion of regime change only days after George W. Bush's inauguration.[3] Powell sought to divert the more aggressive course of action, instead advocating the return of inspectors, as well as a retooling of the sanctions regime over Iraq, what he called "smart sanctions." He had long placed great faith in such measures. In 1990, he had urged giving the sanctions strategy more time to work in the approach to the first Gulf War, and he believed they had been instrumental in bringing an end to white rule in South Africa. He saw Iraq as a problem to manage, not as an imminent threat. The secretary believed UN sanctions and inspections had kept Iraq weak, isolated, and in check, and no new evidence showed that Iraq had revived its weapons programs. In fact, he was well aware that the most authoritative information and intelligence about Iraq had concluded, contrary to the administration's claims, that Saddam Hussein remained in a box and had been unable to engage in weapons development. Restarting the inspection process would suffice, Powell felt.[4]

Only a few days after September 11, Deputy Secretary of Defense Paul Wolfowitz began pushing for regime change in Iraq in lieu of going after al Qaeda. Powell was alarmed that Bush took Wolfowitz's views seriously. "Ending terrorism is where I would like to leave it," Powell said, "and let Mr. Wolfowitz speak for himself." Powell had already warned Bush after 9/11 that an attack on Iraq would jeopardize the international support he had worked to assemble for the war in Afghanistan. He doubted America's allies would support an abrupt change of focus to Iraq. "They'll view it as a bait-and-switch," he warned Bush. "It's not what they signed up to do." The chairman of the Joint Chiefs, Gen. Hugh Shelton, also strongly opposed Wolfowitz, fearing an attack on Iraq would unnecessarily alienate many countries whose cooperation was essential for successful operations in Afghanistan. Powell expressed his exasperation to Shelton over Donald Rumsfeld's and Wolfowitz's single-mindedness about Iraq. "What the hell, what are these guys thinking about?" he asked. "Can't you get these guys back in the box?"[5]

The stampede to war depended upon provoking a wave of mass public hysteria about Iraq. The administration continued to make the case, vividly with Condoleezza Rice's "mushroom cloud" analogy, that Iraq had weapons of mass (WMD) destruction and was preparing to use them. Bush, too, luridly invoked the image of mushroom clouds over American cities in speeches during the autumn of 2002. While Iraq's nuclear program had been dead for a decade, Rice's and Bush's alarmist talk convinced many that Hussein presented an imminent nuclear threat to the American homeland. To make the case for war to the American people, the administration stretched the rationales to include weapons of mass destruction and alleged Iraqi ties to al Qaeda and 9/11. Rumsfeld and Dick Cheney persistently alleged that al Qaeda operated out of Iraq, and Bush also linked Iraq to 9/11. Some polls showed that 70 percent of the American public accepted this assertion, and many thought the 9/11 hijackers were Iraqis, when in truth most were Saudis.[6] Powell told Bob Woodward that he considered these charges absurd and saw no linkage between 9/11 and Hussein. Although Powell would ultimately resort to linking al Qaeda with Iraq publicly in February 2003, he initially dismissed Cheney's fixation with demonstrating a possible Iraq–al Qaeda link, no matter how tenuous the evidence.

Astonishingly, much of the news media accepted and repeated these rationales without serious analysis. Venerable publications such as the *New York Times* reported as fact the disinformation fed to it by administration sources and did much to contribute to the climate of mass hysteria. This lack of debate was crucial to establishing the justifications for war. Bush and his chief advisers feared that an actual debate eliciting more accurate information and closer scrutiny of the arguments would jeopardize these flimsy rationales. Whether or not Iraq had WMD was incidental. Administration leaders wanted a war with Iraq not only because they believed it would be easy but also because they believed it would bring about the birth of a "New Middle East"—one where Arab states would embrace American values, pursue friendly relations with Israel, and assist Washington's strategic objectives in the region.

In the months leading up to the war, Powell remained on the margins while his own administration made its case for war with Iraq. Increasingly, the administration embraced large-scale social engineering for the entire Middle East, marking a radical departure from the kind of cautious realism Powell had championed throughout his career. But he eventually signed on to the war against Iraq, and any differences he had with other administration officials had more to do with the best means, not necessarily the ends, of going to war. Powell did not want to avoid a war against Iraq; rather, he wanted the war against Iraq in 2003 to be as close as possible to a rerun of the 1990–1991 buildup, whereas Rumsfeld and Cheney dismissed the previous conflict as irrelevant. They preferred to ignore the United Nations and broader international concerns.[7]

In his 1995 memoir, Powell seems almost to have anticipated the dilemma he faced in 2002. He said he enjoyed being challenged by subordinates. Powell told his men that if they thought something was wrong, it was their obligation to speak up. "When we are debating an issue," he wrote, "loyalty means giving me your honest opinion, whether you think I'll like it or not." Disagreement at that stage stimulated him. "But once a decision has been made, the debate ends," he wrote. "From that point on, loyalty means executing the decision as if it were your own."[8]

In early August 2002, as the war in Afghanistan continued, Powell expressed to Bush his reservations about what would be America's most ambitious overseas endeavor since Vietnam. Again, Powell was not against going to war with Iraq per se, but he had serious misgivings about the way in which the administration was proceeding. He wanted Bush to consider seriously the big issues at stake in Iraq, without the usual objections from Cheney and Rumsfeld. Powell, according to an account he shared with Woodward, had deep misgivings about the administration's obsessive focus on Iraq. He naively held out hope that the Iraqi military would intervene and overthrow the Baathist regime. He wanted Bush to understand that an assault on Iraq would likely be much more difficult than the intervention in Afghanistan. Americans would end up running Iraq. Could anyone in the administration truly guess for how long? "You will become the government until you get a new government," Powell warned Bush. "You are going to be the proud owner of 25 million people. You will own all their hopes, aspirations and problems. You'll own it all."[9]

Powell urged Bush to consider the potential repercussions an attack on Iraq would have in the Arab world. The region could be destabilized. A war could have implications for neighboring countries and even oil prices. The costs of occupying and rebuilding Iraq would be immense, certainly larger than the administration had been saying. Moreover, how would the United States measure success? He bluntly told Bush, "It's nice to say we can do it unilaterally, except you can't." The United Nations was one way to put together the necessary coalition, Powell offered. "You can still make a pitch for a coalition or UN action to do what needs to be done." He suggested that skillful diplomacy would achieve much of what Bush wanted, but he left the meeting uncertain that Bush had grasped everything he had said. Indeed,

Bush later indicated to Woodward that he had not given much thought to what his secretary of state had shared with him.[10]

Some critics have argued that neoconservative dogma was also a major factor in the drive to war. Powell believed the neoconservatives had created a virtual cell where they echoed each others' views. On the subjects of Iraq and the Middle East, Wolfowitz had his own perceptions of reality, and he tended to castigate as intellectually dishonest anyone whose worldview did not conform to his.[11] He had strong ideological beliefs not always supported by facts and a history of pressuring intelligence agencies to issue reports to reflect his hopes and views more closely. He also embraced conspiracy theories pushed by right-wing think tanks, never fully accepted that al Qaeda was behind 9/11, and dismissed the focus on Bin Laden. Contrary to almost all available evidence, he became convinced that Iraq was behind both 9/11 and the earlier World Trade Center bombing in 1993. Some officials concluded that Wolfowitz existed in an "alternate reality." Others observed Wolfowitz's penchant for denying unpleasant or inconvenient facts that did not sit comfortably with his views.[12]

Rationalization had replaced analysis. The intelligence agencies were politicized to provide justifications for the most ambitious military adventure since Vietnam. Powell had little confidence in the intelligence Cheney sent via his chief of staff, Scooter Libby. Powell told Bob Woodward that Cheney had a penchant for selecting obscure, ambiguous pieces of information on Iraq, then, by applying biased judgment, transforming them to fit his preconceptions.[13] Some found the CIA analysis so bad that it amounted to little more than talking points in favor of war with Iraq. Even the intelligence community's senior analyst for the Middle East, Paul Pillar, acknowledged that the administration selected, or "cherry-picked," unrepresentative raw data to make its case. "The administration used intelligence not to inform decision-making, but to justify a decision already made," Pillar asserted. Preformed policy drove intelligence rather than vice versa.[14]

The Failure of Diplomacy

The way the administration made the case for war with Iraq and the way the war was ultimately waged also represented a dismal failure of diplomacy, one for which Powell has received much criticism. Some critics have argued that the attack on Iraq constituted one of the most serious diplomatic failures in recent American history. Political capital accrued immediately after 9/11 that could have gone into pressing for solutions to a number of international problems, such as the Israeli-Palestine conflict, North Korean nuclear ambitions, or the India-Pakistan enmity, was spent instead on Iraq.

Powell's principal problem as secretary of state was that he never established control over foreign policy, and the rush to war with Iraq only further marginalized him. Throughout his four years as secretary, he was frequently frustrated by the freelance foreign policy carried out by the vice president, secretary of defense, Pentagon officials, and White House staff. Often, Powell could not obtain even the most basic information about who was conducting foreign policy. He seemed to lose control of the administration's foreign policy completely, with Rumsfeld, Cheney, Rice, and even John Bolton making pronouncements that normally would have been the domain of the secretary of state. He did a poor job of protecting the State Department's prerogatives against assaults from the Pentagon. Rumsfeld persistently undercut his efforts, frequently making pronouncements on diplomatic matters, often timed just before a Powell address or public appearance. He was repeatedly taken aback by both the frequency and the tenor of the pronouncements by other members of the administration. And, he objected to the rhetorical hyperbole so much in use during the run up to the war with Iraq.

In August 2002, Powell thought he had won a victory for the diplomatic track by securing presidential support for taking the administration's case against Iraq to the United Nations. He consulted with Tony Blair's foreign secretary, Jack Straw, who warned that only the UN route would make it possible for the prime minister to support Washington. Much to Powell's dismay, Cheney declared in an August 26, 2002, speech before the Veterans of Foreign Wars that Iraq undoubtedly possessed chemical and biological weapons, as well as a nuclear program, and that Hussein would share them with al Qaeda. Based on his own intelligence sources, Cheney proclaimed, "Simply stated, there is no doubt that Saddam Hussein now has weapons of mass destruction [and] there is no doubt that he is amassing them to use against our friends, against our allies and against us." Newspaper headlines the next day screamed about the vice president's warning that the threat of a nuclear attack from Iraq justified a preemptive strike and that the speech represented a virtual declaration of war.[15]

Cheney's speech troubled Powell, who viewed it as a preemptive strike against *him*, steering Bush away from the diplomatic track. He described it as a move to dominate the administration's foreign policy. He revealed to Bob Woodward that he felt undermined by Bush. He was baffled that the president had allowed Cheney to deliver such a speech. He later discovered that Cheney had run the idea for the speech past Bush, who had not reviewed it in detail. The speech sparked alarm in Powell's former colleagues from the previous Bush administration, such as Brent Scowcroft, James Baker, and Lawrence Eagleburger, all of whom went public with their concerns. Some thought that these elder statesmen spoke for the former president; some thought they voiced Powell's own misgivings. Powell took the extraordinary step of calling Scowcroft and thanking him for speaking out against his own administration's policies.[16]

Relations between Cheney and Powell thereafter fell to new lows. They confronted each other over Iraq at Camp David in early September, and some observers believed that Powell's resentment of the vice president had reached a boiling point. Powell found Cheney in a state of war fever. Like Wolfowitz, Cheney had become fixated on Iraq to the exclusion of all else. Powell still thought the UN option remained the best course to build a genuine coalition, but Cheney told Powell he wanted to act unilaterally and staunchly opposed involving the United Nations. Cheney repeated that Hussein presented an imminent threat, and Powell responded that a war in Iraq might not prove as effortless as the vice president assumed.[17]

Powell was playing for time against difficult odds. He initially used the UN route effectively, convincing Bush to make an address there on September 12, 2002. This was seen as a Powell victory. He and Blair appeared to be working in tandem because the prime minister had also been urging Bush to go to the United Nations. Powell subsequently enjoyed another hard-won victory with a 15–0 vote in November for UN Security Council Resolution 1441, which renewed the weapons inspections in Iraq. This was seen as a huge diplomatic success for Powell, who may have hoped that such international pressure would force Hussein to back down.

In September 2002, Powell distributed a memo to the cabinet making the case that the Iraq project's long-term success depended on international support. He argued that all diplomatic options should be exhausted in order to build legitimacy for the administration's case if war became unavoidable. He believed Cheney grew increasingly alarmed that the diplomatic path would succeed and deprive the administration of a war in Iraq.[18] To go to war, the administration also had to preempt the UN inspections process and the diplomatic track favored by most of America's allies. In a reprise of his dilemma during the 1991 Gulf War, Powell discovered, all too late, that the diplomatic options, sanctions, and inspections process could never be given sufficient time to work because the administration feared that they would preempt the march to war.

Powell badly misread the diplomatic scene. He seemed to have assumed that other nations would ultimately follow the American lead if they were convinced the train was leaving without them. But, with the lone exception of Britain, other members of the UN Security Council remained unconvinced by American claims about Iraq. If America truly wanted to lead, it had to lead by example, and other nations had to feel confident of her claims. Instead, the American march toward war in Iraq created great anxiety worldwide, even among the closest U.S. allies.

Powell failed to persuade key allies, such as France and Germany, of the arguments for war in Iraq. The French genuinely saw it as a terrible idea and feared that a war and occupation would turn into a quagmire. Even for the ever-faithful Blair, alliance with the administration was less than easy. Bush was so unpopular with the British public that Blair's close association with him proved a catastrophic political liability.[19] The administration believed every country should align its foreign policy with U.S. objectives. From the administration's perspective, the only thing that mattered in the international arena was support for a war against Iraq. At one point, even Powell, in a fit of pique, became furious with the French for daring to question the U.S. desire for a war. But the French, along with other nations, felt abused by Powell's lack of candidness about his own motivations and objectives. Increasingly, Powell failed to take into account the difficulty of winning the support of governments whose peoples remained overwhelmingly opposed to a war in Iraq.

Relations with France deteriorated badly during Powell's tenure. He could not prevent Iraq from completely dominating U.S.-French relations. This was a failure of more than diplomacy. Powell and many of the pundits simply could not accept that European leaders like Jacques Chirac and Gerhard Schröder sincerely opposed an invasion of Iraq. French officials had legitimate misgivings and felt deeply betrayed by Powell's late-in-the-day support for war. A major crisis in the Atlantic alliance occurred, and the tone of relations became bitter. At one point, Rice acknowledged the administration's desire to "punish" France for its refusal to submit. The approach to war unleashed mass hysteria and lurid conspiracy theories directed at traditional allies. This bitterness reached a peak of absurdity when "French fries" became "freedom fries" and pundits like the New York Time's Thomas Friedman warned that France was becoming "our enemy."[20] The French were baffled. They had felt snubbed by the United States after 9/11, when the Bush administration balked at greater French cooperation. French officials had offered forces for an American-led campaign in Afghanistan and were astonished when their offer was rejected. To the French, U.S. officials were simply not interested in French assistance or French opinions.[21]

During Powell's time at State, German-American relations also deteriorated to the lowest point since World War II. The Germans, too, had legitimate reservations about the administration's case for war, and German chancellor Gerhard Schröder felt deeply betrayed. Cheney jeopardized Schröder's standing when, only weeks before the German elections in September 2002, the vice president's rhetoric seemingly forecast an inexorable path to war with Iraq. Cheney's speech provoked dismay in Germany. His remarks made it clear to the Germans that the administration believed there was no other choice but war. Cheney had not bothered to clear his speech with the State Department, perhaps anticipating Powell's warning that his remarks might have major repercussions for other countries who had cooperated with the United States thus far, particularly Germany.[22]

Powell's position, at least that which he revealed to Bob Woodward, was closer to Schröder's than Cheney's. Schröder argued that Afghanistan and the challenge of terrorism should be higher priorities than Iraq and that Afghanistan should be stabilized first. Schröder feared that Afghanistan could descend into chaos if the Bush administration lost interest and raced off to a war with another Muslim country. Moreover, Schröder could not understand why all other issues, from securing Afghanistan to German-American relations, should be subordinated to the Bush administration's exaggerated sense of insecurity and single-mindedness on Iraq.

Schröder was in no way convinced by Washington's exaggerated claims about Iraq. As would be revealed later, both the United Nations and German intelligence had a much better idea of Iraq's capabilities than did the United States. Schröder believed that Bush had committed to consulting with him on Iraq, and Cheney's speech was an unwelcome surprise. When Schröder began to distance himself from the administration, Bush accused Schröder of playing politics, of pandering to public opinion to win an election, something, Bush argued, no leader should ever stoop to. When Schröder won reelection in September, Bush refused to make the customary congratulatory phone call, and Rice accused Schröder of poisoning U.S.-German relations. Rumsfeld, ignoring the German contributions to the war in Afghanistan, equated Germany with Libya and Cuba and, standing on German soil, thanked "New Europe" but said nothing about Germany's contributions. Overlooked in much of the wrath directed at Schröder was the fact that the German chancellor had taken immense political risks at home by dispatching a large support group to Afghanistan, and, as surely Powell, Bush, Cheney, and Rumsfeld must have known, by providing the administration with crucial and accurate intelligence from Iraq.[23]

During a meeting with Bush at the White House on January 13, 2003, Powell received further confirmation of the death of the diplomatic track. Bush had already revealed to the Saudi ambassador, Prince Bandar bin

Sultan, his determination to go to war, and yet he had not informed his own secretary of state. Bush told Powell he had no faith in the inspections, as Powell had suspected all along. The UN track had been used merely for political reasons to convince the American public that all options had been exhausted. Powell impressed upon the president the consequences of choosing war. "You sure?" he asked Bush. "You understand the consequences?" Bush never asked for Powell's assessment, and Powell surmised that Bush did not care to know. Powell still thought the diplomatic path could succeed, but observers found him "semidespondent." America was going to war, a war he still thought was avoidable, and many would die. Powell told Woodward that while Bush was absolutely convinced of the war's correctness and morality, Powell remained plagued by doubts. Sadly, Powell never shared these misgivings with the American people. When Bush made it clear that he was merely informing Powell of the decision he had already made, the secretary fell in line. "Are you with me on this?" Bush asked. "I think I have to do this. I want you with me." Powell replied, "I'll do the best I can. Yes, sir, I will support you. I'm with you, Mr. President."[24]

The Bush administration cared little for diplomacy. But Powell never made an effective case, either to the White House or to the American people, that American goals could be achieved through negotiation rather than bluster and coercion. Bush made it known that there was no way to avoid going to war. Anything else done along the diplomatic or UN track would be mere window dressing. Powell rationalized that he would play out the diplomatic hand, but he seems to have misread Bush's intentions. Powell held to the false hope that he could pull a rabbit out of his hat, but the diplomatic option was clearly dead and probably had been from the very beginning.

Despite Powell's struggle to keep the diplomatic track open, his commitment to diplomacy was often episodic, when many problems could have been avoided with more comprehensive efforts. Some judged that his heart was never in it. Former secretary of state James Baker had traveled to forty-one countries prior to the 1991 Gulf War. Powell rarely visited any in the lead-up to the Iraq War, and when he did, he seemed to deliberately avoid the subject of Iraq.[25] Powell later argued that his presence was needed in Washington as a counterweight to the neocons, but there is little evidence that he had any success against them.

Although Powell continued to act on the belief that greater consensus could have reinforced and legitimized the American position, the failure to put together a real coalition had lasting consequences. At some point, he may have accepted that the administration was unalterably committed to war and would have to make do with its "coalition of the willing." He claimed that the other thirty countries constituted a legitimate coalition.[26] Powell's diplomatic travails over Iraq, together with his inability to obtain substantive support from other nations, contributed to the war plan's failure. The administration's failure to create a genuine coalition or to include the United Nations further undermined its objectives during the occupation debacle. The disdain for diplomacy meant that the tens of thousands of allied troops the administration had counted on never materialized, although an argument can certainly be made that the war plan, as conceived by the Pentagon, with its insufficient planning for the postwar occupation, was doomed all along, even if more countries had contributed. The hasty push for war left most countries dubious of U.S. claims about Iraq. Instead of the anticipated participation of Germany, France, Russia, and other NATO partners, as well as contributions from Arab nations, the administration had to work with a roster featuring Micronesia, the Marshall Islands, Palau, and Tonga.[27] The war was essentially seen as a unilateral U.S. campaign, lacking international sanction, support, or legitimacy.

The Failure to Plan

Many of the problems arising during the occupation of Iraq resulted from the lack of thorough planning for the invasion. The military plan itself was flawed in its conception because it failed several of the Powell Doctrine's essential tests. It did not match America's capabilities with its goals. The invading force was too small to achieve even the most modest degree of postwar stability. Rumsfeld's desire to be seen as a "transformational" steward of the Pentagon did not allow for the commitment of sufficient resources to occupy a country of twenty-five million people. The effort was also hampered by inflexible notions about planning. The administration's dogmatic ideological rigidity prevented it from making the necessary adjustments when problems arose. Worried about these matters, Powell took the extraordinary step of calling the commander assigned to lead the invasion, Gen. Tommy Franks, on September 5, 2002. He explained his concerns. "I'm going to critique your plan up at Camp David," he told Franks. "I've got problems with force size and support of that force, given such long lines of communication." Franks and Rumsfeld did not have much respect for Powell's reservations. "Colin Powell was the free world's leading diplomat," Franks later recalled. "But he no longer wore Army green. He'd earned his right to an opinion, but had relinquished responsibility for the conduct of military operations when he retired as the chairman of the joint chiefs in 1993." Although only eight years younger than Powell, Franks dismissed him as being "from a generation of generals who believed that overwhelming military force was found in troop strength—sheer numbers of soldiers and tanks on the ground."[28]

Franks, eager to please Rumsfeld, went along with the defense secretary's desire to prove that the days of half-million troop mobilizations were a thing of the past. Wolfowitz largely drove the war planning, reassuring Congress that fewer peacekeeping forces would be needed for Iraq than had been deployed to the Balkans. He argued that the Pentagon's favorite Iraqi exile, Ahmad Chalabi, along with his "Free Iraqi Forces," would be sufficient.[29] Powell thought Wolfowitz's ideas strategically unsound and even naive. He remained apprehensive about exaggerated projections of American military supremacy that, to him, defied all logic. "This is lunacy," Powell thought. He observed that everyone was acting as if the United States had been attacked by Iraq and had to rush to respond. He recognized this was a war of choice. "This is not as easy as it is being presented," Powell subsequently warned Bush. "Take your time on this one."[30]

Powell's military career, particularly his experience in Vietnam, gave him flesh-and-blood exposure to the costs and consequences of war. It troubled him that the Bush administration had so few senior officials with combat experience and yet so many who saw military intervention as the solution to every problem. Powell was never eager to commit troops to battle. He felt strongly that lives should not be risked unnecessarily. The absolute least that the civilian officials could do was be certain of the reasons for war. To Powell, it was simply unacceptable that young men and women would have to die in combat merely for civilian politicians to prove their toughness. His 1995 memoir revealed this as one of his core convictions.[31] He was no pacifist, but he understood that war was not always the best choice—an understanding he had voiced during the Clinton administration's debates over Bosnia, at which, despite holding the position of chairman of the Joint Chiefs, Powell openly expressed his misgivings. He feared that those who had never experienced combat often had an unrealistically antiseptic view of war, seeing it as a kind of game.[32] "It's pretty interesting," observed Gen. Anthony Zinni, a senior adviser to Powell and a former chief of the U.S. Central Command, "that all the generals see it the same way, and all the others who have never fired a shot and are hot to go to war see it another way."[33]

Given these apprehensions, why was Powell not more outspoken about the flawed military planning? As a four-star general, former chairman of the Joint Chiefs, and father of the Powell Doctrine, he possessed an informed perspective about planning for war. Instead, officials with far less experience controlled the planning. During his activist stint as chairman under Bill Clinton, he rarely shrank from offering his opinions, privately or publicly, often on matters outside his immediate purview. This history made his failure either to express public misgivings or to exercise greater influence even more curious.

He had previously contended that the military should never apologize for going in "big" if that was what was required for success. "Decisive force ends wars quickly and in the long run saves lives," he said. Whatever threats America faced in the future, he claimed in 1995 that he intended to make such rules the bedrock of his counsel.[34] He must have known that the Pentagon was embarking upon a poorly planned war, with too few troops to accomplish even the most modest objectives (such as securing Iraqi arms depots), too few allies, and a cultural and historical ignorance of the country they would be occupying and the peoples living in it. Perhaps Powell, too, got caught up in the false optimism. Perhaps he was merely following his commander in chief. Yet, as chairman of the Joint Chiefs, he had been part of the decision making at the end of the first war with Iraq in 1991. His views then were that it would require a large force merely to remove Iraqi troops from Kuwait. Anything beyond that, he believed, would be flirting with a potential quagmire. Americans should enter and leave as soon as possible, without taking on the daunting task of actually occupying and reinventing Iraq. Nothing had changed in the interval that should have altered these conclusions.

Moreover, what about the so-called lessons of Vietnam? Powell had based much of his career on his perception of what that war had meant. His 1995 memoir devoted many pages to this subject, and his critique of American blunders in Vietnam remains relevant. He had once criticized the Vietnam-era Army for rationalizing that "[i]f it ain't working, pretend it is, and maybe it will fix itself." He claimed to have been appalled by what he saw as the docility of the senior military leadership during Vietnam. The United States misunderstood the nature of the war; it failed to study the realities of Vietnamese history and culture; it overestimated its own capabilities. Powell recognized that despite official assessments, the mission in Vietnam overwhelmed the Johnson administration and the military. It simply proved more complex than the Pentagon and the Joint Chiefs had ever anticipated.[35]

Was Powell, along with much of the administration, condemned to repeat many of the errors of Vietnam? Did Vietnam offer insight into what the United States was embarking on in Iraq? And, if it did, was Powel in a position to raise this point? The administration fought hard to quash any comparisons, and the very mention of the Vietnam analogy was perceived as so polarizing that no such questions could be raised with respect to Iraq. Yet, did the Bush administration understand Iraq? Did it know enough about the country to which it was sending thousands of troops? Did it know sufficient Iraqi, or Middle Eastern, history? Did Americans understand that Iraqi traditions, views, language, culture, values, and history differed profoundly from their own? Moreover, the challenges of Iraq demanded a hardheaded and realistic assessment of U.S. national interests. But Powell's desire to be loyal to Bush revealed a lack of clear thinking about the consequences for American interests. Just what *would* be the costs and consequences of such an ambitious undertaking? When the occupation went wrong, what would be gained by merely staying the course? Moreover, did the administration understand the United States' own limitations? As with Vietnam, Washington failed to take the broader view: what would be achieved by images of Americans fighting in a small country, provoking thousands of civilian deaths? It was not a pretty picture to contemplate, and most officials seemed to avoid it. When it came to the Middle East, knowledge seemed to have been put through an ideological filter. Middle East policy had become a hotbed of ideological and polemical struggle. Powell acknowledged as much in his final meeting with Bush in January 2005 when he warned that the administration had internalized hard-line Likud dogmas.

In his 1995 memoir, Powell harshly criticized America's Vietnam-era leadership for bowing to groupthink pressure and keeping up the pretense of the war in Vietnam's necessity. He referred to this as "the conspiracy of illusion."[36] Yet, when confronted with a similar challenge, Powell performed no better. He, too, acted as if the uniformed military had no role beyond accepting illusions about Iraq and the Middle East and going off to war. Moreover, he failed to anticipate the consequences for the armed forces. The all-volunteer military would shoulder the entire burden. The administration would not dare to call for a draft. Doing so would provoke a more rigorous and unwelcome examination of the arguments for war. Powell had long expressed concerns about shared sacrifice, once lamenting that the costs of Vietnam "were perceived as if they were happening only to the military and their families, people unlucky enough to get caught up in a messy conflict; they were not seen as sacrifices shared by the country for a common purpose, as in other wars."[37] At the first sign of trouble, the administration faced calls for more troops. Just as in Vietnam, some believed that, merely by sending more troops, many of the problems of Iraq would be better addressed. Just as in Vietnam, this was a mirage, as Powell must have known.

To Powell's increasing frustration, Rumsfeld also sought to become chief diplomat. In February 2003, Rumsfeld gave a speech in New York, "Beyond Nationbuilding," arguing that Iraq would have to adhere to his new military model: minimalism. Neoconservative polemicists once again hailed his "transformational" vision, but the planning for the war failed to draw upon the recent experiences in Kosovo and Bosnia and the many innovations there in peacekeeping, occupation, and reconstruction.

Throughout his career, Powell demonstrated little interest in postconflict operations. Perhaps he feared that it would give civilians yet another temptation to use the military for purposes he did not support. In reality, however, postconflict operations, such as stabilization, reconstruction, and even nation building, were becoming every bit as important as fighting and winning wars. Recent history had shown that U.S. administrations, whether they wanted to or not, had been confronted with the challenge of reconstructing postconflict societies.

The absence of a real understanding of Iraq and its history complicated this challenge. Despite the U.S. foreign policy obsession with Iraq since 1990, few in the administration actually knew much about the country and its peoples, and those who did were swiftly marginalized. Considering that the war and the reconstruction of Iraq would be one of the most ambitious projects in American history, the disdain for expertise was particularly mindless. The problems did not arise from a lack of warnings about what might happen. Many such warnings were ignored. Incomprehensibly, few senior officials seemed concerned about what was likely to happen after the invasion, in what many were warning would be America's most ambitious overseas project since Vietnam. Senior officials fell into the trap of listening only to assessments that most closely matched their own prejudices and illusions.

As far back as 1998, fears that the Iraqi regime would disintegrate had provoked Gen. Anthony Zinni, at Centcom, to begin working on a postwar plan, "Desert Crossing." Zinni warned that postwar reconstruction would be a massive challenge, and he thought a reconstruction plan should complement any military plan. Zinni feared his plan for Iraqi reconstruction had been unfairly tainted by association with the Clinton administration. Under Powell, the State Department's Bureau of Near Eastern Affairs recruited Iraqi exiles and organized seventeen committees to focus on postwar planning, headed by the State Department's Thomas Warrick and his "Future of Iraq Project."[38]

Powell, nevertheless, lost the battle over the future of Iraq to the Pentagon when, on January 20, 2003, Bush signed National Security Presidential Directive No. 24. Bush refused to heed Powell's objections and those of the specialists at State and instead granted authority for postwar Iraq to the Pentagon. Despite its new responsibilities, the Pentagon's Office of Special Plans, headed by Douglas Feith, did little. The Pentagon opposed State Department experts assisting with the planning for postwar Iraq. Rumsfeld,

Wolfowitz, and Cheney did not want specialists challenging their beliefs. They disdained the messy details of postwar planning and insisted upon outsiders loyal to the Pentagon and the Iraqi exile and neocon favorite, Ahmad Chalabi. Rumsfeld and Cheney deemed Warrick insufficiently loyal to Chalabi and banished him from the planning process.[39]

Many have argued that the Iraq War was fought and lost in Washington before a single shot had been fired. The administration existed in a highly insulated environment, circumscribed by its own doctrinaire aversion to careful planning and nation building. Perspectives grounded in expertise faced hostility. When a number of moderate or nonpartisan think tanks, including the Army War College, produced reports backing Powell's call for more thorough planning, he gained no leverage. Whenever anyone at Centcom asked about postwar planning and reconstruction issues, they were told, "Mr. Wolfowitz is taking care of that." When the Council on Foreign Relations offered its services to the administration on postwar planning expertise, a meeting with Rice was disrupted by one of the right-wing think tank participants she had insisted attend: "Wait a minute. What's all this planning and thinking about postwar Iraq?" He turned to Rice. "This is nation building, and you said you were against that. In the campaign you said it, the president said it. Does he know you're doing this. Does Karl Rove know?"[40]

The administration grew increasingly hostile toward those who contested its rosy scenarios. In February 2003, Army Chief of Staff Gen. Eric Shinseki testified before the Senate Armed Services Committee that securing postwar Iraq would require several hundred thousand troops. Many outside of Rumsfeld's closed circle shared the general's concerns, but Wolfowitz promptly contradicted Shinseki.[41] In April 2003, the administration projected that total postwar planning costs would be less that $3 billion. When Budget Director Lawrence Lindsay predicted $200 billion he too was reprimanded and persuaded to retire. Shinseki and Lindsay had violated the administration's policy of concealing the true costs and sacrifices from the American public. Purging Shinseki and Lindsay sent the clear message that candor would be costly.

Few in the administration, other than Powell, seemed sufficiently concerned about the postwar details needed to ensure that U.S. forces would succeed. Cheney told the nation that American troops would be greeted as liberators. When a friend of Cheney's warned him that American forces were likely to get bogged down in Iraq, Cheney replied, "They're going to welcome us. It'll be like the American army going through the streets of Paris. . . . The people will be so happy with their freedoms that we'll probably back ourselves out of there within a month or two."[42] But Cheney and Rumsfeld had made several enormous miscalculations. They embraced the fantasy of training six thousand Chalabi followers as the "Free Iraqi Forces" to fight alongside U.S. forces and provide the vanguard of a future Iraqi government led by Chalabi himself. This dissolved into recriminations when Chalabi could muster only seventy men.[43] Most importantly, the administration also failed to anticipate or accept the many warnings of inevitable sectarian strife.

It was becoming clear to Powell that the kind of wishful thinking he had witnessed in Vietnam and so often scorned in his 1995 memoir now applied to Iraq. Since no one anticipated difficulties, the administration had few ideas about what to do when problems inevitably arose. Few seemed to understand that using a military occupation as the instrument of liberation could make things difficult long after, particularly in terms of establishing the legitimacy of a new Iraqi government.[44] Even Powell eventually embraced wishful thinking and dubious rationales about the war. For example, only days before the invasion, he confidently predicted publicly that Iraq's oil revenues would be sufficient to cover most of the costs of occupation and reconstruction.

Powell at the United Nations: Making the Case for War

Powell decisively threw in his lot with the pro-war faction with his dramatic speech before the UN Security Council on February 5, 2003. In what some called Powell's "Adlai Stevenson moment"—referring to John F. Kennedy's UN ambassador's dramatic presentation before the United Nations during the Cuban missile crisis—the administration dispatched Powell to the Security Council to make the case for war. Even Bush saw him as the best person in the administration to present its position. "You have the credibility to do it," Bush told him. Powell was reportedly flattered by Bush's confidence in him.[45]

The administration understood that ongoing UN inspections would undermine the justification for war. The inspections had to be short-circuited, and the move toward an invasion had to begin before the inspections rendered an attack unwarranted. Cheney feared Powell might once again be steering Bush in a multilateral direction and that his speech carried the risk of brokering a last minute compromise short of war. The vice president viewed the UN course as delaying the inexorable path to war, and he urged Powell to examine his chief of staff Scooter Libby's homemade intelligence portraying lurid conspiracies connecting the 9/11 plotters to Iraq.

Not wanting to taint his UN presentation with Cheney's "B" squad intelligence, Powell wisely cast such material aside, but he was later criticized for the intelligence he did include, intelligence that subsequently provoked investigations by a Senate committee and a report by the chief of U.S. weapons inspectors. Paradoxically, Powell had much experience with intelligence. He knew more about the subject than any previous secretary of state. In 1988, he and George Shultz, having become aware of the degree to which the intelligence agencies were having difficulty coping with the changes in the Soviet Union, simply ignored much of it.

Powell spent all day on February 1 at CIA headquarters going over intelligence, including raw intercepts. What he discovered troubled him. The intelligence had been so politicized that no one knew its context or origins. He found much of it flimsy and suggestive, not as concrete as he expected, not the "slam dunk" CIA director George Tenet had promised. He wanted hard evidence and was dubious of much of what he saw. Parts of the material he decided to use were of doubtful origin. He knew much of it was shaky, but he made do with what he found. "Based on everything we ourselves knew, we had doubts going in," recalled Powell's former chief of staff Col. Lawrence Wilkerson, who accompanied Powell to the CIA. "And after that day I don't believe Powell felt any more comfortable about the intell on Iraq."[46] Powell never shared his misgivings with the American public. Instead, he swallowed his doubts and went ahead preparing his address. Powell's public statements during this period stand at odds with the private reservations he conveyed to Washington Post reporter Bob Woodward and with misgivings he admitted to ABC's Barbara Walters two and a half years later, after he had left the administration and as American forces were fighting and dying in Iraq.[47] To further complicate matters, in the fall of 2007 Powell defensively told an interviewer, "I didn't know [the intelligence] was flawed. Everybody was using it. The CIA was saying the same thing for two years. I gave perhaps the most accurate presentation of the intelligence as we knew it—without any of the 'Mushroom clouds are going to show up tomorrow morning' and all the rest of that stuff. But the fact of the matter is that a good part of it was wrong, and I am sorry that it was wrong."[48]

A hysterical media frenzy preceded Powell's presentation, with the American broadcast networks using administration-inspired color-coded alerts to warn of the imminence of terrorist attacks, presumably from Iraq. Whatever Powell's objectives, his presentation raises unsettling questions about his judgment and motives. Powell, who claimed to be uncomfortable with rhetorical hyperbole, could not resist resorting to it himself. It was a lamentable performance. Read today, his presentation seems astonishingly alarmist. Heard in February 2003, with the color-coded terrorism alerts going full throttle, his remarks only added to the climate of mass hysteria. Parts of the speech were overblown, and while he never laid out convincing evidence of ties between Iraq and al Qaeda, he implied that they existed. A close analysis of the speech reveals that he repeatedly conflated the two subjects, linking Iraq to international terrorism twenty-six times. Casting aside warnings from throughout the bureaucracy regarding the administration's claims about Iraq and nuclear weapons, he mentioned nuclear weapons or programs twenty-five times, chemical weapons thirty-nine times, and biological weapons thirty-six times.[49]

This address, which Powell once considered the capstone of his career (he appended the speech to the end of a recent paperback edition of his memoir), has been thoroughly discredited. The basic premise of his presentation—that Iraq presented an imminent threat to world peace—proved false, as the French and others who warned against the rush to war had consistently contended. His presentation was deeply misleading, based upon selected intelligence, innuendo, and flimsy evidence.[50]

A few days later, Hans Blix, head of the United Nations' weapons inspections in Iraq with immense credibility in Europe and throughout the world as an able and impartial statesman, challenged Powell. "Since we arrived in Iraq," Blix told the Security Council, "we have conducted more than 400 inspections covering more than 300 sites." Throughout all of the inspections, no convincing evidence was revealed that Iraq had weapons of mass destruction, or WMD. Powell responded angrily to Blix's presentation. "These are all tricks that are being played on us," he said in frustration. He endured another affront when French foreign minister Dominique de Villepin received a thunderous ovation at the United Nations following a rousing antiwar speech to the Security Council. Witnesses observed that only Nelson Mandela had ever been so enthusiastically cheered. For all of Powell's anger at the United Nations and the French, it was later revealed that UN inspectors more clearly understood Iraq's weapons programs than the Bush administration. Substantial documentary evidence reveals that the rigorous system of weapons inspections was far more effective than Powell claimed. The UN's International Atomic Energy Agency and its director Mohamed El Baradei, both frequent targets of the administration's vituperation, received the 2005 Nobel Peace Prize for their efforts.

Loyalty was a word heard frequently when discussing Powell. It became the chief rationale when analyzing the dichotomy between his public support for Bush administration policies and his presumed private misgivings. Powell had maintained his public silence about his misgivings out of loyalty to Bush, but his public silence denied the American people the opportunity to weigh the potential costs and consequences of an invasion of Iraq. Powell's public statements and the public record of his remarks and comments during four years as secretary of state are frequently at variance with his revelations expressed to Woodward. He failed to boldly challenge the administration's course in the way Cyrus Vance did with his resignation in 1980 or Shultz had with his many threats to resign. Powell had once memorably suggested at the Naval Academy that even junior officers should resign if they felt strongly about administration policies. But he more often demonstrated loyalty to Bush than to the American people, even on matters over which he claimed to be strongly at odds with the president. By some accounts he wanted to resign as early as 2002 but feared it would hurt Bush's reelection chances. Powell could have taken a stand at several other moments. He could have contested the mindless cronyism that occurred in Iraq. The staffing of so much of the Coalition Provisional Authority (CPA) with rank amateurs and political hacks reportedly incensed him.

As the administration was predicating the most ambitious overseas endeavor since Vietnam upon wishful thinking and rationalization, not analysis, Powell had staked his continued support for the policy upon a series of rationales that do not hold up under closer scrutiny. By adhering to the official line, he held on to his job until 2005, but he also did an immense disservice to the men and women in uniform. The general might have served them far better by resigning in protest against the administration's ill-conceived war. By doing so, he might have dramatized the importance he placed on the diplomatic option and the fate of the armed forces. It would have proved his most powerful weapon. But, unlike Shultz during the Reagan administration, it was a weapon Powell proved uncomfortable wielding. Powell once rationalized, "Senior officials cannot fall on their swords every time they disagree with a President."[51] To some, matters of war and peace should be the exception to that rule, but Powell seemed to have rationalized his actions with the assumption that he could fight the good fight. He shared with Tony Blair the illusion that it was better to be Bush's friend in the hope of maintaining some degree of influence. Both egregiously overstated their influence with the White House; paradoxically, however, both may have undervalued their ability to alter a policy about which they later claimed to have misgivings. Richard Armitage conceded that there was considerable truth in an assessment by a friend from Congress who charged that Powell had deluded himself and become an enabler, giving crucial political cover to the administration's more extreme policies.[52]

In any event, the White House might well have welcomed Powell's threatening to resign. "The president doesn't like him very much," a member of the Senate Foreign Relations Committee observed. "If Powell threatened to resign, the president would say, 'go to hell.'"[53] Moreover, Powell never disagreed with the ends of the Iraq policy, only the means. He saw himself as a servant of power. "He's the president, and he decided and therefore it was my obligation to go down the other fork with him," Powell told associates after the war began.[54]

Some critics have argued that Powell, owing to his military career, was inclined to respect rather than challenge power. This overlooks the extent of his insubordination in 1993 regarding gays in the military. His behavior in the Clinton administration complicates the loyalty argument. He left Clinton with the belief that he might resign. He went public with his misgivings. Some thought him insubordinate. He certainly used his political capital more aggressively in 1993 during the gays in the military controversy and during the debate over Bosnia, neither of which was nearly so consequential as war in Iraq.

In late April 2003, former speaker of the House Newt Gingrich, addressing an audience at the neoconservative American Enterprise Institute, essentially called for Powell's resignation, demanding "bold, dramatic change" at the State Department. This was a remarkable statement, coming from someone known to be close to Rumsfeld. Obviously Gingrich was not acting on his own, and the address signaled the Pentagon's next move to take over many of State's functions. All the more remarkably, the White House remained silent, merely offering a canned defense of Powell issued by a spokesman rather than the president himself. Powell, like Shultz before him, might have been galvanized by the threat to him. Moreover, he could have used the threat of his resignation tactically. Given his immense standing, Powell was perhaps the only person in the country in a position to raise the very doubts he claimed to have. His resignation, or at least the threat of it, could have slowed the march toward a war he privately confessed to be poorly planned and based upon trumped-up pretexts. There were precedents. In the past century, secretaries of state such as Cyrus Vance and William Jennings Bryan had resigned over matters of principle, and several other secretaries of state had at least threatened to resign over matters large and small. In the approach to the invasion of Iraq, Powell's onetime counterpart as British foreign secretary, Robin Cook, resigned from Blair's cabinet in a dramatic speech in the House of Commons over the impending war.

In the end, Powell acquiesced to a path he himself had conceded was deeply flawed. Because Powell did not make a persuasive case for the alternative foreign policy vision he claimed to have, Bush escaped the need to acknowledge there were alternatives to his unilateral path. Powell entered office with more political capital than any secretary of state in recent times, but his goal seemed to be to shepherd that capital, rather than spend it in pursuit of the objectives he claimed to hold dear.

The invasion of Iraq went ahead on March 19, 2003, and appeared to proceed with almost effortless success. Many hailed the capture of Baghdad in just three weeks as the product of a new form of warfare, and over the summer of 2003, Rumsfeld continued to receive good press. Self-anointed military pundits cited his 135,000 troops as a demonstration of his military genius. Emboldened by such praise, Rumsfeld remained fixated on this number for fear that any departure from it would undermine his "transformational" legacy. But U.S. success was short-lived. The triumphalism was grotesquely misplaced as American troops settled in for a long occupation of Iraq. The invasion began a chain of events with disastrous consequences, mostly for Iraq but also for the United States. The overthrow of Saddam Hussein was not the end of the war but merely the beginning of a new, more complex conflict.

The realities of Iraq did not match the administration's blueprint for military transformation. The administration's messianic illusions of reinventing the Middle East ran headlong into regional and global realities. Ignoring all warning signs and based on both an overestimation of U.S. capabilities and unfounded confidence in his administration's abilities, Bush ignored the details of how difficult it would be for the United States to transform Iraq. The administration had studiously avoided a full airing of actual costs and consequences of the endeavor for fear of eroding public support. Thus, the actual reasons for going to war, as well as the tremendous sacrifice that would be required to fulfill even the most modest American objectives in Iraq, were obscured and never discussed. Instead, the nation was subjected to an irrelevant debate about Iraqi culpability for 9/11 or possession of nonexistent WMD, when it should have been discussing what goals it had in Iraq, how they might realistically be achieved, and at what cost and consequences. Powell had a reputation for asking these sorts of questions. He apparently had misgivings and intermittently raised such questions behind closed doors. He gave the president the benefit of his guarded and private counsel. Still, the larger national interest suffered immensely for his decision not to air these concerns more openly.

Bush never grasped the magnitude of the looming debacle in Iraq and never seemed focused or engaged enough to make the tough decisions required to stave off disaster. As Powell had warned him, the transformation of Iraq was a far more complicated task than anticipated. Administration officials had failed to give sustained thought to what it would truly involve. The United States had neither committed sufficient troops nor provided the means to address genuine Iraqi grievances. A pervasive ignorance of Iraq's history and that of the region led only to imperial fantasies. "Because Bremer and his colleagues in the CPA and the Bush administration never grasped history," observed Larry Diamond, a consultant to the CPA in Baghdad, "they could not anticipate how viscerally much of Iraq would react to an extended occupation."[55] In one of its least excusable blunders, the Pentagon had not provided enough troops to guard even a fraction of the many munitions dumps all over Iraq. The United States found it could not secure these arms depots, which were subsequently looted to make the so-called improvised explosive devices (IEDs). One U.S. general in Iraq warned that it was like trying to secure all of California with only 150,000 troops.

As in Vietnam, the insurgency refused to follow the Pentagon's script, and senior officials were slow to adjust. Despite efforts to rationalize that al Qaeda directed the insurgency, U.S. intelligence understood plainly that it had deep local roots. Chairman of the Joint Chiefs of Staff Gen. Richard Myers conceded that al Qaeda sympathizers comprised only a small percentage of the insurgents, most of whom were Iraqis hostile to the U.S. occupation. Undeterred, Bush increasingly conflated 9/11 with Iraq, calling Iraq the central front in the war on terror.[56]

The ideological—almost theological—adherence to unilateralism guaranteed that the unilateralists' chief project would fail. It was always difficult for an administration so steeped in neoconservative ideology to see the realities of Iraq. There had been many grandiose illusions and many unrealistic fantasies but very little hardheaded analysis or follow-through. The failed assumptions demonstrated a naiveté at the heart of the entire enterprise. The administration's devotion to ideological purity meant that it could never admit mistakes or seriously assess its performance; thus, it could not accept help or even suggestions about changing its approach.

At the end of their study of the Iraq War, *Cobra II*, Michael Gordon and Bernard Trainor reached conclusions supporting the much-maligned Powell Doctrine. Of all the mistakes Bush and his advisers made, several stood out as the most grievous: "They did not bring the right tools to the fight and put too much confidence in technology. They failed to adapt to developments on the ground and remained wedded to their prewar analysis even after Iraqis showed their penchant for guerrilla tactics in the first days of the war. They presided over a system in which differing military and political perspectives were discouraged. Finally, they turned their back on nation-building lessons from the Balkans and other crisis zones."[57]

The ideological commitment to unilateralism also prevented the Bush administration from placing sufficient expertise on the ground in Iraq. An administration opposed to peacekeeping, nation building, and long-term deployments found itself in a quagmire, in part because of its doctrinal rigidity. Few Americans knew the language, culture, or history of Iraq. Few CPA employees had even the minimum professional skills necessary for postconflict reconstruction. They often lacked experience and judgment and simply could not comprehend or cope with the challenges they faced. The incompetence and ineptitude of the CPA became legendary. The CPA's own inspector general saw it as a dumping ground for political operatives and campaign volunteers. State department officials with experience in such matters or even UN specialists could have aided considerably, but the administration put a premium on stands such as opposition to abortion and support for capital punishment.[58] The challenge of rebuilding Iraq simply overwhelmed the administration. The arrival of Proconsul L. Paul Bremer in April 2003 was a concession that the war plan had failed. There would be no early withdrawal. But the administration proved inept at choosing competent administrators with a knowledge of Iraq. Bremer, too, soon came to realize that, for all of the optimistic forecasts, no amount of Iraqi oil revenue or seized Baathist assets was going to come even remotely close to covering the costs of the war, occupation, and reconstruction.

While one war was being fought in Iraq, another was fought in Washington. The Bush administration was at war with itself. Officials seemed confused in public, and their explanations of the war grew increasingly incoherent. In private, there were angry clashes among senior officials. At one point, Cheney, feeling the pressure, stuck a finger in Powell's chest and said, "If you hadn't opposed the Iraqi National Congress (INC) and Chalabi, we wouldn't be in this mess."[59] The State Department continued to battle the Pentagon, and the infighting reached new levels of dysfunction. "Bureaucratic tribalism exists in all administrations, but it rose to poisonous levels in Bush's first term," observed neoconservative polemicist Francis Fukuyama. "Team loyalty trumped open-minded discussion, and was directly responsible for the administration's failure to plan adequately for the period after the end of active combat."[60] Recriminations followed. Officials accused each other of wishful thinking and hostility to dissenting opinions. The whole enterprise seemed to suffer from a lack of accountability, and Bush, shifting the blame while facing a tough reelection campaign, asserted that Bremer's occupation botched Iraq. Eventually, Bremer began dealing with Powell, who told a staff meeting at State, "We have one priority. That priority is Iraq. What Jerry Bremer asks for, Jerry Bremer gets, and he gets it today."[61]

The diplomatic fallout from the administration's rush to war, as well as the decision to award postwar reconstruction contracts only to American firms, many with close ties to the administration, left lasting resentments and impeded the limited efforts to broaden the rebuilding effort. Moreover, one of the obvious problems with the American occupation, largely misunderstood in Washington, was that it never had legitimacy in the eyes of the Iraqis or the world.

The spring of 2004 marked a low point in the American occupation as full-blown insurgencies erupted in the Iraqi cities of Najaf, Fallujah, and Baghdad. Powell reportedly said privately that not only were U.S. forces bogged down in a full-scale guerrilla war in Iraq, but they were losing it. It now seemed increasingly unlikely that the handover of power from the CPA to the Iraqi governing council would happen. The Iraqi governing council threatened resignation, and the CPA's last hope, Ayatollah Ali al-Sistani, rejected the American timetable. The administration remained dogmatically hostile to international assistance of any kind, even when it had become increasingly apparent that such internationalization might be the last hope for its flailing policy.

In desperation, some members of the administration turned to the despised United Nations to rescue the misadventure in Iraq. "We are trying to put this issue in Kofi Annan's lap and let him run with it," a senior Bush administration official admitted.[62] The United Nations had numerous advantages the CPA did not possess: it had a talented staff of experienced personnel with knowledge of the region, its languages, and its peoples, and, most importantly, it had experience with nation building honed from recent operations in Kosovo, Bosnia, and East Timor. The United Nations also had a legitimacy that the United States, seen in the region as an imperial occupier, could not match.

With Powell's surreptitious backing, UN Secretary General Kofi Annan dispatched to Baghdad seasoned diplomat and former Algerian foreign minister Lakhdar Brahimi, a man recognized as perhaps the greatest living international negotiator. Brahimi had served two years as UN special representative in Afghanistan and was widely hailed for his successful mediation at the 2001 Bonn conference establishing the post-Taliban government. In UN circles, it was widely recognized that the Bush administration policy in occupied Iraq was confused and reactive, too focused on military solutions to clearly political problems. The United Nations had not compromised itself by backing Iraqi favorites as the United States had with Chalabi. Many outside the administration understood that multilateral peacekeeping and nation building had compiled a superior record of achieving lasting transformations to unilateral efforts. The State Department acknowledged that it was becoming increasingly dependent upon Brahimi to prepare Iraq for elections. One State Department official conceded, "We're very dependent on him to develop a plan—and then help legitimize it among Iraqis." The White House seemed to be acquiescing. At one point, when Bush was asked specific questions about Iraq's politics, he shocked many in his administration when he replied that it would be "decided by Mr. Brahimi."[63] But any UN role was a bitter pill for many to swallow, and Bush administration's ideological coloration meant that it could not decide whether it wanted to utilize or undermine Brahimi. It was no secret that Cheney and Rumsfeld remained dogmatically opposed to Brahimi's rescue mission.[64]

Brahimi's proposed reforms—such as calling on the United States to support confidence-building measures, criticizing the detainee policy of the occupation, and questioning the scope of de-Baathification—met with predictable hostility from the administration, and he was subjected to withering criticism and attacks by right-wing polemicists. Still, he succeeded in convincing various Iraqi factions to be patient and assisted the Iraqis in making necessary adjustments, forging a consensus on the composition of an interim government, allowing for Bremer to flee Iraq at the end of June, and diverting attention from the administration's many blunders during a heated presidential campaign.[65]

Resignation

One year after his UN speech, Powell admitted in February 2004 that had he then possessed the information he currently had about Iraq, he would have supported the war less enthusiastically. Many observed that as the 2004 elections approached, Powell appeared to be going through the motions. "I don't think he's fighting, and I can't understand why," observed one of Powell's former colleagues from the first Bush administration. Increasingly, throughout 2004, it was widely predicted that Powell would not be retained long in a second Bush term. Many speculated that Rice would replace him, but only after Bush's reelection so as not to unleash Powell or concede that anything was even remotely amiss with Bush's foreign policy.[66]

The April 2004 release of Bob Woodward's *Plan of Attack* compounded Powell's problems. Woodward's revelations about Powell's purported misgivings about the war and his true feelings toward Cheney, Rumsfeld, Rice, Wolfowitz, and Bush himself further imperiled his position in the administration. Powell grew increasingly defensive in public. He was quick to claim that he had not misled anyone with his many public statements leading up to the invasion. But, throughout the spring of 2004, revelations piled upon revelations about Iraq's lack of WMD and the manipulation of intelligence.

Many of the doubts Powell privately claimed he harbored at Langley in February 2003 were now coming out. He conceded to friends that he felt betrayed by the CIA. He now doubted much of what the CIA had ever told him. Bush's impatience with Powell was also starting to show, and he grew testy when asked about his secretary of state.[67]

It had become increasingly apparent to Powell that the script for George W. Bush's administration would not run like that of Reagan's. In the Reagan administration, the pragmatically inclined faction of George Shultz, Frank Carlucci, and Colin Powell created a team that triumphed over a coterie of more hawkish officials. Shortly after Bush's reelection in November 2004, he announced that Rice would replace Powell. Even some of Rice's aides had conceded that she should have long since resigned as national security adviser, but in an administration where loyalty was prized above all else, she was rewarded with appointment to the State Department.[68] "With this," the *Economist* reported, "the administration's most famous malcontent is making way for a fierce loyalist."[69]

Although Powell left the impression that he was resigning of his own volition, he later told close friends and associates that he had in fact been fired. During Powell's waning days at State, he had a final meeting with Bush. In early January, he was summoned to the White House and after several awkward minutes, Powell realized Bush had no idea why he was there. Bush summoned White House Chief of Staff Andrew Card, but none of the three knew why the meeting had been called. Powell may have suspected the vice president had set him up for one last humiliation, but he also surmised that this might be his last opportunity to meet alone with Bush. Powell spoke his mind to the president, unencumbered by the restraints of the past four years. Powell wanted Bush to know that he believed the administration lacked a strategy for fighting the war in Iraq. The administration was focused more on public relations and winning the battle for U.S. public opinion. The invasion of Iraq was still being conflated with September 11 since the latest rationale for the war held that the American homeland would be best defended on the streets of Iraq. Powell bluntly told Bush that the Pentagon had accrued too much power in the administration and had dominated foreign policy during the previous four years. He lashed out at Undersecretary of Defense Feith as a "card-carrying member of the Likud Party." He urged the president to consider a new strategy and to find new advisers to carry it out. No one ever spoke to Bush this way. If Powell truly felt so strongly, it was a discussion he should have had with Bush two or three years before, when it might have been more decisive.[70]

The Iraq War turned out to be Powell's undoing, and his reputation was one of the war's casualties. His goal of emerging as the George Shultz of the administration lay in ruins. His tenure at State will more likely be compared to that of Alexander Haig or even William Rogers. He and his aides would forever claim that they had made a difference, but they had arrived in January 2001 with high hopes and departed in January 2005 with precious few achievements.

Powell resigned as secretary of state nearly three decades after the fall of Saigon. His career was in many ways bookended by the wars in Vietnam and Iraq. Powell left behind a polarization not seen since Vietnam, the consequences of which, particularly for the all-volunteer military, could not yet be imagined. In his memoir written a decade before, Powell had been especially critical of Lyndon Johnson's actions during Vietnam. Recalling Johnson's decision not to run for reelection in 1968, Powell felt that "packing it in and going home to the ranch was not an option available to career officers, or to American draftees, for that matter."[71] But the kind of agonizing and self-flagellation that Vietnam-era officials like Johnson and Robert McNamara had engaged in was not for Powell. In public, he seemed untroubled by the mess left behind in Iraq. He resumed his lucrative speaking schedule, joined the board of several companies, and bought a new Porsche. Back on the lecture circuit, he was much in demand for his witty performances. The largely appreciative audiences often came away impressed by his sense of humor.

Powell's Record at State: An Assessment

Powell's record as secretary of state was one of opportunities missed. Few secretaries of state entered office with such a strong public reputation. He had hopes of becoming another George Marshall, or at least another George Shultz. Moreover, few secretaries of state had an opportunity like that which 9/11 presented. As had been the case following World War II, the nation awaited the promotion of a viable foreign policy consensus. Having entered office with more prestige and public good will than previous secretaries of state, the events of 9/11 gave him the opportunity to shape the global architecture to his vision. But, he failed to seize the opportunity after 9/11 to build a sustainable foreign policy.[72] Perhaps no one could have succeeded, given the political and bureaucratic context in which he worked. Still, Powell had arrived at State with a strong reputation and seemingly unlimited reserve of good will and political capital. When he first addressed the State Department on January 22, 2001, there was a widespread feeling of optimism. Powell's arrival not only augered well for the State Department but seemed to portend that the new administration would take diplomacy seriously.

At the time of Powell's departure four years later, some lamented the many opportunities missed. He had arrived claiming to be a champion of diplomacy, but in the end, his loyalty to Bush prevailed over his own professed values.[73] "In another administration, Powell might have been a great secretary of state," observed veteran diplomatic correspondent John Newhouse. "However, not since William Rogers, who served in the first Nixon administration, has a secretary of state been rolled over as often—or as routinely—as Powell."[74] Like Tony Blair, Powell mistakenly assumed that becoming Bush's friend would lead to influence. Both Powell and Blair failed to understand that when it came to foreign policy, Bush was not the only relevant player in his administration. Despite the cult of personality erected around the president after 9/11, Bush proved woefully out of his depth as commander in chief. Vice President Cheney's unprecedented power, particularly over foreign affairs, meant that for all of Powell's efforts to court Bush, his views ultimately counted for little.

Assessed against the high hopes of January 2001, many issues simply went unaddressed. Measured against Powell's own public statements, many of the objectives he brought to the office were left unattained. It would be difficult to recall an administration where diplomacy was used so sparingly and so ineffectively. The diplomatic failures of the administration loomed large and ultimately had major ramifications for the war in Iraq. Powell's inability to gain the support of important allies such as Germany, France, Turkey, and the Arab states increased U.S. burdens, adding to the difficulty of obtaining a real commitment of money or troops for Afghanistan and Iraq. As he had feared, the single-minded focus on terrorism and the Iraq War had sucked all of the oxygen out of the foreign policy agenda. The war in Afghanistan had been bungled, in part owing to Bush's notoriously short attention span. Bush simply grew bored with the details of shoring up Afghanistan and became consumed with going to war in Iraq.

The Iraq War left the administration diplomatically isolated and inattentive to other pressing international issues. The few achievements in foreign policy that the administration could claim at the end of its first term, such as relatively stable relations with Moscow and Beijing, were more the unintentional byproduct of the distractions of 9/11 than the results of Powell's active diplomacy. Powell's efforts in the Middle East and North Korea had largely gone for naught. The Atlantic alliance suffered its most severe crisis since its inception. Latin American countries felt ignored and embittered. Even Africa, where Powell had staked much hope for a new approach, languished on the back burners of the administration's agenda. Paradoxically, most problems, from Iraq to North Korea to Iran, could only really be addressed in concert with other nations, which remained ideologically anathema to the administration. The disappointment many felt over Powell's tenure at State resulted in part from their high expectations. Some felt vaguely betrayed that he had staked his reputation on the case he presented before the United Nations. We now know that privately, he too harbored many doubts about the arguments he made for war.[75]

Since his resignation, Powell has become a figure of considerable controversy. He is remembered as much for his self-assured support for the war, as demonstrated in his UN speech, as for the qualified and entirely private misgivings he leaked to Woodward. "I'm the one who made the television moment," Powell said in an interview after his resignation. "I was mightily disappointed when the sourcing of it all became very suspect and everything started to fall apart. The problem was stockpiles. None have been found. I don't think any will be found . . . I will forever be known as the one who made the case." Eight months later, he revealed to Barbara Walters that his UN speech would remain a "blot" on his career, which was "painful" for him to accept. "I'm the one who presented it on behalf of the United States to the world," Powell said. It "will always be a part of my record."[76]

Powell's foreign policy vision, as he had defined it during his confirmation hearings in January 2001 and in numerous public addresses thereafter, was stillborn. His stint as secretary did not achieve a union of realism and selective multilateralism. His support for the war in Iraq damaged his reputation for realism. Any genuine realist could have observed that, in Iraq, there never were any "good" options. But Powell had proved useful to Bush in one important way. He had provided the administration with a moderate and realist front for policies that were quite unrealistic in their conception and incompetent in their execution. "They turned out to be among the most incompetent teams in the postwar era," observed neoconservative activist Kenneth Adelman. "Not only did each of them, individually, have enormous flaws, but together they were deadly, dysfunctional."[77] While on most of the major issues of his four years—North Korea, relations with Europe, the response to 9/11, the war in Iraq—Powell had often been the odd man out, he consistently provided the administration with useful political cover, or window dressing, for its policies.

The Iraq debacle revealed that, regardless of all the trumpeting of raw force, the United States simply did not possess the military power or the public enthusiasm to pursue such a grandiose objective as reinventing another society in the image of the United States. The American people are usually uncomfortable seeing themselves in such imperial terms. They also traditionally possess a powerful aversion to overseas crusades. The way in which Bush led America into the war, inflating the threat Iraq presented, sowing mass hysteria, and conflating Iraq with 9/11, enabled the administration to launch its invasion. These very same tactics, once they were exposed for what they were, also led to the inevitable unraveling of public support for the war.[78]

A war to transform Iraq was a far greater undertaking than those responsible for it had ever imagined. To have come even remotely close to some arbitrary and minimalist measure of success would have required a level of nuance and diplomatic creativity that proved largely alien to the Bush administration. Moreover, as events over Powell's four years at State revealed, military power can never be the sole means of achieving foreign policy objectives, most of which are ultimately political in nature. American power has traditionally rested on several factors. Military power is one, but economic and political power and moral example are also relevant. The damaged relations with allies and the many rejections of diplomacy were obvious. On strictly military grounds, however, the intervention in Iraq also raised serious questions about American military power.

Powell's achievements as secretary were meager. He will more likely be compared with other "failed" secretaries of state, such as William Rogers, Cyrus Vance, and Alexander Haig, than with the more commanding figures whose legacies reveal substantial achievements, such as Henry Kissinger, George Marshall, and Dean Acheson. Although expectations of him as he entered office were higher than for any secretary of state in recent times, he never articulated a realist foreign policy vision that would have stood as an alternative to neoconservative illusions about unilaterally reinventing the world. He failed to demonstrate how a realist foreign policy could be utilized in promoting America's strategic interests or even in defending democratic ideals or human rights. This was Powell's tragedy. It was also America's.

Notes

1. George Packer, *The Assassins' Gate: America in Iraq* (New York: Farrar, Straus and Giroux, 2005), 46.

2. Author interview with Col. Lawrence Wilkerson, September 20, 2007.

3. Ron Suskind, *The Price of Loyalty: George W. Bush, the White House, and the Education of Paul O'Neill* (New York: Simon and Schuster, 2004), 74–76.

4. Colin Powell, "Briefing for the Press Aboard Aircraft En Route Brussels," February 26, 2001, www.state.gov/secretary/former/powell/remarks/2001/953.htm; Bill Keller, "The World According to Powell," *New York Times Magazine*, November 25, 2001.

5. Bob Woodward, *Bush at War* (New York: Simon and Schuster, 2002), 61.

6. James Risen, *State of War: The Secret History of the CIA and the Bush Administration* (New York: Free Press, 2006), 92–102; Richard A. Clarke, *Against All Enemies: Inside America's War on Terror* (New York: Free Press, 2004), 241–42; John Newhouse, *Imperial America: The Bush Assault on the World Order* (New York: Alfred A. Knopf, 2003), 35.

7. Newhouse, *Imperial America*, 42.

8. Colin Powell, *My American Journey* (New York: Ballantine, 1995, 2003, paper), 309.

9. Quotations and the account of the Bush-Powell meeting are taken from Woodward, *Bush at War*, 332–34, and Woodward, *Plan of Attack* (New York: Simon and Schuster, 2004), 149–53.

10. Woodward, *Plan of Attack*, 152–53, 292.

11. Risen, *State of War*, 72.

12. Clarke, *Against All Enemies*, 30, 95, 231–33; Packer, *The Assassins' Gate*, 116–17.

13. Woodward, *Plan of Attack*, 292.

14. Quoted in Paul Pillar, "Intelligence, Policy, and the War in Iraq," *Foreign Affairs* (March/April 2006): 17–18.

15. Woodward, *Plan of Attack*, 163–64.

16. Woodward, *Plan of Attack*, 163–67; Ivo Daalder and James Lindsay, *America Unbound: The Bush Revolution in Foreign Policy* (Hoboken, NJ: Wiley and Sons, 2005), 136.

17. Woodward, *Bush at War*, 345–53.

18. Packer, *The Assassins' Gate*, 104; Woodward, *Plan of Attack*, 157, 175–76.

19. Philip H. Gordon and Jeremy Shapiro, *Allies at War: America, Europe, and the Crisis over Iraq* (New York: McGraw-Hill, 2004), 146; Robin Cook, *The Point of Departure* (London: Simon and Schuster, 2003), 49–50, 104–5.

20. Gordon and Shapiro, *Allies at War*, 124, 127; Anatol Lieven, *America Right or Wrong* (New York: Harper Collins, 2004), 168.

21. James Mann, *Rise of the Vulcans: The History of Bush's War Cabinet* (New York: Viking Press, 2004), 304.

22. Daalder and Lindsay, *America Unbound*, 136.

23. Daalder and Lindsay, *America Unbound*, 187.

24. Woodward, *Plan of Attack*, 270–71.

25. Daalder and Lindsay, *America Unbound*, 188.

26. Larry Diamond, *Squandered Victory: The American Occupation and the Bungled Effort to Bring Democracy to Iraq* (New York: Owl Books, 2005), 311.

27. Daalder and Lindsay, *America Unbound*, 168.

28. Quoted in Tommy Franks, *American Soldier* (New York: Regan Books, 2004), 394.

29. Daalder and Lindsay, *America Unbound*, 167.

30. Quoted in Woodward, *Plan of Attack*, 22.

31. Powell, *My American Journey*, 281, 314.

32. Woodward, *Plan of Attack*, 78.

33. Quoted in Newhouse, *Imperial America*, 48.

34. Powell, *My American Journey*, 421.

35. Powell, *My American Journey*, 100–101, 451.

36. Powell, *My American Journey*, 100, 144.

37. Powell, *My American Journey*, 125.

38. David L. Phillips, *Losing Iraq: Inside the Postwar Reconstruction Fiasco* (New York: Westview, 2005), 37.

39. Daalder and Lindsay, *America Unbound*, 164; Woodward, *Plan of Attack*, 283–84.

40. Packer, *The Assassins' Gate*, 112, 117–20.

41. Diamond, *Squandered Victory*, 285.

42. Robert Draper, *Dead Certain: The Presidency of George W. Bush* (New York: Free Press, 2007), 178.

43. Packer, *The Assassins' Gate*, 128.

44. Diamond, *Squandered Victory*, 281.

45. Woodward, *Plan of Attack*, 291.

46. Author interview with Col. Lawrence Wilkerson, September 20, 2007.

47. Steven R. Weisman, "Powell Calls His UN Speech a Lasting Blot on His Record," *New York Times*, September 9, 2005; Woodward, *Plan of Attack*, 299–300.

48. For Powell's interview with Walter Issacson, see www.despardes.com/FEATURES/20070911-colin-powell.htm.

49. Colin Powell, "Remarks to the United Nations Security Council," February 5, 2003, www.state.gov/secretary/former/powell/remarks/2003/17300.htm.

50. Craig Whitney, ed., *The WMD Mirage: Iraq's Decade of Deception and America's False Premise for War* (New York: Public Affairs, 2005).

51. Powell, *My American Journey*, 297.

52. Woodward, *Plan of Attack*, 433–34.

53. Quoted in Michael Steinberger, "Misoverestimated," *American Prospect*, April 1, 2004, www.prospect.org/cs/articles?articleId=8853.

54. Woodward, *Plan of Attack*, 414.

55. Diamond, *Squandered Victory*, 301.

56. Daalder and Lindsay, *America Unbound*, 168, 175; Packer, *The Assassins' Gate*, 245.

57. Bernard E. Trainor and Michael R. Gordon, *Cobra II: The Inside Story of the Invasion and Occupation of Iraq* (New York: Pantheon, 2006), 497–98.

58. Daalder and Lindsay, *America Unbound*, 173; Packer, *The Assassins' Gate*, 200; Diamond, *Squandered Victory*, 289.

59. Quoted in Packer, *The Assassins' Gate*, 146.

60. Quoted in Francis Fukuyama, *America at the Crossroads: Democracy, Power, and the Neoconservative Legacy* (New Haven, CT: Yale University Press, 2006), 61.

61. Packer, *The Assassins' Gate*, 396, 327.

62. Daalder and Lindsay, *America Unbound*, 179.

63. Diamond, *Squandered Victory*, 246, 255.

64. L. Paul Bremer, *My Year in Iraq* (New York: Simon and Schuster, 2006), 279.

65. Diamond, *Squandered Victory*, 256–58.

66. Steinberger, "Misoverestimated," www.prospect.org/cs/articles?articleId=8853.

67. Woodward, *Plan of Attack*, 440, 166.

68. Risen, *State of War*, 3.

69. "Bush Makes Room for Rice," *Economist*, November 16, 2004.

70. Quoted in Packer, *The Assassins' Gate*, 444–45.

71. Powell, *My American Journey*, 120.

72. Flynt Leverett, "Illusion and Reality," *American Prospect*, August 13, 2006, www.prospect.org/cs/articles?article=illusion_and_reality.

73. George Gedda, "Colin Powell: Four Tumultuous Years, Focus on the Powell Legacy," *Foreign Service Journal* 82, no. 2 (February 2005): 32–40.

74. Newhouse, *Imperial America*, 24.

75. Author interview with Col. Lawrence Wilkerson, September 20, 2007.

76. Thomas E. Ricks, *Fiasco: The American Military Adventure in Iraq* (New York: Penguin, 2006), 407; Weisman, "Powell Calls His UN Speech a Lasting Blot."

77. David Rose, "*Now* They Tell Us: Neo Culpa," *Vanity Fair*, November 3, 2006, www.vanityfair.com/politics/features/2006/12/neocons200612.

78. Anatol Lieven, "A Trap of Their Own Making," London Review of Books, May 8, 2003, www.lrb.co.uk/v25/n09/liev01_.html.

CHAPTER 8

~

Conclusion

Colin Powell's career was unique in recent U.S. history. Over the course of a quarter century, he held senior appointments in the Pentagon, the White House, the U.S. Army, and the Department of State. He was even a national political figure, thought of by millions as a dream candidate for either vice president or president in 1988, 1992, 1996, and 2000, often courted by both Republican and Democratic nominees. The range of appointments he held between 1987 and 2005, such as national security adviser, chairman of the Joint Chiefs of Staff, and secretary of state, has no parallel in modern American history. In many ways it was a career of paradoxes, one of remarkable successes and, at the end, perplexing failures.

Powell will be seen as one of the more successful national security advisers (1987–1989), one who helped restore the National Security Council's place in foreign policy after the debacle of Iran-Contra and who played a key role in improving U.S.-Soviet relations and helping influence the Reagan administration's shrewd response to Mikhail Gorbachev's bold initiatives. His conduct as chairman of the Joint Chiefs (1989–1993) during the first war with Iraq was extraordinary. Few who recall that conflict will forget Powell's commanding presence or the compelling story of his reluctance to go to war and his efforts to find a solution to the conflict short of armed conflict. Nor will many soon forget the excitement surrounding his flirtation with a possible presidential bid during the last months of 1995.

Had Powell remained true to his desire to stay out of public life, the narrative of his career would have ended on a decidedly different note. But the

bitter and polarizing discord that the George W. Bush administration's foreign policy provoked will guarantee that Powell's tenure as secretary of state
(2001–2005) will continue to fascinate historians and the public. There
will long be speculation and controversy about his role. "When Powell was
a general he was very political, involving himself in matters not usually the
domain of the chairman of the joint chiefs," observed former Pentagon official Lawrence Korb. "But when he was secretary of state, he behaved more
like a general, more or less accepting the decisions of others. It's simply.
baffling."[1]

Although he sought to portray himself as a qualified dissenter, he will
always be linked to the war in Iraq. His February 2003 UN speech made
the administration's case for invading Iraq and did more to build support for
war than the actions of other U.S. officials. Yet, the speech was ultimately
revealed to have been riddled with inaccuracies, exaggerated claims, and, at
points, outright falsehoods. It gravely damaged Powell's reputation.

There is certainly more to Powell's career than Iraq, as this account has
demonstrated throughout. He was, by most accounts, a conscientious public
servant. But Powell's career demonstrates that decency is rarely enough in
public life. Powell showed formidable political skills in advancing his career.
His path was meteoric, helped along by powerful mentors, good timing, and
an extraordinarily positive press. Perhaps owing to this, he did not develop
the necessary political skills that might have helped him survive in the
George W. Bush administration. He often lacked the hardness and ruthlessness to succeed in an administration where power was vested in hidden
places, where senior officials did not hesitate to undermine and humiliate
colleagues. The Bush administration had complex, often unseen hierarchies,
whereas Powell came from an institutional culture with clear lines of authority. He often became entangled in an environment where things were not
what they seemed. At times, he appeared hopelessly out of his political and
bureaucratic depth.

Powell's career also paralleled the rise of the neoconservatives as a factor
in American foreign policy. This was one of the tragedies of his career. He
became their foil, their scapegoat for all that they believed was wrong with
American foreign policy. They could not forgive or forget his role over two
decades. In the Reagan administration, he became associated, first, with
Frank Carlucci, deemed by the neocons as "soft" owing to his prior service
in the CIA during the Carter years, and, second, with Secretary of Defense
Caspar Weinberger, known for his cautious doctrine and lukewarm support
for Israel. Then, in 1987 and 1988, the neoconservatives castigated Powell,
Carlucci, and Secretary of State George Shultz for seeking rapprochement

with Gorbachev and thus "betraying" Reagan's legacy as a hard-line ideologue. The neocons were convinced that the Reaganite struggle against communism had been won through a policy of military confrontation and ideological crusading. Powell, who became part of the pragmatic troika (along with Carlucci and Shultz) that pushed hard for negotiations and a revival of détente, may have had a different interpretation.

After the 1991 Gulf War, a mythology developed among neoconservatives that by arguing against taking the war to Baghdad, the cautious Powell had frittered away the military's victory. During the Clinton administration, one of the few administration policies with which some of the neoconservatives agreed was the use of American military power in the Balkans, something Powell staunchly opposed. Finally, between 2001 and 2005, Powell became the chief target of their vituperation over a host of issues, such as relations with Ariel Sharon's Israel; policy toward North Korea; relations with China, Europe, and Russia; the response to 9/11; and the Iraq War. Powell understood that to succeed, the neoconservative's objectives required mass support from the American people for imperial crusading. Powell shrewdly concluded that such a departure from American traditions was not likely and that the inflation of threats and the sowing of mass hysteria would only have a transitory effect. Sadly, despite Powell's astute critique of the neoconservative dilemma, he proved incapable of offering a compelling alternative to such grandiose fantasies.[2]

To make even the most preliminary assessments of Powell's tenure in Foggy Bottom, one must analyze his achievements alongside previous secretaries of state. The most influential of the modern era, such as Charles Evans Hughes, George Marshall, Dean Acheson, and Henry Kissinger, left a mark on the diplomacy of their times. The least successful, such as William Rogers, Cyrus Vance, and Alexander Haig, failed for various reasons, perhaps the one commonality being that they did not enjoy strong relations with the presidents they served and were thus easily marginalized.

Powell was in no way a novice to the job of secretary of state. He possessed a strong resume for this appointment. He had served as the military aide to the secretary of defense for three years, where he observed the struggles between the Pentagon and State for influence over Reagan's often rudderless foreign policy. He served as deputy national security adviser under Frank Carlucci for a year, then held Carlucci's job for the remainder of the Reagan presidency, where he worked closely with Secretary Shultz. His four years as chairman of the Joint Chiefs gave him further perspective on the uses of American power and intervention, as well as on the turf wars within the Washington Beltway. Moreover, Powell was temperamentally well suited to the duties of the nation's chief diplomat, as he demonstrated during the Carter mission to Haiti in 1994.

Under normal circumstances, a successful secretary of state must persuade the president, the cabinet, other nations, and the American people of his proposed course of action. Of course, the years 2001 to 2005 were hardly normal, with the administration's penchant for ideological conformity and frequent denial of reality. Nor was the character of the Bush administration normal, with secret powers vested in the vice president's office and the Pentagon's aggressive assertion of power over foreign policy. Moreover, the administration's embrace of neoconservative ideology departed radically from Powell's brand of realism. Powell, perhaps alone among senior administration officials, understood the unreality of Bush's foreign policy. For example, he remained dubious of the neoconservative illusion that a nation like the United States, with an all-volunteer military, could constantly threaten to fight simultaneous wars against all comers and remain credible. He believed America led most effectively by example, not coercion. Unlike some of his colleagues, he understood that gratuitous hostility to other nations was counterproductive and that it was important not to gloat, because the subtle camouflaging of diplomatic successes often made it easier to repeat them.

As secretary of state, Powell proved uncertain about how best to make use of the vast political capital he had accumulated throughout his career. Over the course of his nearly two decades in the public eye, Powell had accrued much good will and public trust. The American people seemed willing to give him the benefit of the doubt, even when they disagreed with him on specific issues. The assumption often was that Powell was speaking truth to power from within the White House. How often he did so remains unclear. Moreover, how much truth mattered in the ideologically inclined George W. Bush administration is debatable. In any event, Powell repeated Tony Blair's misjudgment of seeking to build a relationship with Bush, when Donald Rumsfeld and Dick Cheney may have been equally, and in some cases more, important in foreign policy.

Few senior officials were more a product of American institutions than Colin Powell. Having entered the army in 1958, during the Eisenhower administration, he resigned from government service in 2005 having spent forty of those forty-seven years in either the army or the federal bureaucracy. Powell was shaped by these institutions in ways other recent secretaries of state, most of whom came from the corporate or academic worlds, could not have been. Other than having adopted much of Weinberger's doctrine as his own, Powell's main contribution was that of a servant of power, rather than an innovator.

During his rise, and particularly at the time of the publication of his 1995 memoir, Powell became known for his sharp criticisms of the civilian and military leadership during the Vietnam War. In retrospect, he was too quick to criticize the mistakes of the Vietnam generation of policymakers, mistakes that Powell and his colleagues in the Bush administration were mindlessly determined to repeat. It is certainly tempting to see Powell as a paradox, a man who devoted much of his career sounding warnings about the possibility of "another Vietnam" only to observe, and in at least one conspicuous instance aid, his colleagues in marching into an ill-conceived war in the Middle East.

Powell's career also paralleled troubling trends in American foreign policy, such as the growing tendency toward government secrecy, the relentless growth of executive branch power, and the recurrent use of fear and apocalyptic rhetoric to stir public apprehension about real or imaginary threats. His career coincided with the tremendous increase of presidential power at the expense of congressional power. Although he maintained generally good relations with Congress, he rarely suggested that it should have much of a role in foreign policy. Some, such as Cheney, made no effort to conceal their staunch advocacy of unrestricted presidential powers. Yet the founders of the American republic feared that the executive branch would most likely start wars and thus vested this power in the legislative branch. Moreover, some institutions were certain to bear the burden of the tremendous growth of presidential powers in making war. The military, for example, was left to carry out the objectives of an interventionist-inclined executive branch without sufficient checks and balances. Powell's predecessor as chairman of the Joint Chiefs, Adm. William Crowe, once cautioned Powell that presidents liked to launch wars because almost all presidents believed the truly great ones had fought successful wars.

In one capacity or another, Powell was involved in almost all major American military engagements over the past four decades. This included, as a soldier, the Vietnam War, but he also saw military service in Cold War hotspots such as West Germany and South Korea. As a Pentagon adviser, he was involved in the ill-fated deployment to Lebanon, the U.S. invasion of Grenada, the air strikes against Libya, and the covert war against Nicaragua. As chairman of the Joint Chiefs, he planned and oversaw the interventions in Panama, Iraq, and Somalia and opposed the same in Bosnia and Haiti. The wars in Afghanistan and Iraq occurred on his watch as secretary of state, the last ultimately contributing to his resignation.

Powell's rise to prominence as a public official coincided with the end of the Cold War, the decline of Europe and the Soviet Union as the central focus of U.S. strategy, and the rise of the Middle East as the most important region in American geopolitical thinking. Powell's subsequent career as a senior official was curiously linked with events in the Middle East and, more specifically, the Gulf region. Powell claimed that Jimmy Carter's mishandling of the Iranian hostage crisis in 1980 had pushed him into the Republican Party. He voted for Ronald Reagan in that year's presidential election and later became one of the rare black officials in the Reagan administration, holding a favorable position for promotion and advancement. The bombing of the U.S. Marine barracks in Lebanon in October 1983, while Powell was a military aide to Secretary of Defense Caspar Weinberger, led to Weinberger's proclamation of the doctrine that evolved into the Powell Doctrine. The Iran-Contra scandal, which erupted after the Reagan administration launched an ill-conceived and naive scheme to trade arms to Ayatollah Khomeini's Iran for hostages held in Beirut, resulted in Powell's return to Washington as Frank Carlucci's deputy at the NSC, which in turn led to his replacing Carlucci the following year. Four years later, while he was chairman of the Joint Chiefs, the Gulf War with Iraq transformed Powell into a much-celebrated national figure and gave him presidential aspirations in the mid-1990s. The attacks of September 11, certainly linked to America's policies in the Middle East, and the subsequent war in Iraq beginning in 2003 provided a coda to Powell's career. For all the links between Powell's rise and American involvement in the Middle East, U.S. intervention there after 2003 ultimately led to Powell's undoing as a statesman.

Despite these experiences, did Powell actually have a clear understanding of the Middle East or develop a coherent U.S. policy toward the region? Like so many senior officials with influence over American foreign policy during these years, Powell was not an expert on this troubled region. With the exception of his passages about the 1991 Gulf War, he said little about the Middle East in his 1995 memoir. Moreover, Powell aside, there has been little official or public understanding of America's myriad problems in the Middle East, as we cling ever tightly to preconceived notions about the region and its peoples. That the Middle East has become an obsessive, yet vexing focus of the last five administrations is not surprising in light of Washington's incorporation of Israeli strategic designs into U.S. foreign policy and the insatiable thirst for Middle Eastern oil. But, when discussing the Middle East, Washington politicians and pundits often reveal a reluctance to think seriously about the realities, costs, and consequences of American empire, particularly in the Middle East.

Mikhail Gorbachev once posed the question to Powell, "What are you going to do when you've lost your best enemy?" This question consumed much of Powell's post-1989 career. Yet, during Powell's career, America was increasingly drawn into a classic security dilemma. The greater the American military establishment, the less secure America actually perceived itself to be, in part because it so frequently launched military interventions to address its perceived challenges and also because it resorted to the inflation of threats to justify high levels of military spending. With every act of intervention, from Lebanon, to Libya, to Saudi Arabia, to Afghanistan, to Iraq, the United States created new circumstances that led to new and different problems and challenges and, in many cases, further interventions.

After a quarter century pursuing a more vigorous post-Vietnam strategy, America found itself more isolated, more despised. Paradoxically, the more America has flexed its military muscles, the more it has been exposed as essentially powerless. Military power has proven largely useless in addressing many of the challenges of the nation, both abroad and at home. Colin Powell may not be the chief reason for this dilemma, but as a senior military and civilian official in the past four administrations, he does bear some responsibility. More importantly, Powell struggled with the most essential test for a statesman: distinguishing between the nation's true national interests and the temptations of empire. Or, as John Quincy Adams once prophetically cautioned, distinguishing between genuine national objectives and the temptation to go in search of monsters to destroy.

Notes

1. Author interview with Lawrence Korb, March 17, 2006.
2. Fred Kaplan, *Daydream Believers: How a Few Grand Ideas Wrecked American Power* (Hoboken, NJ: Wiley and Sons, 2008); Jacob Heilbrunn, *They Knew They Were Right: The Rise of the Neocons* (New York: Doubleday, 2008).

~

Bibliographical Essay

A good place to begin a bibliographic discussion of Colin Powell is with his memoir, *My American Journey* (New York: Ballantine, 1995, 2003), which contains his own account of the events of his life from his birth in Harlem in 1937 to his decision not to run for president in 1996. The 2003 Ballantine edition of the memoir also includes an appendix featuring Powell's February 5, 2003, address before the United Nations—an address he has since disavowed. An excellent concise treatment of Powell's life and tenure as secretary of state is F. Erik Brooks, "Colin Powell," in *American Statesmen: Secretaries of State from John Jay to Colin Powell*, ed. Edward S. Mihalkanin (Westport, CT: Greenwood Press, 2004). A much longer and more sympathetic, but equally good, treatment is Karen DeYoung, *Soldier: The Life of Colin Powell* (New York: Alfred A. Knopf, 2006).

Vietnam is an important part of Powell's story. The best concise survey of the Vietnam War remains George Herring, *America's Longest War: The United States in Vietnam, 1950–1975* (New York: McGraw-Hill, 1986). H. R. McMaster, *Dereliction of Duty: Lyndon Johnson, Robert McNamara, the Joint Chiefs of Staff, and the Lies that Led to Vietnam* (New York: Harper, 1997), is valuable for understanding the interaction of the Joint Chiefs with the Lyndon Johnson administration and the framework through which Powell drew his lessons from the war. James Westheider, *Fighting on Two Fronts: African Americans and the Vietnam War* (New York: New York University Press, 1997), explores the ambivalence many African Americans, Powell included, felt about fighting in Vietnam while the civil rights struggle raged at home. John Hellmann, *American Myth and the Legacy of Vietnam* (New York: Columbia University Press, 1986), addresses how Americans have processed the many meanings of Vietnam. Also useful is Jerry Lembcke, *The Spitting Image: Myth, Memory, and the Legacy of Vietnam* (New York: New York University Press, 1998). Powell himself claimed to have been influenced by reading Bernard Fall, *Street without Joy: The French Debacle in Indochina* (Mechanicsburg, PA: Stackpole Books, 1961, 1994). James Mann, *Rise of the Vulcans: The History of Bush's War Cabinet* (New York: Viking Press, 2004), provides insight into Powell's early life, experiences in Vietnam, and career in Washington in the 1970s.

More than one thousand books have been written about Ronald Reagan's administration since his departure from office. Unfortunately, many of them are published or subsidized by conservative think tanks and amount to little more than paeans aimed at burnishing Reagan's historical reputation. The Reagan years also produced an extraordinary number of memoirs, but only a few are worth mentioning. Alexander M. Haig Jr.'s *Caveat: Realism, Reagan, and Foreign Policy* (New York: MacMillan, 1984) is useful for understanding the problems of Reagan's foreign policy during the administration's first year, but it also reveals problems with Reagan's foreign policy management that plagued the administration throughout its eight years. Robert C. McFarlane, *Special Trust* (New York: Cadell and Davies, 1994), contains much about foreign policy between 1983 and 1986, including accounts of Lebanon, Nicaragua, and the Iran-Contra scandal. George Shultz's *Turmoil and Triumph: Diplomacy, Power, and the Victory of the American Ideal* (New York: Simon and Schuster, 1993) is the most detailed account of Reagan's foreign policy in the years from 1982 to 1988. For insight into the defense buildup, Caspar Weinberger, *Fighting for Peace: Seven Critical Years in the Pentagon* (New York: Warner Books, 1990), covers the years 1981 to 1987 and includes a full text of Weinberger's November 1984 speech before the National Press Club, which became known as the Weinberger Doctrine. Although he is a staunch Reagan loyalist, Michael K. Deaver's *Behind the Scenes* (New York: William Morrow, 1988) reveals more than he intended in his story of media management and presidential image shaping. The controversial memoir by Reagan's second White House chief of staff, Donald Regan, *From the Record: From Wall Street to the White House* (New York: Harcourt Brace Jovanovich, 1988), pulled back the curtain on the inner workings of the Reagan White House, revealing much of the chaos at the heart of the administration, as well as its dependence on an astrologer. Constantine C. Menges, *Inside the National Security Council: The True Story of the Making and Unmaking of*

Reagan's Foreign Policy (New York: Simon and Schuster, 1988), is a generally favorable insider portrayal of Reagan's foreign policy.

Scholarly and reportorial explorations of the Reagan administration, with some discussion of foreign affairs, include Michael Schaller, *Reckoning with Reagan: American and Its President in the 1980s* (New York: Oxford University Press, 1992), which is the best concise treatment. Sean Wilentz, *The Age of Reagan: A History, 1974–2008* (New York: Harper, 2008), is the most up-to-date account. Among the best larger assessments are Lou Cannon, *President Reagan: The Role of a Lifetime* (New York: Public Affairs, 2000), and Richard Reeves, *President Reagan: The Triumph of Imagination* (New York: Simon and Schuster, 2005). David Ignatius, "Reagan's Foreign Policy and the Rejection of Diplomacy," in *The Reagan Legacy*, ed. Sidney Blumenthal and Thomas Byrne Edsall (New York: Pantheon Books, 1988), and David E. Kyvig, "The Foreign Relations of the Reagan Administration," in *Reagan and the World*, ed. David E. Kyvig (Westport, CT: Praeger, 1990), offer concise overviews. More specific assessments of Reagan's foreign policy include Frances Fitzgerald, *Way Out There in the Blue: Reagan, Star Wars and the End of the Cold War* (New York: Touchstone, 2000), which uses the theme of Star Wars to imaginatively explore Reagan's foreign and defense policies, with insightful profiles of Reagan and his advisers.

William M. LeoGrande, *Our Own Backyard: The United States in Central America, 1977–1992* (Chapel Hill: University of North Carolina Press, 1998), provides a thorough analysis of Reagan's policies in Central America, while Robert Pastor, "The Centrality of Central America," in *Looking Back on the Reagan Presidency*, ed. Larry Berman (Baltimore: Johns Hopkins University Press, 1990), and Susanne Jonas, "Reagan Administration Policy in Central America," in *Reagan and the World*, ed. David E. Kyvig (Westport, CT: Praeger, 1990), are more concise treatments. Robert Lieber, "The Middle East," in *Looking Back on the Reagan Presidency*, ed. Larry Berman (Baltimore: Johns Hopkins University Press, 1990), Philip S. Khoury, "The Reagan Administration in the Middle East," in *Reagan and the World*, ed. David S. Kyvig (Westport, CT: Praeger, 1990), and William Quandt, *Peace Process: American Diplomacy and the Arab-Israeli Conflict Since 1967* (Berkeley: University of California Press, 2005), examine Reagan's Middle East policies. Mark P. Logan, *The Reagan Doctrine: Sources of Conduct in the Cold War's Last Chapter* (Westport, CT: Praeger, 1994), and James M. Scott, *Deciding to Intervene: The Reagan Doctrine and American Foreign Policy* (Durham, NC: Duke University Press, 1996), investigate the Reagan Doctrine and covert operations. Michael T. Klare, *Beyond the "Vietnam Syndrome": U.S.*

Interventionism in the 1980s (Washington, DC: Institute for Policy Studies, 1982), examines the many interventions in the wake of Vietnam.

The Iran-Contra affair has encouraged a lively scholarship. The most thorough assessment remains Theodore Draper, *A Very Thin Line: The Iran-Contra Affairs* (New York: Hill and Wang, 1991), but Peter Kornbluh and Malcolm Byrne, eds., *The Iran-Contra Scandal: The Declassified History* (New York: The New Press, 1993), is a useful supplement, complete with many of the key primary documents from the scandal. David J. Rothkopf, *Running the World: Inside the National Security Council and the Architects of American Power* (New York: Public Affairs, 2005), discusses the scandal from the perspective of the National Security Council. John Tower, Edmund Muskie, and Brent Scowcroft, *The Tower Commission Report* (New York: Times Books, 1987), remains an essential source for understanding the scandal, but it should be supplemented with the more critical account by the Iran-Contra special prosecutor, Lawrence Walsh, *Firewall: The Iran-Contra Conspiracy and Cover-Up* (New York: W. W. Norton, 1997), as well as Walsh's *Iran-Contra: The Final Report* (New York: Random House, 1994). Senators William S. Cohen and George Mitchell, in *Men of Zeal: A Candid Inside Story of the Iran-Contra Hearings* (New York: Penguin Books, 1989), offer insight into the congressional investigations.

For works touching on various aspects of U.S.-Soviet diplomacy, the Reagan-Gorbachev relationship, and the summit meetings between the two leaders, several personal accounts are worth mentioning, such as Jack Matlock Jr., *Reagan and Gorbachev: How the Cold War Ended* (New York: Random House, 2004), and George Shultz, *Turmoil and Triumph: Diplomacy, Power, and the Victory of the American Ideal* (New York: Simon and Schuster, 1993). The memoir of Chairman of the Joint Chiefs of Staff William J. Crowe Jr., *The Line of Fire* (New York: Simon and Schuster, 1993), reveals the military's thinking during the waning years of the Cold War. The best brief scholarly exploration is the essay by Michael Schaller, "Reagan and the Cold War," in *Deconstructing Reagan*, ed. Michael Schaller et al. (New York: M. E. Sharp, 2007). Perhaps the best thorough scholarly analyses of these events are Raymond L. Garthoff, *Détente and Confrontation: American-Soviet Relations from Nixon to Reagan* (Washington, DC: Brookings Institution, 1994), Garthoff's *The Great Transition: American-Soviet Relations and the End of the Cold War* (Washington, DC: Brookings Institution, 1994), and Frances Fitzgerald, *Way Out There in the Blue: Reagan, Star Wars and the End of the Cold War* (New York: Touchstone, 2000).

The Colin Powell papers at the Ronald Reagan Presidential Library in Simi Valley, California, contain documentation related to his tenure as deputy national security adviser under Frank Carlucci (1986–1987) and as national security adviser in his own right (1987–1989). Currently, approximately more than a quarter of the collection has been processed and is available to researchers. The Reagan Library also has a rich collection of oral histories of officials relevant to the Powell story, such as Carlucci, Caspar Weinberger, and George Shultz.

For the foreign and defense policies of the George H. W. Bush administration, several memoirs have appeared. George H. W. Bush and Brent Scowcroft, *A World Transformed* (New York: Vintage Books, 1999), is a joint memoir focusing mostly on the end of the Cold War and the war in the Gulf against Iraq. Their account features a remarkable and lucid explanation of why that administration did not continue on to Baghdad to overthrow Saddam Hussein in March 1991. James Baker, *The Politics of Diplomacy: Revolution, War and Peace, 1989–1992* (New York: Putnam, 1995), offers much detail about American diplomacy during these years. H. Norman Schwarzkopf, *It Doesn't Take a Hero* (New York: Bantam, 1993), largely discusses the military aspects of the Gulf War. As for scholarly accounts, Steven Hurst, *The Foreign Policy of the Bush Administration: In Search of a New World Order* (London: Cassell, 1999), is a solid overview. For assessments of the Gulf War, see Bernard E. Trainer and Michael R. Gordon, *The Generals' War* (Boston: Back Bay Books, 1995), Rick Atkinson, *Crusade: The Untold Story of the Persian Gulf War* (New York: Houghton Mifflin, 1993), and Bob Woodward, *The Commanders* (New York: Touchstone, 1991). Powell is known to have cooperated closely with Woodward, sometimes giving him hundreds of hours of interviews. Although Woodward's methods are controversial and his books should be read with extreme caution, his works must be taken very seriously as an account of how Powell himself would like to be portrayed.

Evaluations of aspects of Powell's tenure as chairman of the Joint Chiefs of Staff include Dale R. Herspring, *The Pentagon and the Presidency: Civil-Military Relations from FDR to George W. Bush* (Lawrence: University Press of Kansas, 2005). Andrew J. Bacevich's *American Empire: The Realities and Consequences of U.S. Diplomacy* (Cambridge, MA: Harvard University Press, 2002) and *The New American Militarism: How Americans Are Seduced by War* (Oxford: Oxford University Press, 2005) are absolute "must reads." Russell Weigley, "The American Civil-Military Cultural Gap," in *Soldiers and Civilians: The Civil-Military Gap and American National Security*, ed. Peter D. Feaver and Richard H. Kohn (Cambridge, MA: MIT Press, 2001), are also important contributions. Powell's papers as chairman of the Joint Chiefs of Staff can be found in the manuscript collections at the National Defense University Library at Fort McNair in Washington, D.C.

Memoirs focusing on foreign and defense policy during the Clinton years include Madeleine Albright, *Madam Secretary* (New York: Miramax Books, 2003), Warren Christopher, *Chances of a Lifetime: A Memoir* (New York: Scribner, 2001), and Bill Clinton, *My Life* (New York: Vintage, 2004). The two best assessments of Clinton's foreign and defense policies are David Halberstam, *War in a Time of Peace: Bush, Clinton, and the Generals* (New York, Scribner, 2001), and William G. Hyland, *Clinton's World: Remaking American Foreign Policy* (London: Praeger, 1999). To provide the necessary context, these accounts should be supplemented with Lester H. Brune, *The United States and Post–Cold War Interventions: Bush and Clinton in Somalia, Haiti, and Bosnia, 1992–1998* (Claremont, CA: Regina Books, 1998). Biographies of Clinton by John F. Harris, *The Survivor: Bill Clinton in the White House* (New York: Random House, 2005), and Joe Klein, *The Natural: The Misunderstood Presidency of Bill Clinton* (New York: Broadway Books, 2002), include some discussion of Clinton's foreign policy. For a discussion of Powell's presidential boomlet in 1995, see Bob Woodward, *The Choice: How Bill Clinton Won* (New York: Simon and Schuster, 1996).

Powell's speeches, media appearances, and public statements as secretary of state can be found at the Department of State website: www.state.gov/secretary/former/powell/remarks. John W. Dietrich, ed., *The George W. Bush Foreign Policy Reader: Presidential Speeches with Commentary* (London: M. E. Sharpe, 2005), includes a selection of Bush's most important foreign policy statements during the first term. Assessments of the Bush administration's foreign policy are numerous and include Fred Kaplan, *Daydream Believers: How a Few Grand Ideas Wrecked American Power* (Hoboken, NJ: Wiley and Sons, 2008), Ivo Daalder and James Lindsay, *America Unbound: The Bush Revolution in Foreign Policy* (Hoboken, NJ: Wiley and Sons, 2005), Stefan Halper and Jonathan Clarke, *America Alone: The Neo-Conservatives and the Global Order* (Cambridge: Cambridge University Press, 2004), James Mann, *Rise of the Vulcans: The History of Bush's War Cabinet* (New York: Viking Press, 2004), Robert Jervis, *American Foreign Policy in a New Era* (London: Routledge, 2005), and John Newhouse, *Imperial America: The Bush Assault on the World Order* (New York: Alfred A. Knopf, 2003). Alexander Moens, *The Foreign Policy of George W. Bush: Values, Strategy, Loyalty* (Aldershot, UK: Ashgate, 2004), offers a sympathetic assessment. William Quandt, *Peace Process: American Diplomacy and the Arab-Israeli Conflict Since 1967* (Berkeley: University of California Press, 2005), focuses on administration failures in the Middle East, as does Tanya Reinhart, *The Road Map to Nowhere: Israel/Palestine Since 2003* (London: Verso, 2006). Studies of the influence of the neoconservatives include Anne Norton, *Leo Strauss and the*

Politics of American Empire (New Haven, CT: Yale University Press, 2004), Jacob Heilbrunn, *They Knew They Were Right: The Rise of the Neocons* (New York: Doubleday, 2008), and Francis Fukuyama, *America at the Crossroads: Democracy, Power, and the Neoconservative Legacy* (New Haven, CT: Yale University Press, 2006). A lucid effort to understand Bush's personality and how it influenced policy is Jacob Weisberg, *The Bush Tragedy* (New York: Random House, 2008).

Insider accounts that pay some attention to Bush's foreign policy include Richard A. Clarke, *Against All Enemies: Inside America's War on Terror* (New York: Free Press, 2004), Ron Suskind, *The Price of Loyalty: George W. Bush, the White House, and the Education of Paul O'Neill* (New York: Simon and Schuster, 2004), Joseph Wilson, *The Politics of Truth* (New York: Carroll and Graf, 2004), and George Tenent, *At the Center of the Storm: My Years at the CIA* (New York: Harper Collins, 2007). The events of 9/11 are thoroughly addressed in *The 9/11 Commission Report: Final Report of the National Commission on Terrorist Attacks upon the United States* (New York: Norton, 2004). The Bush administration's foreign and defense policies after 9/11 are the focus of Bob Woodward, *Bush at War* (New York: Simon and Schuster, 2002). Glenn Kessler, *The Confidante: Condoleeza Rice and the Creation of the Bush Legacy* (New York: St. Martin's Press, 2007), is also a useful account. For an analysis of the major intelligence failures of these years, see James Risen, *State of War: The Secret History of the CIA and the Bush Administration* (New York: Free Press, 2006), and Craig Whitney, ed., *The WMD Mirage: Iraq's Decade of Deception and America's False Premise for War* (New York: Public Affairs, 2005), which is a collection of documents on the widespread misuse and abuse of intelligence. For comparisons of Vietnam and Iraq, see Robert K. Brigham, *Is Iraq Another Vietnam?* (New York: Public Affairs, 2006), and Lloyd C. Gardner and Marilyn B. Young, eds., *Iraq and the Lessons of Vietnam: Or, How Not to Learn from the Past* (New York: The New Press, 2007).

Memoirs and eyewitness accounts about the war in Iraq include Tommy Franks, *American Soldier* (New York: Regan Books, 2004), L. Paul Bremmer, *My Year in Iraq* (New York: Simon and Schuster, 2006), Larry Diamond, *Squandered Victory: The American Occupation and the Bungled Effort to Bring Democracy to Iraq* (New York: Owl Books, 2005), David L. Phillips, *Losing Iraq: Inside the Postwar Reconstruction Fiasco* (New York: Westview, 2005), George Packer, *The Assassins' Gate: America in Iraq* (New York: Farrar, Straus and Giroux, 2005), and Anthony Shadid, *Night Draws Near: Iraq's People in the Shadow of America's War* (New York: Henry Holt, 2005). The most comprehensive study of the military operations during the invasion of Iraq is Bernard E. Trainor and Michael R. Gordon, *Cobra II: The Inside Story* of the Invasion and Occupation of Iraq (New York: Pantheon, 2006), which should be supplemented with Seymour Hersh, *Chain of Command: The Road from 9/11 to Abu Ghraib* (New York: Harper Collins, 2004), and Thomas E. Ricks, *Fiasco: The American Military Adventure in Iraq* (New York: Penguin, 2006). Bob Woodward's *Plan of Attack* (New York: Simon and Schuster, 2004) and *State of Denial* (New York: Simon and Schuster, 2006) come closest to offering Colin Powell's point of view.

For assessments of the damage the Iraq War did to allies and alliances, see Philip H. Gordon and Jeremy Shapiro, *Allies at War: America, Europe, and the Crisis over Iraq* (New York: McGraw-Hill, 2004), David Andrews, ed., *The Atlantic Alliance under Stress: U.S. European Relations after Iraq* (Cambridge: Cambridge University Press, 2005), Elizabeth Pond, *Friendly Fire: The Near-Death of the Transatlantic Alliance* (Washington, DC: Brookings Institution Press, 2004), and Julia E. Sweig, *Friendly Fire: Losing Friends and Making Enemies in the Anti-American Century* (New York: Public Affairs, 2006). Chris Patten, *Not Quite the Diplomat* (London: Penguin Books, 2005), is a revealing insider account by the former European commissioner for external relations. For accounts focusing largely on Anglo-American relations during Powell's tenure at State, see James Naughtie, *The Accidental American: Tony Blair and the Presidency* (London: Macmillan, 2004), Con Coughlin, *American Ally: Tony Blair and the War on Terror* (London: Politico's Publishing, 2006), and Christopher Meyer, *DC Confidential: The Controversial Memoirs of Britain's Ambassador to the U.S. at the Time of 9/11 and the Iraq War* (London: Weidenfeld and Nicolson, 2005). For an exploration of the administration's muddled Korea policy, see Chae-Jin Lee, *A Troubled Peace: U.S. Policy and the Two Koreas* (Baltimore: Johns Hopkins University Press, 2006).

Index

~

About the Author

Christopher D. O'Sullivan teaches history at the University of San Francisco. He is the author of *Sumner Welles, Postwar Planning, and the Quest for a New World Order*, which won the American Historical Association's Gutenberg-e Prize in 2003, and *The United Nations: A Concise History*. He served as the keynote speaker at the United Nations' sixtieth anniversary celebrations in 2005. He is a fellow at the Center for International Studies at the London School of Economics and was a recent Fulbright visiting professor of the history of American foreign policy at the University of Jordan, Amman.

DATE DUE

HIGHSMITH 45230